HOW TO BE A MAN

HOW TO BE A MAN

John Birmingham
&
Dirk Flinthart

DUFFY & SNELLGROVE
SYDNEY

Published by Duffy & Snellgrove in 1998
PO Box 177 Potts Point NSW 1335
dands@magna.com.au

First edition 1995
Revised and expanded second edition 1998
Reprinted 1998

The information given in this book is not intended to be taken
as a replacement for parental advice. No responsibility is taken on
the part of the publisher for accidents resulting in incorrect usage
of this book, or its instructions. For maximum safety please
remain in a hotel and order room service at all times.

Cover design by Alex Snellgrove
Typeset by Cooper Graphics

Printed and Bound by Griffin Press Pty Ltd

ISBN 1 875 989 28 5

CONTENTS

In memory of Elizabeth Burch, 1944-1997, who raised men and women alike with grace, patience and love.

INTRODUCTION

SO, HERE WE ARE, RAPIDLY approaching the end of the millenium. It's a scary thought isn't it, lads? So far as I'm concerned, it's all been science fiction since 1984 anyway, but there's something about the year 2000 that really puts the willies down your spine.

It's been a hell of a century, though. We've gone from horse and cart to space shuttle, from Maxim gun to H-Bomb, from pen and inkwell to word processor. And think of the grounds we've made in social progress – women have the vote, women have careers, women are legally part of the military, women are running governments ... hang on! Can anyone else see a pattern here?

Indeed. For although the 20th century has been a century of unparalleled misery for the greater body of the world's population, for some, at least, it has been a century of liberation.

Both sexes have new roles, new parts to play. Often, these new roles conflict with the older, more traditional activities associated with gender, making it difficult to manage both at once. Quite wisely, women have dealt with this by whining ferociously. 'How can I be expected to have a career and still raise children?' has been the catchcry of the modern feminist. And as a result, men are cooking, men are raising children, and doing a hundred other things their grandfathers would have laughed themselves stupid about.

Naturally, this kind of thing has put pressure on the traditional masculine role as well. The thing is, men aren't quite so well organised as women in terms of whinging, whining, and throwing their weight around until things go their way. In fact, all over the world men are standing around with stupid, glazed expressions on their faces wondering what the hell has been happening and who's going to fix it.

That's not going to work. The longer you go on standing still, the bigger the head start the babes have got on you, lads. In fact, if you hang around here much longer, they'll be gone, out of sight, and you'll be left holding a half-empty stubbie and scratching your bum along with a couple of billion other relics of a bygone era. The 20th century is *over*. The Battle of the Sexes has come and gone, and you, sir, are in the uncomfortable position of having come second.

Therefore, if the Man of the 21st Century is going to happen at all – if men the world over are going to convince women to stand still long enough to procreate the next generation of humankind – those men are going to need an ace up their sleeves. And that ace isn't going to be some white-livered mineral-water sipping tree-hugging goddam paisley-tied pony-tailed brown-bread and sprouts Sensitive New Age Rubbish, either. Nor is it going to be a return to the Great Hairy-chested Mammoth-slaying days of beer, footy, and pregnant women chained barefoot in the kitchen, unfortunately. No, if Men are going to survive as a viable force in the next century, they're going to have discover anew the one thing Men have always done better than women, and probably always will: *cheating*.

That's right. Bending the rules. Ducking to the last chapter in the Great Book of Life to find out whodunit in advance. Slipping an ace to the bottom of the deck. Hiding a horseshoe in the boxing glove of romance. Dropping chloral hydrate into the gin fizz of gender equity ...

That's where this book comes in. The authors, Birmingham and Flinthart, have extensive and extremely degenerate experience in the realms of cheating. Birmingham in particular is a noted sleazeweasel, a devilish, sweating brute of a man who uses up women like some people use toilet paper. He is the Free Willy Clinton of the journalistic world – yet he manages to write bestselling books, pin his vastly overinflated expense accounts upon the long-suffering pockets of perfectly respectable publishing firms, and to marry a hyper-babe with a six figure salary of her own. I'd call that a role model, wouldn't you?

What about Flinthart? Well, in *The Tasmanian Babes Fiasco* Birmingham describes him as a kind of combination Errol Flynn and Timothy Leary, with a streak of larceny and treachery a mile wide. Those who know him will tell you quite honestly that if only half the stories are true, the man belongs either in an institution or at the bottom of the Brisbane River, his feet in a bucket of concrete – not shacked up in a lush tropical hide-away with a babe who makes the young Jane Seymour look like Yoda. Care to guess which of those two places he really is?

The pair of them are liars, swine and cheaters born – and yet both of them seem to be leading disgustingly cushy existences. The kind of life you know you deserve for yourself. The model 21st Century Man's life.

What's wrong here? What's going on? *What do these two know that you don't?*

Aha. Well, that's what you're here to find out.

Read it, keep it handy, use it whenever you find yourself in doubt as to where you stand in the Brave New World. Draw on its wisdom. Build on it – share it with your brothers in confusion. But for God's sake, don't tell the women about it, or we're all in trouble.

Commander Harrison Biscuit, RAN (ret'd)

CHAPTER ONE

Hygiene, Manners & Clothes: becoming a Smoothie.

§

ON THE LIST OF HOW these things rate with the female half of the world, hygiene is most important of the three, followed closely by manners. Clothing rates a distant third.

§

HYGIENE: MEAN 'N' CLEAN KEEPS 'EM KEEN.

FOR THE PURPOSES OF THIS book, we're going to assume you fall within the normal boundaries of blokehood. You know enough to shower daily, brush your teeth after meals, and pick the fattest, slowest moving lice from your body. If this description doesn't apply to you, no amount of reading is going to be of assistance.

So let's move straight on to all those international hygiene trouble spots.

• **CHEESY FEET.** Man, these are really *disgusting*. The boys in the locker room might think it's kind of funny that you smell like you've been wearing dead weasels for socks, but think how *she'll* feel when it comes time to slip off the hush puppies and make with the horizontal folk dancing. No kinky toe-sucking antics for you my friend. Unless …

There are things you can do to minimise the problem. First and foremost – wear only shoes made of leather or canvas. Vinyl, plastic, and any of the other vile petrochemical substitutes act like nasty Bulgarian saunas, stewing your feet in their own juices. And get rid of any of your older shoes which have begun to resemble a petrie dish. Give them a Viking funeral if you were really attached to them … but get rid of them.

Same goes for your socks. It isn't easy to find pure cotton socks, and they don't wear as long as the nylon and orlon and rayon stuff, but they do help move the moisture away from your feet. In winter, wear nice woollen socks for warmth. Never, never leave dirty socks balled up in your shoes. They'll go for your jugular when released.

If your feet still smell, buy some of those charcoal-impregnated insoles down at the chemist. They're not too expensive, and they do make a difference when used properly.

Finally, you can treat the feet themselves. Skin infections and fungus may be contributing to their Living Dead aroma. A good dose of Tinea medication to the area may help. Give your feet a wash immediately upon taking your shoes off, too. You might also try bathing your malodourous plates in hot vinegar to help eliminate odours and weird skin stuff. And before your feet go into their shoes, give them a quick puff of a commercial foot powder. It will help keep them dry.

Your best bet of all is to try going barefoot more often. Tarzan's feet never smelt unless he'd trodden in some monkey shit or something.

• **DEATH BREATH.** Talk about your passion-killers! The worst thing is, most people will never tell you that you smell like you've been eating your own dick cheese. You'll just have to work out the problem by their grimaces and watering eyes and the way they constantly back away from you.

Short term Death Breath, caused by scarfing down Limburger and pickled onions or the like, can easily be dealt with by a quick brushing, followed by a strong mouthwash and a breath mint. However, real Doggy Breath – the kind that follows you around like a black cloud of doom – is tougher to deal with.

Good oral hygiene may help. Brushing your teeth after every meal, flossing, cleaning tongue and gums – these are all Good Ideas anyway. If you've neglected them so far, clean up your act you filthy swine. Take up gargling with an antiseptic mouthwash too, just for good measure. A mouthwash which contains zinc may be desirable.

Diet can help. Crank up your intake of fresh fruits, vegetables, and natural grains, wind back on the booze and barbecues. Eating fresh parsley is supposed to help, as is chomping into the odd lemon if you can take it like a man. Take chlorophyll tablets and try some antacids.

If you've gone through all these remedies and you're still curdling milk at fifty paces, there may be a serious underlying medical or dental problem. Take your foul exhalations to a doctor, pronto!

§

YOU CAN HAVE AN AFFECTION for a murderer or a sodomite, but you cannot have an affection for a man whose breath stinks – habitually stinks, I mean. – *George Orwell*

§

• **PITS OF DOOM.** Some women claim to be aroused by a whiff of natural male scent, but they are unanimous in saying they prefer the smell of clean sweat to the grotesque reek of a genuinely rancid bod. So it pays to shower, lads.

Regular and frequent bathing is the single best answer for real rankness. Keep your clothing clean, too – especially socks, jocks, and T-shirts. There is no law saying you *have* to wear your favourite white T until it turns grey and falls from your body in shreds. Stick to natural fibres, especially cotton and linen. Close-woven silk doesn't breathe quite as well as these two, but it won't contribute to the pong problem nearly so much as nylon, rayon, orlon, dacron, or L. Ron.

Diet is also of assistance here. Although you may not realise it yourself, the day after a night of gorging yourself on garlic bread and stuffed mushrooms, you could wither an army of vampires just by pointing your armpits towards Transylvania. Again, if you move towards a correctly balanced diet, with lots of fruit, grains and vegetables you may well improve your personal odour. Losing excess weight and improving your fitness and stamina will also decrease the amount of sweating you do, which will certainly help. It'll probably mean less horrified gasps from the babes and more lights-on rumpy-pumpy too.

Deodorants or antiperspirants are kind of a necessity if you're going to make it through a typical working day and remain relatively civilised. There is a difference between the two. Experiment with a few different brands until you find one that seems to work for you.

• **GAS! GAS! GAS!** – Okay. We'll refrain from the more obvious fart jokes. After all, serious, voluminous, pungent flatulence is no laughing matter. Well not much anyway. It's normal to fart upwards of twenty times a day, and release a litre or more of methane into the atmosphere. (Though it's not environmentally sound. Methane is an even more efficient Greenhouse gas than carbon dioxide.) And while most of your boys will be fairly innocuous, one or two will have real penetrating power ... enough to knock the canary off its perch.

First thing to look at is diet. Certain foods are known fartstarters, especially in combination. Bananas and peanut butter. Guinness and garlic. Popcorn and anything. Rich, creamy foods like heavy pasta sauces can promote indigestion and lead to abnormal bacterial activity in the gut. Keep an eye on your own diet, and stay away from any of the killer combinations, especially when you're expecting your social life to become active. At any rate, you're not going to be much good in the sack if the best you can manage is to lie there, groaning in the dark and holding the taut skin of your overstretched belly while trying to digest a whole suckling pig.

As usual, the 'healthy diet' rule holds. Fruits, veges, grains ... you know the drill. Plenty of dietary fibre helps – though don't overdo it, as this can be fartogenic in its own right. With a good diet, regular exercise and the right amount of fibre, your 'problem' should subside to normal, EPA sanctioned levels. If it doesn't – well, you might consider seeing a doctor.

• **ZITS.** It's estimated that 80% of adolescents cop a dose of acne at some stage. In some cases, it can linger well into adult life. Fortunately, it mostly just goes away after a couple of years.

The best remedy is cleanliness. Wash your face twice a day with unscented or medicated soap to prevent the build-up of oils on the skin. Rinse thoroughly with warm water. Don't do the face-washing thing so often that it dries out and irritates your skin, though.

Non-prescription medications containing benzol peroxide may help control the average case of zits. Stop using the medication if it causes excessive dryness, chapping, or irritation.

Don't worry about the food side of things. The idea that stuff like chocolate, cheese, or greasy fried McFood causes zits has been discredited by reasonable research. However, in some people, it may be possible for certain foods to cause brief flareups. So we're back to the healthy diet thing yet again …

For persistent and severe cases of acne, go visit the doctor. There's some real kick-arse zit medications available these days, although you should regard them as a last resort.

• **STD – AND WE'RE NOT TALKING TELEPHONE CALLS!** Yup – STD is the approved acronym for any of the diseases you get by having careless sex with people even more careless than you are. Stands for 'Sexually Transmittable Disease', and it'll kill your sex life stone dead quicker than that copy of Pauline Hanson's biography on the bedside table.

Note that bit about 'Sexually Transmittable'. You get these things by having sex. Not from toilet seats, or borrowed underwear, or anything else. There's a whole range of exciting diseases you can catch this way, ranging from the very mildly annoying all the way up to the completely fatal. It is therefore in your interest to avoid catching them.

Aside from total celibacy, the single best method of avoiding STDs is through the use of the Condom. As

'And remember,' said Jill's father, 'never re-use a condom.'

irritating as they may be, only the most foolish and irresponsible of blokes – or those immersed in genuinely monogamous, long-term relationships – will unsheath the love python without one of these critters in place. (If you're not certain how this is done, read the manufacturer's instructions. Then practise a few times. It's not that tricky.)

If you have been careless though, there are things to watch out for. Any unusual discharge from your penis, pain or difficulty in urination, any recurrent or persistent sores, warts, or odd growths in the genital region – and it's off to the dick doctor for you.

Take heart. Most STDs are quite curable – and those that aren't, such as Herpes, can generally be lived with. AIDS is the real bummer, so to speak. No cure, extraordinarily long incubation period … and in the end, it's a truly depressing way to die.

If you are diagnosed with an STD, your doctor will advise you as to your next course of action. You'll need to round up all your recent sexual partners, though, to let them know of your status, and to encourage them to get a checkup for themselves. And naturally, it's only good manners to refrain from sex until your illness has run its course.

CLOTHING THE OUTER MAN

FRIENDS, IT TAKES A VERY special breed of man to wear the unwearably camp junk foisted on us by newspapers, magazines and insufferable French wankers such as the evil Gaultier. Think about it: your girlfriend doesn't really pretend to be a super model, does she? Sure, when she's out on the town, she'll crank things up a notch or two – but for the most part, if she's got any sense, she's got her own 'look', and she knows it.

That, gentlemen, is what you are striving for. Your own personal 'look'. It has to seem unforced and natural, but should also be neat, clean, and if not tidy and elegant, at least raffishly disarrayed. To achieve it, you'll need to consider not only your own physical characteristics, but your budget, and your requirements at work and at play. It's a big ask, and most men never achieve it on their own. In fact, there's a theory which suggests that were it not for marriage most men would front up at the office in some variation of cum-stained, thread-worn tracky dacks and an 'I'm with Stupid' T-shirt.

HOW TO CHOOSE A SUIT

The business suit is still, by and large, the uniform of the gainfully employed Man. These days, a lot of jobs may not require it – but you can bet that almost all the really well-paid ones do. Get in, get yours early. Look like a million bucks and who knows? Maybe someone will mistakenly think you're worth it.

You could buy a cheap suit but then, as the saying goes, you'd have to wear it. Cheap suits are a bad idea. If you check the rules on making money and finance, you'll find a section which advises against buying on credit, and suggests avoiding the purchase of depreciating assets. Well, a good suit transcends those rules. Spend the money, because a cheap, shiny, baggy suit will impress nobody but the Russian mafia.

How do you spot a cheap and nasty suit? First of all, the name means nothing. Lots of famous designers license out their name or trademark to other manufacturers. As a result, famous-name suits can be every bit as shoddy as the cheap Filipino ripoffs. In fact, they may well be one and the same.

Check for wrinkles. Grab a handful of suit fabric and give it a good scrunching. If it stays wrinkly, it's probably a cheap, shoddy suit. Wrinkling around the seams in the fabric is a very bad sign indeed. It frequently indicates not only cheap fabric, but cheap, glued-seam fabrication. Don't wear one of these pieces of shit. You'll look as though you're going to your own funeral. Best way to spot glued or fused fabric? Rub the lapel between your thumb and forefinger. If the layers of cloth move slightly over the top of one another, the lapel has been finished by hand, which is what you want.

Now check the fabric under a good strong light. You're looking for uneven weave and loose or missing threads. These are not a good sign either. Count the stitches while you're there. A good suit should have at least five stitches per centimetre of seam.

When you're done checking the fabric, you can give your prospective suit a good eyeballing. Do the jacket and trousers match completely? Remember, a lot of stuff is made piecemeal by starving Third World slaves. The jacket and trousers may have been made in entirely different countries. Under no circumstances should you encourage these shit pot antics.

The shoulder of your suit should sit neatly when you wear it, and the line of the seam should be flat, not bulgy. The lapel and collar should lie neat and flat too. Wherever two pieces of fabric come together – at the shoulders, on the back, under the arms – the patterns should match up. There should be a generous amount of cloth under the arms – so that when you lift your arm the neck of the coat does not shoot up to your ears and

§

Girls Like You To Dress Well For Them

It's the first night. I've bagged this boy I've been keen on for ages. He gets up the next morning and asks if he can borrow ten bucks and an old T-shirt. So I give him an old red one. Anyway he rings up later that day and says we're going out to this really nice restaurant on Wednesday night. He won't tell me the name because it's a surprise. I thought, great. So Wednesday night I get cleaned up. Pour myself into my finest glad rags. Everyone in the house is saying, 'Oh wow! You look nice'. The guy rings up and says we're going to Rocket in Potts Point and to meet at a pub beforehand. So I head off to the pub and he's waiting there for me but he's wearing my crappy red T-shirt. It's about ten years old, right? But we head off to dinner. The following night he comes over. He's a chef and he's been at work all day. In the kitchen, over the oven and steam, in my red T-shirt. And he pops over, still wearing it. Won't have a shower. Just takes the red T-shirt off. The next night we're all going to see the Plunderers at the Annandale. We're going to meet Mark there. And sure as hell he's easy to spot because there he is playing pool in my red T-shirt. He wore that fucking thing till it virtually fell off his back three weeks later. Then we broke up. – *Nikki*

§

make you look like a crooked real estate agent or Richard Nixon.

Inside the suit, the lining should go all the way down the sleeves and at least halfway down the back. In the trousers, the lining should go at least halfway down. Check the buttons on your jacket, too. They should be well made, and firmly attached. Three buttons on the front of the coat is trendy at the moment, but two is just fine. Ensure the fly in the trousers is neatly, discreetly tucked away under the drape of the fabric.

If you've come this far, you can be reasonably sure the suit you're investigating is a goer. There's more to the matter than simple cost versus quality, though. There's the nature of the fabric itself, for example. For a working, travelling suit, it may be acceptable to suffer a little polyester – but personally we'd stick to worsted wool, linen, and silk or silk blends. They always look better.

In terms of colour, brown is to be avoided at all costs. They were very popular with old Soviet Union's politburo and look where it got them. They were very lucky not to swing by their thumbs because of those brown suits and you should be in no rush to emulate them. For work, charcoal, dark grey, and dark blue to navy are perfectly acceptable. Lighter colours, such as beige and olive, work best in the summer months. Black is for funerals or a life in crime. White is best left to those career professionals in the security and intelligence services who might actually have cause to lounge around cocktail bars on the Ivory Coast. Plaid suits are utterly unacceptable, unless you happen to be a sportswriter,

The way you wear your suit is important.

in which case they're probably an improvement on whatever you're wearing now. You can get away with a Prince of Wales check, narrow vertical stripes or very small herringbone patterns, if you must.

Length is important. With your arms at your side, the sleeves of your suit should end at the narrowest part of your wrist. Your shirtsleeves should end no more than 2cm past that point. The crease in your trousers should gently 'break' when the trouser bottom is resting on the top of your shoe. Whether or not your trousers have cuffs is a personal choice. But they should have no more than two pleats on each side – any more and you'll look like an unemployed gigolo.

The way you wear your suit is important too. A well-tailored suit should hang off a man like a fine and beautiful mistress, not some rumpled, insane old bag lady. Wear the trousers a little high, and have the cuffs let out some. Keep your jacket buttoned, and your tie drawn tight. Your legs will magically lengthen, and you'll get that whole elegant 1940s Cary Grant thing going. If you want the serious, competent look, think dark suits only. Waistband of the trousers fractionally below the waist. White shirts and no novelty socks. Your multinational corporate sorts are rarely impressed by the sight of Homer Simpson climbing out of your black Italian lace-ups to smack himself in the head and say, 'D'oh!'

If you're in doubt about how to buy a good suit, head for David Jones and tell the nice man what you want and how much you can afford to pay. They even have their own label suits which are pretty good value, we suppose. If you'd prefer not to be a bit of a loser however, just remember that each large city will have its own legendary tailor, such as Zink's of Sydney. Spend the extra dough (you're looking at about $1200 to $1500 minimum) and you *will* make out like a bandit with both the Board of Directors and the hot babe in reception.

THE DILEMMA OF SHIRTS

• **WHITE IS BEST. BLUE IS OKAY. NOTHING ELSE IS ACCEPTABLE WITH A SUIT.** Coloured shirts with white collar and cuffs are a reminder that fashion is something so horrible we can only bear to look at it for a very short time.

• **COTTON WORKS.** Stick with it. In a moment of florid formal grandeur, you might consider fine Irish linen, or even silk – but for most of us, cotton is more than adequate.

• **GET YOURSELF MEASURED UP PROPERLY,** and buy shirts that fit in an exact size. Don't mess around with generic X and L and S things; these are shirts for the proles, and you are an individual. Have the measuring process repeated every year. Be especially careful with the neck measurements. Collars should fit snugly, but not tightly.

• **YOUR SLEEVE SHOULD END ABOUT 12CM UP YOUR WRIST FROM THE TIP OF YOUR THUMB.** As mentioned before, it should extend about 2cm past the end of your jacket when your hands are by your sides.

• **THE COLLAR SHOULD RISE ABOUT A CENTIMETRE OR SO PAST THE BACK OF YOUR JACKET COLLAR.** Good, solid stitching around the outer edges of the collar will help it remain rigid – but the stitching should be subtle enough to remain nigh-invisible. The two sides of the collar should meet under the chin and make a nice vee shape. Pulling it together with your necktie is cheating, and makes both shirt and tie look funny.

• **YOU NEED ABOUT 15CM OF FABRIC THAT HANGS BELOW WAIST LEVEL TO TUCK INTO THE TROUSERS.** Don't overdo it, but for pity's sake, don't neglect this either or you'll have shirt tails flapping around everywhere and will very quickly come to resemble a drunk at an Irish wake or, even worse, you will look like you've just rogered the work experience girl in the stationary cupboard.

Upmarket department stores are good places to buy shirts too – the staff usually know what they're doing but won't bully you. If you're feeling confident Polo/Ralph Lauren stores are especially good for tall men.

THE TIES THAT BIND

Here are the two tie knots you really must know. The bottom of the tie should end up fully covering the buckle of your belt. If you're tall, it could hang even lower. James Bond wouldn't trust a man who couldn't tie one of them, but we can't remember which. Sorry.

HALF WINDSOR

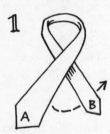

Situate the tie so that the end 'A' is longer than end 'B' and cross 'A' over 'B'.

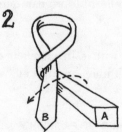

Bring 'A' up around and behind 'B'.

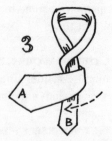

Bring 'A' up around front, over 'B' from left to right.

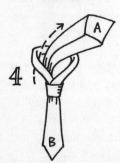

Pull 'A' up and through the loop.

Bring 'A' down through the knot in front.

Using both hands, tighten the knot and draw up to collar.

FULL WINDSOR KNOT

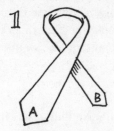

1

Situate the tie so that the end 'A' is longer than end 'B' and cross 'A' over 'B'.

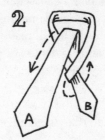

2

Bring 'A' up through loop between collar and tie; then back down.

3

Pull 'A' underneath 'B' and to the left.

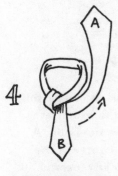

4

Pull 'A' back through the loop again.

5

Bring 'A' across the front from left to right.

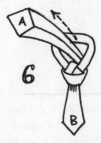

6

Pull 'A' up through the loop again.

7

Bring 'A' down through the knot in front.

8

Using both hands, tighten the knot and draw up to collar.

The Windsor and the half-Windsor will see you through all everyday tie situations. When you need a bow tie – which is rarely – you can buy a cheap, pre-fixed one. Or you can decide not to look like a complete Barry and master this near forgotten art. It will make you look like Superman if you do it with a formal white shirt and a tux or dinner suit, or like an utter feeb if you do it with anything else at all ...

BOWTIE

(Note. First you have to actually buy a genuine bow tie. Nothing else will work.)

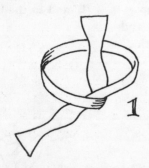

Place the bow tie around
your neck, situating it so that
end 'A' is longer than end 'B'.
Cross 'A' over 'B'. Bring 'A'
up and under the loop.

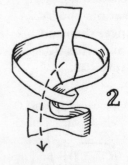

Now double 'B' over itself
to form the front base
loop of the tie. Loop 'A'
over the center of the
loop you just formed.

Holding everything in place,
double 'A' back on itself and
poke it through the loop
behind the tie.

Adjust the tie by
tugging at the ends of it
and straightening the
centre knot.

Now, as for the appearance of your tie: bow ties are always black. There is no other kind, no matter what anyone may try telling you. Bow ties do not spin, flash, blink, spurt water or feature idyllic scenes of Tahitian beach life. Are we clear on this?

For your standard business-type tie, colour is less important than width. Here again, we harken back to the 1970s, the Time that Taste Forgot. Remember when ties were nearly as wide as doonas? Well, if you do, you won't thank us for reminding you. And if you don't, think yourself lucky and, try very hard not to bring those dark days upon us once more. If your tie is wider than ten centimetres at the broadest, it is *too fat!* Skinny ties are pretty stupid-looking too, by the way. And string ties are the exclusive preserve of slack-jawed yokels who become excited at the thought of sexual congress with aliens and/or livestock.

When you're buying a tie, make sure it's a good one. If it was made off-centre, it may be impossible for you to situate the knot in the middle of your neck, as you should. When you're buying it, drape the middle of the tie over one wrist and let the two ends dangle as they will. The small end should land smack in the middle of the fat end. (If not, it's a screw-up. Don't buy it.) If it passes this test, try tying it around your neck. It should hang comfortably and look good.

In wearing a tie, it's more important to match patterns and fabrics with your shirt and jacket than it is to match colours. Plain shirts call for a patterned tie, and vice versa – although it is recommended the patterns and colours stay relatively muted. If you have an old school tie, or a college tie, wear them only where there will be some decided advantage in it for you; in the waiting room of the more expensive sort of brothel for instance. Alternately, you could just burn them.

In terms of fabrics, it's easy. Slick, smooth suits need a slick, smooth tie. On the other hand, tweeds, corduroys and heavy wools want nice rough, tweedy neckties. Don't mix up the two styles. It's horrible.

The easiest place to buy a good tie is Grace Brothers or David Jones. Their house label, pure silk numbers are excellent value. The *best* place to buy a good tie is Italy.

EVERYTHING YOU NEEDED TO KNOW ABOUT SHOES

• **NEVER BUY GREY SHOES.** They're too light for all your dark trousers, and they'll make all your lighter trousers look grubby. Grey shoes suit only race touts, policemen and the better breed of pimp.

• **LEATHER FOR BUSINESS.** Come to think of it, it's leather for jogging and pleasure too. Canvas is okay for a pickup basketball game, and scuffing around the neighbourhood in blue jeans and a pullover – but under no circumstances are vinyl or plastic ever acceptable. See also; foot odour.

• **WING-TIPS WORK NICELY FOR BUSINESS.** Black is best. Brown limits your wardrobe drastically.

• **PLAIN CAP-TOE AND PERFORATED CAP-TOE SHOES, IN BLACK – OR OCCASIONALLY, BROWN – ARE FOR BIG BUSINESS.** These are dressy, *important* shoes. You can wear these with your tuxedo and be completely safe.

• **TASSELLED LOAFERS ARE COMFORTABLE AND CONVENIENT.** They're also highly suspect, the sort of thing one would expect to find under a pile of stripey shirts, old school ties and plaid jackets at some proto-fascist arsefuckers convention. We wouldn't recommend them with a suit, not for anyone under fifty-five anyway.

• **LONG SOCKS SHOULD BE WORN WITH YOUR SUIT.** That way, nobody gets a flash of skinny, hairy calf when you cross your legs. Long socks should not be worn with shorts after you leave school.

THE CASUAL STUFF

Having disposed of the white-collar uniform of suit, tie, shirt and foot-crushers, we can now spare a few words on what you're going to wear elsewhere. Remember, we're trying to give you a touch of class, a little style …

> §
>
> **BEWARE OF ETHNIC CLOTHES**
>
> Nobody ought to wear a Greek fisherman's cap who doesn't meet two qualifications:
> 1. He is Greek.
> 2. He is a fisherman. – *Roy Blount jnr*
>
> §

- **THE ONLY LEISURE SUIT IS A TUXEDO.** Damn the torpedoes, full steam ahead! Tuxedoes have class. They have elegance. They can suggest all kinds of things about their wearers, depending on their condition. Get yourself measured up, and get one decent tux. Then wear it to death. The thing with a tuxedo is this: at any formal or even semi-formal occasion, the man with a tux is not overdressed. The moment he saunters through the door and orders his first martini, *every other man in the room begins to look shabby*. The trick is to be that guy.

- **HATS ARE DEAD.** They are no longer part of a wardrobe. They are part of a costume. The only exception to this is the very necessary sun hat, or a thick, knitted winter woollen cap. Baseball caps are for stupid Americans who don't know any better because of the collapse of their education system – or for people who play baseball.

- **ALWAYS CONSIDER THE REST OF YOUR WARDROBE WHEN BUYING CLOTHING.** There's no use in buying a grand, Byronic white shirt with enormous puffy sleeves and a tie-up front unless you've got the tight black trousers and decent pirate boots to match.

- **IF YOU'RE SHORT ON MONEY, STICK TO A NARROW RANGE OF COLOURS.** That way, everything you own will go with most everything else. If you stick to muted earth-tones, like tans and greens, you'll be able to wear the same stuff pretty much all year round.

- **JUMPERS SHOULD NEVER BE SKINTIGHT.** Make sure you have room to move comfortably. And cardigans are for people over sixty. Stick to good wool, cashmere, or alpaca for your jumpers. Synthetics are quite nasty. Try not to wear polo-necks, unless you're doing it under a sports coat. And even then, don't.

- **A COUPLE OF PAIRS OF BLACK CHINOS WILL TAKE CARE OF MOST OF YOUR CASUAL NIGHTS OUT.** White and beige are reasonable alternatives for summer, but grey will just make you look like you forgot your jacket.

- **BELTS SHOULD BE DONE UP TO THE THIRD HOLE.** They should also be no wider than five centimetres, no narrower than three. Big, chunky buckles work only with blue jeans, ten gallon hats, and if you're dating your cousin.

- **CUBAN HEELS ARE FOR CUBANS.** Only.

- **DON'T SKIMP ON THE REG GRUNDIES.** There will come a time when someone else looks at them, and at that time, it is not desirable that she should either laugh, or gasp in horror. If you want to wear nifty patterns, stick with boxer shorts. Jockeys should be plain, and preferably coloured. It is a sad fact that no man can keep white underwear in that condition for more than three minutes. When your underwear develops its first, minute hole, or when the elastic doesn't spring back with a crisp snap any more, it is no longer underwear. It is now a paint rag.

- **HAIR IS IMPORTANT.** Neat and clean beats everything else, including blow-waves, mousse, and your own personal stylist. If you've got good hair, treat it well. Wash it every three or four days with a mild shampoo, and a matched conditioner. The length you choose to wear it is your problem, although hair any longer than collar length looks really, really dodgy with a suit. (And ponytails are only for cheerleaders.)

- **IF YOU'RE LOSING YOUR HAIR, FOR THE LOVE OF GOD, DON'T TRY TO DISGUISE IT.** Wigs and toupees are nothing short of embarrassing. Hair-weaves and hair transplants almost always come off looking dodgy as hell. And please, please, stay away from Comb Over. If you're thinning on top, the simple answer is to pull out the clippers, and get a Number Four buzz-cut. And buy some more sunblock.

MANNERS MAKETH THE MAN

POLITENESS AND COURTESY ARE TWO different things. Politeness is a kind of social code. You use it when you meet strangers, or when you're put into a potentially difficult situation. By behaving politely, you tell the other people in any given situation that you are a civilised being. That way, they know what to expect from you, and can transact their business with a minimum of fuss.

Politeness, being a recognisable social code, can be taught. But not by us. If you must get into the detail, go and buy one of those books by Adelaide Snapsphincter. Otherwise just stick to the rules you learned as a kid, don't grab for things that aren't yours, stay reasonably quiet, and you'll be fine.

Courtesy, on the other hand, can't be taught. You have to genuinely possess some degree of fellow-feeling towards other human beings in order to be courteous. The simple rule of courtesy has always been the same, though: treat others as you would like to be treated. If you can remember that, and practise it even in the most informal and irreverent of circumstances, you'll be right.

RANDOM MANNERS

• **WOMEN, LIFTS AND DOORS.** Most women over fifty like you to let them go first through a doorway. Otherwise it's tricky. The general rule is to act just as you would with aother man – whoever's closest goes first. In

§

BE GENTLE, PLAY NICE

You know how little boys bash up the people they really like? Well it's funny, they don't really change. You get a bunch of guys and a new girl comes into their circle, they'll start fighting and jostling each other, thinking this is attractive. A blonde triathlete beauty queen came into my circle of friends and the guys went mad for her, one guy in particular. And she'd shown some interest in him. We all went out one night and as he didn't quite know how to go about wooing this super model he decided, in drunken desperation, to fall back on an old standard. He said to a mate next to him, 'Lets go crash-tackle the guys up front.' He meant me and the new girl. His mate later told the ambulance crew he'd never seen a flying tackle like it. They just mussed my hair but this drunken fool accelerated to top speed and speared into this other girl like he was defending a one point margin in a rugby World Cup. A thirty-stone Samoan would have been proud of him. It drove this girl about four feet in the air then into the ground. It took all the skin off her elbows and knees, tore her expensive Laura Ashley dress to shreds and knocked her unconscious for about fifteen minutes. And all because he really liked her. – *Emma*

§

a restaurant try not to sit down and start vacuuming up the free breadsticks before your date has even slipped off her coat. (Although you shouldn't make a point of standing around like a goose until she's seated).

• **THE WINE WAITER.** If you think tasting the wine before you allow the waiter to pour it is outdated, you're right. Wine-making techniques have improved a lot since the nineteenth century, and today only about one bottle in a thousand goes off. So it's cool to just tell them to pour it. If it's bad you can still send it back. (Bad wine tastes really bad, like vinegar.) If you're not a wine expert and you're not sure if the wine's off, it probably isn't. And if the idea of 'getting the wine wrong' terrifies you, ask the waiter what they would recommend with the dish you have ordered.

§

HOW TO BEHAVE IN A BROTHEL

Guys who come in and are really nervous are very nice. But guys who come in who are rude and arrogant and who put their feet up all over the furniture and who, after meeting a group of ladies say things like, 'Is that it? Got any more', those are very unpleasant guys. I mean, the ladies are people too. Young men trash waiting rooms pretty regularly and I wish they wouldn't. You come in and the bowl of Minties is strewn everywhere. Paper and half chewed Minties spat out on the carpet. Very unnecessary. They pop a Mintie in their mouth and the girls come to meet them but instead of swallowing they spit! Horrid.

The perfect young man would come in and say hello and would not demand a drink immediately when we are in the middle of explaining the prices and how he's going to meet the women. The young gentleman would listen attentively to you rather than staring at the TV. When the perfect young man is introduced to the ladies he often says hello and politely introduces himself back. When he chooses a lady in a line-up he thanks the other ladies for their time and indulgence. Then he pays.

In the room the perfect young gentleman should take his guidance from the lady. She knows what she is doing. She is

HOW TO MAKE A SPEECH

Most of us have to do this at some time or other in our lives. It can be as simple as saying a few words at a friend's birthday party, or as fraught as delivering a eulogy or pitching a multi-million dollar project to the CEO of a major Mafia-backed construction firm. For most people, they're all equally terrifying. Public speaking, which ranks way up in the top ten phobias, gets easier with practice, but most of us don't get much practice so the trick is to prepare carefully beforehand ...

- **WHO'S YOUR AUDIENCE AND WHAT'S THE OCCASION?** Keep your speech relevant and appropriate to the situation at hand. Do the wedding guests *really* need to hear every gynaecological detail of the groom's tequila drenched visit to a three dollar Mexican whorehouse?

not there to rip him off or give him a tough time. She will give him a very good service and look after him if he is polite. But if he's obnoxious and arrogant he is immediately going to put her in a bad mood and she is not going to want to look after him as well as she should and can.

A proper young man will avoid being overly demanding and aggressive. The lady is a person, not a rubber dolly and should not be tossed around like one. He should certainly ask for anything he wants. But if she says he can't do something or that something hurts and he should stop, listen and take heed.

If he finishes before his time is up he is quite welcome to try again but most gentlemen prefer to sit and relax, have a massage or another drink.

When leaving he should avoid kicking the walls in. There is no need for groups of young men to pile into the street like a football team on a grand final binge. There is no need to be raucous and loud. It's just a matter of being polite.

Safe sex is not a negotiating position and a proper gentleman would never attempt to make it one. It would do them no good anyway. Nor should a gentleman stick his tongue out at or into a lady, at any time. It is the height of bad manners. — *Kaz*, receptionist at *A Touch of Class*, Sydney

§

During formal, busines engagements, stick to business. Clever, trained speakers can mix 'n' match to good effect. But if you're not one of these, keep it short and simple.

- **GET YOUR POINT ACROSS.** That means you should be looking at establishing no more than three or perhaps four main points in the entire speech. People can't handle a lot more without taking notes.
- **KEEP YOUR LANGUAGE SIMPLE.** High rhetoric is for professionals. Stray outside your own natural speech patterns and vocabulary, and you're asking for serious embarrassment. Don't worry about sounding downmarket; it's far, far better to deliver a simple speech well than to cock up a masterpiece.
- **REHEARSE.** Write the whole thing down, time it, and deliver it in front of a mirror, watching yourself. Get rid of the stupid gestures, like running your fingers through your hair, sticking your hands in your pockets, playing with your tie, or whatever. Decide what you're going to do with your hands — grasping the lectern, if one's available, is a good idea — and stick with it. Keep practising it until the speech runs smoothly.
- **BRING NOTES.** Even if you've got the thing memorised down to the smallest detail, carry palm cards with the main points outlined on them. If you're not a seasoned public speaker, chances are that at some time, you will run out of steam, notice the audience watching you, and forget everything you meant to say. When that happens, cough slightly, have a drink of water, and consult your palm cards. Then pick up where you left off.
- **SPEAK SLOWLY AND LOUDLY.** Normal patterns of speech will be impossible to understand at the back of the audience. Enunciate your words clearly, and try to project your voice to the person at the farthest corner of the room — even if you've been given a microphone.
- **MAKE EYE CONTACT.** As you make your speech, don't stare at the ceiling, or bury your face in your notes. Let your gaze drift over the audience. Direct your words to individuals — first one, then another.

    It's spooky talking to a sea of blank faces, but the good news is that most of them actually want you to succeed. A decent joke will usually get a better response from a crowd than from just one listener.
- **KEEP IT SHORT.** Unless you've been engaged to speak for a specific period of time, any speech longer than five minutes is too damned long. If you had really fascinating material, you could consider stretching that to seven or eight minutes ... but chances are you'll lose your audience by then, unless you really know what you're doing.

HOW TO PROPOSE A TOAST

Informal toasts are easy. They usually crop up at the beginning of a meal or celebration. Someone raises a glass and says the local equivalent of cheers. Everyone clinks glasses, and a lot of booze disappears.

More formal toasts usually involve a short speech honouring someone or another, and usually get done at the end of the meal, when everyone still has a little wine in their glasses. Better yet, they can be done at dessert, when the champagne arrives.

The toaster stands and makes their speech. At the end, they say 'I now propose a toast to …' and everyone except the toastee rises to their feet. They repeat the name of the toastee (or title – 'The Bride' for example) touch glasses and sip. Non-boozers: toasting with water is supposed to be bad luck. Just touch an empty glass. Or get some orange juice.

Now, supposing you're the toaster; what are you going to say? Well, first, keep it short. Three or four sentences will do. You're talking to people who've just had a big meal and a lot of wine. If you run off at the mouth, they'll probably assume you're drunk, and ignore you. Or fall asleep.

Don't get carried away by your own wit, either. Chances are you've had a few glasses. Trust us: whatever you were thinking of saying isn't

§

NEVER ADMIT TO FARTING

Never admit to farting even if there are only two of you. If this is really going to make you look like a liar, a flustered pretence of searching for an imaginary gas seepage between the floorboards with the attendant turning up your own nose in disbelief at the horrid smell is a proper demonstration of innocence preventing blame and embarrassment. This ruse will of course be understood by other fair-minded farters. – *J.P. Donleavy*

§

nearly as funny as you thought it was. If people start slapping their thighs, pointing and laughing it's probably because your fly is undone. Say something pleasant and friendly. Keep it simple, avoid clichés if you can, and smile.

FARTING, BELCHING AND VOMITING

These things happen. You've got to know how to deal with them.

• **SMALL BURPS MAY BE DISCREETLY RELEASED BEHIND A NAPKIN.** But gigantic, earth-shattering eructations are never acceptable outside of belching contests on an all-male fishing trip. If you eat slowly, chew carefully, and avoid carbonated drinks with your meal, chances are the problem won't arise in the first place.

• **SILENT FARTS ARE PUBLIC PROPERTY.** Never acknowledge them, even if you happen to be one of only two people in an elevator. If you have let out a real toe curler in such a situation, fix the other person with a steely glare and mutter between clenched teeth, 'You filthy little shit.'

• **THUNDERBOLTS ARE A PROBLEM.** Obviously, you're better off controlling them, but if one of them slips out at an inopportune moment, don't make a big deal about it. A simple 'Wups. Goddamn chilli dog,' will do just fine.

• **VOMITING IS NEVER POLITE.** Bean bags, foreign dignatories and first dates are not suitable targets for a geyser of chewed-over carrots and corn. Restrict it to the toilet. Aim for the bowl not the walls. Or take it out to the gutter where you belong.

CHAPTER TWO

Men at Work

§

REMEMBER TO GET OUT OF BED IN THE MORNING

[For] many years I did not recognise that, while it is true that any action may bring unexpected results, it is equally true that so might any lack of action.
– *Donald Horne*

§

What Kind Of Job Do You Want?

IN THE LONG HAUL, IT'S better to take a bad job somewhere you want to be than to be boss hog of some joint you know is going to give you toxic braindeath. Work is going to chew up a huge slice of your life. If you waste all that time and effort on a job you loathe, rest assured you *will not* prosper. The way to success is to do something you genuinely want to do. That way, you got a real reason to get out of bed in the morning.

However, in the short term, any job is better than no job at all. You may have trained for years to be a graphic artist, only to find there's nothing going in that industry. Fine. Don't sit around on your arse feeling sorry for yourself; go get yourself an income washing cars or waiting tables. It's a gig and you'll meet some chicks you might have otherwise missed. It'll also look better on your CV than a year of eating microwave nachos and watching daytime television. More importantly you'll be keeping up the habit of working. Once you get out of the habit of mindless soul-destroying employment tedium, it can be awfully hard to rediscover.

Deciding what you *really* want to do is very tricky. Some people are lucky. The question never occurs to them. Some people take the first real job they get, and hang onto it for the next forty years, hopping off the escalator at the end and onto the pension. These people are known as robots.

Most of us don't really know what we want when we're looking for our first job. That's where further education and training comes in. If tertiary education does nothing else for you, it'll broaden your horizons and options. Eventually though, you have to stop training and studying and start living for real. Your best bet is to jam as much experience as possible into the time you have; study, yes – but take part-time jobs, travel, read, learn a language, hitch-hike, meet people and take interesting new drugs with them. This is the way to find out what's out there. This is the way to find out who you are.

APPLYING FOR A JOB

Almost anything you do well and do regularly can lead to employment. Just by getting out there and doing your thing, whatever it is, you'll make contacts and sharpen your skills. If you're any good at all, there's a solid chance work will find you. Don't sweat it, though. Grab the newspapers

§

Learn self-discipline before it's imposed

A young man needs a few setbacks. A few sits on his arse, a punch on the nose. It seems to me that all the do-gooders have achieved over the last twenty years is getting rid of some of the morals. While I'm a knockabout bloke and yibbedah yibbedah and all that crap, the most important thing is that I'm a man of high principle. I know that where I am today is because of the principles and the discipline instilled in me by my mother and father, by my two years in the army, my years in the police force, and the discipline I had to learn in playing football at the highest level. As far as I'm concerned, if they brought back National Service for every eighteen year old in the country you would not have blokes at Kerford Road Pier with knives down the back of their strides waiting for some person to come along so they can cut their throats.

The advice I would give to young people is if they have an opportunity to do something that involves discipline they should go for it. The best thing you can ever learn is self discipline. The problem with a lot of young blokes goes back many, many years because of the way they were brought up, to bludge on people, to steal and that sort of thing. You can't make bread out of shit. Simple as that. They wouldn't know how to make a bed, or polish their shoes, they wouldn't know how to say please or thankyou. You know why? Because they don't know any better. You gotta feel sorry for them because if you tried to give them a lecture on right and wrong it would just be like water off a duck's back. I'd like to get half a dozen of them to the Rex Hunt school of etiquette. – *Rex Hunt*

§

and look through the ads. If there's anything in your chosen field – excellent! Run up a covering letter, attach a CV, and send it off.

A covering letter should be a simple, introductory document, no longer than a page. Address it to the person cited in the advertisement. Telephone first, to get their exact name and title. Your letter must state who you are, and explain clearly what the job is that you're interested in. If there was a position number or the like on the advertisement, don't forget to use it. Otherwise, cite the title of the job exactly as given in the advertisement.

Once you've said what you're after, you need to say a little bit about why you want the job. Keep it simple, but make certain whoever reads your letter will know that you're very interested in the position, and that they have some idea of why you're interested. The attached CV will hopefully give them an idea of your capabilities. Between these two, with any luck, you'll eventually get a call or a letter summoning you to an interview. More likely, at first, you'll get a simple form letter telling you to fuck off and die. They won't use those exact words of course. They'll probably thank you for your interest and say the position has been filled. Don't sweat it. File the ad, a copy of your letter and a copy of their letter for future reference. This also helps when the dole fascists come a-callin' later asking a lot of nosy, uncomfortable questions about how many jobs you've applied for.

Don't restrict yourself to newspaper adverts. The vast majority of jobs are never advertised in the paper. They're all filled by people with inside running. If you really know where you want to be, try some cold-canvassing. Send a letter of introduction and a CV to *every* potential employer you can. Your letter in this case should simply state who you are, and what your interests are, and explain that you would like to be considered should any positions become vacant which might suit your abilities. In this case, the letter should be directed to the personnel manager – or equivalent – of the organisation. Again, if you can telephone first and get a name and a title, your efforts will look more professional.

If you really want to get out there – and it's not a bad idea – you can visit potential employers in person. Take a current CV, and ask for an appointment. Make it clear you want only a few minutes of their time, and when you get your chance, keep your shit brief and to the point. Do as you would in a letter: introduce yourself, explain your interest in the field of work, and ask whether there are any opportunities available with the company, or whatever. Be polite, and accept a 'no' when you hear it – but make certain you leave a copy of your CV for their personnel files.

While you're grinding your way through this bullshit, it's probably worth your while to check with the employment agencies anyway. We know very, very few people who've actually found work through these useless bastards, but there are other resources there for the plundering. They can help you sharpen your interview and presentation skills, perhaps offer you assistance with finding the right clothing, and help you construct a CV. Usually, they have word-processors and photocopiers which can be used for a minimal cost as well. And they have lots and lots of publications which will tell you pretty much what you're reading here, except they'll crap on much more.

HOW TO WRITE A CURRICULUM VITAE

A CV is a brief, clearly arranged, occasionally fictional document which does nothing more than cover the high points of your career and training to date. An employer should be able to scan it quickly, and get a pretty clear idea of what you can offer. It goes without saying that your CV should be absolutely, spotlessly neat and flawlessly presented, but it's also important not to overdo it. Your best bet is to head to the nearest employment agency, and request a copy of their current model CV, then stick closely to that.

Your CV should be attached to your letter of introduction, in which you express interest in the job. It should not run on from the letter, but be a completely separate document. Stick to standard A4 paper and double-spacing, with at least a 2.5cm margin all round. If you don't have a word processor, or at least a high-grade electric typewriter, avail yourself of the machines down at the employment agency. By the way, don't attach a photograph to your CV unless specifically requested to do so by the employer.

- **PERSONAL DETAILS.** The first section of your CV covers personal details. Offer your name, address, telephone numbers, date of birth and marital status. If relevant, tell them whether you have a driver's licence.
- **CAREER OBJECTIVE.** After the personal details, you should supply a statement of your career objective. Keep it short – two lines, at most – and make sure it's relevant to the job you're applying for. If, for example, you're looking for a year or two of work detailing cars while you study opera, it's probably not useful to tell your employer you're aiming to be the next Luciano Pavarotti. Instead, tell him you want to work your way up to sales, with an eye to eventually running your own car yard, and cite opera in the section under 'Hobbies and Interests'. This is the section of your CV which would be called 'fiction' if you were being honest. If your potential employer believes you have a genuine, long-term interest in the area of employment, your chances of scoring the job are much better. So practise saying you *want* to be a used car salesman until you can do it without pissing your pants from hysterical, gut-clutching laughter.
- **EDUCATION HISTORY.** Following your Career Statement, you should supply details of your education. Secondary matriculation and all tertiary qualifications should be included. Don't bother to mention primary schooling unless you went to a particularly prestigious or outstand-

ing private school. (Or if you happen to know your potential boss went to the same school. Pathetic we know, but worth a shot.) Education details should include the date of your studies, where the studies were undertaken, the level of study you achieved, and the nature of those studies. Again, keep it as brief as possible. If your employer needs to know more, they'll ask you at the interview.

- **EMPLOYMENT HISTORY.** Next up is your employment history. Unless it is as thin as Mr Birmingham's, it should get at least a page to itself. Starting with your most recent employment, work backwards to the start. Supply details of when the work occurred, who you worked for, what position you held, and what your duties were. This should occupy roughly a paragraph for each employer. Don't be afraid to cite part-time jobs, or even any small businesses you may have operated. Your enthusiasm and dedication are as much under the spotlight as your record of relevant employment. Perhaps the most important feature is a nice, steady employment history – not too many long breaks from work, and not too many moves from job to job. Don't try to fake this too outrageously, but it'll help if you can give the impression, however false, that you're a good, solid worker drone just *itching* to grind your way through mindless wage slavery.

- **SKILLS AND ABILITIES.** On a new page, you should cite your demonstrated skills and abilities. It's usual to break your skills into groups such as Cash Handling, Communications and Liaison, Computer Skills, Unarmed Combat, Contraband Smuggling and the like. Under each heading, list the separate things you have learned to do. For example, under Computer Skills, you might list: Able to use Microsoft Word at 80 words per minute; Familiar with Microsoft Windows and Windows 95 operating systems; Capable of using DOS-based systems; Trained in basic maintenance, handling and storage. Hacked into the Vatican's Website and left an obscene image on Home Page. Hmmm, well maybe not that last one, unless you're after a job with some really standout computer geeks. If you find you've got a lot of skills in one particular area, give it a bit more space, but don't list the really minor shit. You want no more than half a dozen lines under each category, so keep it relevant to the job.

- **OTHER STUFF.** The last page tidies up the details. List four or five hobbies and interests. Make 'em up if you haven't got 'em, but do your research, so you can at least sound interested. You want to seem like a well-rounded, socially adjusted individual. List half a dozen or so personal qualities, too. Try things like reliability, punctuality, intelligence, sunny disposition, honesty ... blah blah blah. Don't bullshit too much. Your employer's not really going to pay much attention to these, but if

§

Fantasy job #1: Why the mean streets just got meaner for private dicks.

To be a PI, you can either enrol in a TAFE course which will teach you some retail accounting to run a small business. Or you can do a six month correspondence course. Or you can become a sub-agent to a practising, fully licensed investigator. If you really want to be a private investigator you should ask to be taken on as a sub-agent, basically an apprentice, of a licensed investigator. They would take you on and train you in the office and the field. PI's do insurance work, workers' comp and third party injury and public liability, say when someone falls over in a shopping centre.

Or slips on a milk shake getting out of a lift?

Uhm, right. We do intellectual property, you know trade marks and patents, we do arson investigations, defamation, criminal cases, debt collection, process serving and repossessions. We do a lot of commercial work, for companies having stuff knocked off. There is some domestic work, but it is limited because it is of no benefit with no fault divorce. If you suspected your wife of cheating on you and asked me to find out who she was seeing I could discover that she's been fucked by seven different men every week. It would be of no use to you at all. You cannot use it. Most of our divorce work comes when there is a nasty

He clutched the precious briefcase closer. 'Lesbians! Lesbians everywhere!' he muttered. 'Well they won't be getting their filthy claws into <u>this</u> private dick.'

dispute over property or child custody. In those cases you can use that sort of information to some extent.

Missing persons?

Well there's a few things we can check but that is the province of the police and any investigator who tells you they are a specialist in locating people is a con merchant. In NSW a private investigator has no more powers than any private citizen to get access to that sort of information. ICAC found that many PI's were accessing information from government departments. There was nothing illegal in that at all. But now it is practically impossible to get any information. A private investigator can't even find a witness on behalf of a client in a court case. The various government departments who hold such information say that if you have the permission – in writing – to access the details of the person you are looking for then they can tell you where they are! They are all petrified of ICAC. There's thirty-seven solicitors down there, average age twenty-seven years and four months. They've still got nappies on! They don't know what they are doing mate! And what's more it's a homosexual and lesbian enclave.

Really? ICAC?

Oh shit yes!

I thought they were all at the ABC?

Well there's a lot of them there too. But this doesn't come from me you know. This comes from a very senior police officer who worked down there for two years. The problem is further compounded by the fact that 70% of the lawyers at the DPP are homosexuals and lesbians.

Huh?

You betcha! And then you go further than that. You get the Department of Community Services. That has also been overtaken by feminist lesbians. So you see how the whole system has been infiltrated. – *Robert*, the worried detective.

§

any of them stand out like dog's balls, you can expect to be queried – so don't say you have the courage of a lion unless you're prepared to bungee jump from the 17th floor trying to justify the statement.

The last page is also the place to cite any community or volunteer work you may have undertaken. Community service for minor crimes is not something which comes under this category, by the way. But something like being treasurer of a football club, or organising a church youth group, could look interesting to an employer.

Now you should cite at least three referees – disgustingly decent citizens who are prepared to be contacted by a potential employer, and who are willing to lie through their teeth to the poor deluded fool. Doctors, priests, lawyers, teachers, police officers and the like are your best choices. Check with them first, of course ... because you should supply their name, their current position or status, and a contact phone number for each of them.

Finally, if you have any particularly outstanding work references, it may be worth attaching a copy to your CV. The reference from your last significant job (if there was one) should definitely be attached.

SURVIVING THE INTERVIEW

This is your big shot. If you got this far, you're in the running. Don't mess it up.

- **PRESENTATION COUNTS.** Neat and clean goes without saying. Better still, if you're looking at a job without a specific uniform, try to dress just like the people who are already on the inside. If you look the part, it's easier to play the part.
- **ALWAYS CARRY AN UP-TO-DATE CV TO LEAVE WITH THE EMPLOYER, EVEN IF YOU ALREADY SENT ONE WITH THE LETTER.** If the employer says they've still got your first one, fine. Leave it at that.
- **DO YOUR RESEARCH.** Know what the organisation you're trying to work for actually does. Get a handle on what their needs are, and what their output is. If you don't know, and it's a big company, call them beforehand and ask them if they can send you any information. You can score copies of their annual reports from the Australian Securities Commission and do a name search on the newspaper files at the library.
- **GET THE NAME, AND MOST ESPECIALLY, THE PRONUNCIATION OF THE NAME OF YOUR INTERVIEWER ABSOLUTELY RIGHT.** Use it during the interview. Don't try to stuff it into every sentence, and don't be excessively familiar, but be certain to establish the two-way flow of information. Prepare one or two questions about the company to ask the interviewer.

- **BEFORE THE INTERVIEW**. Try to imagine what kinds of questions you may be asked and prepare answers. If you know anyone on the inside already, ask them for details of their own job interview.
- **ARRIVING TEN MINUTES EARLY FOR THE INTERVIEW IS PERFECT.** More than that and you look anxious. Less than that, and you run the risk of worrying your potential employer. *Never* be late.

§

FANTASY JOB #2. BE A STAR.

People say blokes go into rock and roll because they want to get laid and it's true. There's a lot of power involved. There's power when you're up there in your cowboy boots and your leather pants and your tattoos and the audience is going berko at your feet. In your mind there's no way that you are not not getting laid tonight. That's how my brain worked when I was in a band. Frightening thing was, I did get laid. All the time. The one time I didn't, it sent me over the edge for a week.

I met this girl, this absolute traffic-stopping beauty. We were at some industry party and she said, 'Nice tie', and I thought instantly, 'God she wants to fuck!' I knew no fear, uncertainty or doubt. No woman was too daunting. When it then turned out that we didn't sleep together I just couldn't fathom it. I'd got to a point where I expected to get laid a couple of times a week and I couldn't understand how life could possibly be lived otherwise. I'd had a one hundred per cent success rate for years. I thought I knew she wanted me. I thought I'd picked up the signals. I mean, she had said, 'Great tie', hadn't she? So I'd naturally figured, great, let's do it. But it just didn't happen. I remember getting out of the cab at my place and watching it drive away with her inside. I stood there shaking my head in disbelief. I stood there for ages in the dark. I was flabbergasted! It was only one-thirty on a Friday or Saturday night. I went and scored some drugs instead and stayed bent for a week trying to cope with the rejection. – *C*

§

- **BE POLITE AND FRIENDLY TO EVERYONE IN SIGHT, INCLUDING RECEPTIONISTS, TEA-LADIES, AND PLANT-WATERERS.** You never know who may be sleeping with the boss.
- **USE THAT BODY LANGUAGE!** Face the interviewer directly, and hold an open posture – don't hug your arms to yourself, or sit with your legs crossed. Lean slightly forward, and make eye contact with your interviewer. If you think you're up to it, you might try surreptitiously 'mirroring' the posture and gestures of your interviewer. It's an old trick of psychology. By 'feeding back' their output, you work on an unconscious level to convince them that you're a straight-up dude, just like them. Don't be too obvious about it, though. A lot of people have heard of this one by now.

KEEPING A JOB

LOSING A JOB LOOKS BAD on your CV. Even if you were fired for the most unfair of reasons – even if you undertake and win a heavy legal case against your ex-boss for unfair dismissal – it doesn't really help the blot on your record. Never get yourself fired. Quit, if you must, but never let them kick you out. Even if you're only doing the most mundane and menial of work, still you're building on your base of skills, experience, and most importantly, contacts. Getting a reputation as a lazy slob or a serious troublemaker is like an albatross. Employers are suspicious-minded greedy bastards who close ranks against the workers at every possible opportunity.

Don't give them the opportunity. When you get a job, keep it until you don't want it any more. Here's how.
- **DRESS FOR SUCCESS.** You want to look like everyone else in the place, except maybe a bit neater, a bit fresher, a bit more gung-ho. If you stand out at all, you want it to be for the right reasons – not because of your flashing boob tie.
- **NEVER OFFER A FLAT 'NO'.** If you have to refuse a request of any sort from your employers, the word 'no' should be the last part of your sentence. Think of other things to say, such as 'I'm afraid that with my current workload …' or 'With the upcoming deadline so close …', or 'Without a little extra manpower …'. What you're doing is showing them that while you've got the spirit, there are *good reasons* why you can't take on that little extra task. And believe us, you want to have

very good reasons. These bastards will just take take take until you're a shrivelled little peanut of a worker. It's their thing.

- **GO THE EXTRA MILE.** Isn't that a cringe-making cliché? All it means is this: don't give an average performance. Look for the little extra touch you can add. Don't pack up spot on five and head home. Finish what you were doing, even if it takes another fifteen minutes or so. Get in a little early, and make sure your desk has what it needs for your day's work. Read the documentation. Stay abreast of developments in the field. You're not trying to be an eager beaver. What you're doing is becoming the 'go-to' guy – the first person everyone in the office thinks of when they need something done reliably and well, the bloke the customers remember afterwards and ask for when they come back. You could find this will make you happier, as well as the boss.

- **LEARN THE ROPES.** The best way to score the next job up the ladder is to know everything there is about that job before it becomes available. When your supervisor is on holiday, you want to be the person who gets asked to fill the role on a temporary basis. Watch not only the job, but the person doing it. Are they doing it well? If you got the chance to shoot them in the back of the head, would you do it any differently?

---

§

HATE SOMETHING; IT KEEPS YOU YOUNG.

It does not matter much what a man hates provided he hates something.– *Samuel Butler*

§

OFFICE POLITICS

Every organisation has its official hierarchy of control and command. Concealed like a viper inside that hierarchy is the unwritten, but enormously powerful, system of politics. Who likes who. Who doesn't like who. Who can be relied on in a crisis. Who are the brown-nosers. Who does the fucking and who gets fucked.

Office politics is a brutal, ugly, small-minded game played by brutal, ugly, small-minded people in an environment which forces them to stay in close contact for anywhere up to twelve hours a day. You'll never find a job

§

YOU CANNOT FOOL ALL OF THE WOMEN ALL OF THE TIME

I knew these two girls who went out to lunch one day—they both worked for a big company and didn't know each other very well. Over lunch they began discussing their respective boyfriends and the problems of their relationships only to discover that they were going out with the same guy, who worked in the company too. The clincher was that he'd pulled the same spastic first date gift on both of them, a red dress and a card that chimed 'Lady in Red' when you opened it. When they went back to the office in tears, they told the receptionist on the front desk what had happened only to discover that she too was going out with him. The three of them went down to the carpark and repainted his black SAAB with nail polish, lipstick, hair spray and the company's entire supply of white-out. — *Alison*

§

Rebecca and Julie checked off the entries on their Revenge Agenda. Aldo might have thought they had overreacted by Tippexing his SAAB, but he had no idea of what lay in store. 'We'll teach that two-timing rat to cheat on us,' said Rebecca. 'Yes,' agreed Julie. 'Our vengeance will be furious and terrible to behold.'

where you like everyone in the office (unless it's a very small office indeed) but it's important to minimise your chances of being shafted by some greasy back-stabbing piece of filth. That can turn an otherwise reasonable job into an hellishly stressful experience.

• **DON'T MAKE ENEMIES UNNECESSARILY.** Give everyone a fair chance. Don't jump on the bandwagon just because half the office hates the guy in charge of the filing system. Half the office could be wrong. And the guy in charge of the filing system could be your boss this time next week. Polite and friendly behaviour is vital in the high-stress work environment. Treat your fellow workers with the kind of deference you would offer a valued customer – at least until you know them well enough to dispense with the code of politeness and treat them as genuine friends.

• **BROWN-NOSING IS SELF-DESTRUCTIVE.** Unless your boss is a neurotic, insecure basket case, flattery and bum-licking won't get you very far. Your fellow workers will see it for what it is, and you'll become an object of amused contempt. As often as not, your boss will recognise it too. Smart bosses will take advantage of it, and keep you at hand to get the most out of your pathetic eagerness to please – and you won't move up the ladder.

• **SPEAK YOUR MIND WHEN ASKED.** Hold your tongue at all other times. This is a rule to live and die by in the office. The only times to even consider breaking it are (i) when you've had a ground-breaking, revolutionary idea that you want to present, or (ii) when you are absolutely certain that if you don't speak up, disaster will ensue. And if nobody pays attention in either of those two cases, you should seriously consider alternative employment.

• **DON'T ENGAGE IN COVER-UPS.** Organisations run on information. If something isn't running well, don't try to cover it up or shift the blame. If you can't fix the problem yourself, or with the help of your co-workers, state it as clearly and concisely as possible to your boss, and wait for orders. If you choose to cover your arse today, the problems tomorrow will be all the larger.

• **STAY HONEST.** When asked for an opinion on business matters, always, always give it your straightest, most direct response. If a subordinate or an equal doesn't like your opinion, invite them to suggest alternatives, and see what they've got. If your boss doesn't like your opinion, then you can always point out that he or she is in charge, and has the final say.

• **CHOOSE YOUR FRIENDS CAREFULLY.** The funniest, most popular guy in the office may also be a complete screw-up with a serious drug history. Don't be standing next to Mr Birmingham when he crashes and burns.

• **FULFIL YOUR PROMISES.** Once you've agreed to take on a task, do it to completion and beyond. Don't ever offer excuses. If it turns out you've genuinely overcommitted yourself, come clean and explain the situation. The corollary of this is also vitally important: don't ever make promises you can't fulfil.

• **CUT SOME SLACK.** Everybody has off days. If you step up to bat for a colleague who's made an honest error, or simply just can't keep up for a short while due to some kind of personal difficulties, it will be remembered. Not only will your co-workers value and respect your efforts, but sooner or later, word will reach any halfway intelligent manager. Having the trust and respect of your co-workers is one of the very best ways to put yourself in line for promotion.

HE AIN'T HEAVY, HE'S MY MENTOR

'Mentor' became a bit of a buzz-word in career development seminars a few years back. The word means something like 'wise teacher', and the con-

---

§

FACTORY WORKERS USED TO GET RESPECT

Factories vary. You can't really lump them into one bag. When I went to school forty years ago the idea of going on to university just wasn't part of your thinking. The next best thing was an apprenticeship. They were much sought after and when you got one it was a guarantee that you'd be able to command a good wage, buy a house and provide for your family. There was a different perception in those days. The skilled trades have been devalued now. Years ago there was an appreciation that a tradesman was building something worthwhile. A tradesman was held in higher esteem. It was a well-paid job. The unions were more like lodges and craft guilds. The printers didn't call their union a union. They called it a chapel.

The whole fabric of factory life changes depending on the size of the place you're in. The smaller places are just workshops where you ply your trade for eight hours a day. Then you go home. But the first place I worked in when I left school was a mini-city. There were ten thousand worked there. There'd be blokes flogging cigarettes and condoms out of their own shop inside the factory. There were blokes

---

cept is a simple one that's been around for millennia: when you're the snot nose on the block, hook up with someone you can learn from.

Generally, it's not a formal arrangement, although some organisations do try to set up and encourage mentor/protégé relationships. The best mentor arrangements happen by the unspoken agreement of both parties. You're impressed by the way your mentor-to-be handles

who'd cut your hair in lunch time. And SP bookies. They were always around. It was like a town with its own economy and society.

You probably work with a bigger, more diverse group of people in a factory than you would in a lot of jobs. From the tattooed skinheads through to the bible-reading hymn singers. We've got about thirty on the staff at the moment. I suppose half of them would be from different backgrounds. Fijian, Portugese, Australian, Chilean, English, a really good sort of mix. The bigger factories employ a lot of different types. That place I served my apprenticeship, they had quite a few blind people working there as machine operators. They were totally blind. They'd turn up with their seeing-eye dogs. The dogs would be locked up in the pound, the machinists were led to their stations, and away they went for eight hours. They weren't forced to do that. It was their choice. They could have had a pension and sat at home but they knew what they were doing well enough so that they didn't need their eyes. There were a few slips and a bit of blood occasionally but they obviously enjoyed what they were doing.

Those big places take on all sorts. *To page 42 >*

stuff; and he or she sees in you lots of energy and potential and enthusiasm. Some older people simply enjoy encouraging keen young people. Find one of them.

A good mentor is completely priceless. They're your go-to person. They know the ropes. They've got lines of communication to the echelons above you, but they still remember how it was to be working the salt mines. Ninety percent of your problems they dealt with years ago. Remember this: a mentor is someone who got their current position by doing a job like yours very, very well. You can learn an awful lot from somebody like that.

As often as not, if you put your back into it and demonstrate some enthusiasm for getting the job done properly, your mentor will find *you*. They'll be the person who quietly watches you doing some menial job for half an hour, then strolls over and points out the one, simple, magic trick that makes the job a hundred times easier. Then just as likely,

< From page 41 **Not just the blind people but blokes who are probably a few bob short of a quid too. They were always a source of entertainment for the rest of the workers. I remember one guy, they convinced him that if he stood in a bin he could lift himself off the ground by the rim. This was a great source of entertainment. You always knew where this guy was because there was always a crowd of blokes around him, shouting encouragement. The more they shouted the more he'd try, going blue in the face. I don't know if that sort of thing would go on in a shop or office but it was always happening in a big factory. You could pick the blokes when they started, whether they were going to end up bound and gagged and hanging from a crane.**

If you were sixteen now, would you make a different choice?

Probably, yes. Forty years ago the choices, the opportunities just weren't there. Nowadays there's a lot more options. I don't think I'd completely rule out factory work though, throw my hands up and say 'God, I couldn't do that'. It still offers a good career if you're career minded. You don't have to stay on the floor nowadays. You can go to university and rise up through management within the fac-

they'll stroll away again. Your job is to recognise that person, seize that moment.

WHAT YOU ARE LOOKING FOR IN A MENTOR IS:
- **APPROPRIATE SENIORITY.** If they're too far above your current level, they won't be concerned enough with your job to be of any help to you.
- **APPROPRIATE AGE.** Somebody who's grown old in the job one or two rungs above you is not a mentor. They are precisely the opposite. The person you're looking for is someone capable of steadily – if not rapidly – moving up through merit, and taking you with them.
- **APPROPRIATE ATTITUDE.** A mentor's got to want to *be* a mentor. You can't push someone into the position just because you think they're a likely candidate. A good mentor is the one who shepherds and protects his or her protégé because the protégé is useful, valuable and interesting to them. It's a two-way street. Your mentor will gain from having a

---

tory. I suppose the life of a factory worker is no more boring than the life of an office or shop worker. The grass is always greener. If you're a factory worker you imagine that the office workers are having a great time running around in their good gear all day. But we started a labourer a few months back. He'd worked as a shop assistant for ten years after he left school. And he hated it. He loves being a labourer here because it's so different.

There is still a future in factories. It'll just be different. Nearly all the machinery is computer controlled now. So apprentices will need to be skilled in computer work in the future. When I started, the skilled tradesmen made all the decisions, all the movements. Now the job is done on the disk first. You run it through the computer, watch it develop on screen, make sure it's going okay. Then the computer runs the machine. The operator still has to supervise that process. And not every process lends itself to computerised technology. Occasionally you've got to lay your hands on. That is receding though. I suppose that anyone contemplating an apprenticeship in the future would have to be computer literate. – *John Birmingham Snr.*

§

reliable, enthusiastic, competent subordinate. You gain the benefit of knowledge and a certain amount of protection.

- **APPROPRIATE STANDING.** A mentor is someone who gets real respect inside the office. They're a player in the Big Boys Game. There's no point to attaching yourself to someone who doesn't command that kind of respect from others. Attach yourself to a nobody, become nobody yourself.

HOW TO ASK FOR A RAISE

IF YOU'RE WORKING IN THE public sector, the answer to this one is simple. Don't bother. Government wage and salary packages are controlled by strict rules of seniority rather than productivity. If you want more money, you're going to have to do a different, probably more senior, job.

In the private sector, things are different. Private sector organisations work towards achieving a profit. This is the final motivating factor in the activity of all businesses, companies and corporations. That being the case, the private sector has incentive to offer valuable employees inducements to stay on the team. And that means, if you are one of those valuable employees, from time to time it may be worth your while asking for more money.

Be reasonable about it. You need to know what you're worth. Sniff around, and find out what similar positions pay in similar companies to your own. Estimate what your input is worth to your employer. Are you readily replaceable? Or will filling your spot require training somebody into it for six months? Do you bring to your job any unusual personal skills or qualities? Now don't fool yourself on this; if you haven't put in the goods, you aren't going to qualify for the rewards. If the answers do come out in your favour, though – if it genuinely seems to you that you're worth more than you're getting, front up with a straightforward statement. Let the boss know you understand what you're worth to the company, and that you figure you're not getting a reasonable return on your work. The ball's in the boss's court after that. In most cases you shouldn't ask for a raise until you've been in the job at least a year, maybe more.

Obviously, your timing has got to be good. Going for a raise when the company has just shed half its staff and is undergoing a massive audit is going to get you nowhere. The time to ask for a raise is when the profits are coming in, and you've been in the thick of it. Of course, there are those rare moments when you've got them over a barrel – say, when that massive audit is coming down, and you're the only one who knows the whole book-keeping structure. Asking for a raise at a time like that is asking for trouble, though. You may get your raise in the short term, but rest assured, your opportunism will be remembered …

You also need to have yourself well prepared for the task. At the very least, your boss is going to want to know why you, of all people, should get a raise. You need to have the figures and evidence to hand, so that your argument is immediately clear. There's another kind of preparation necessary too. If you know you're worth more than you're getting, and you know the company can afford it, and your request still gets knocked back, there's a problem. Either the company is badly managed – not knowing or not being prepared to acknowledge the worth of its people – or somebody has it in for you. Smile. Say 'Of course. I understand'. Then start looking for another employer.

WHEN TO QUIT

MOST PROSPECTIVE EMPLOYERS LIKE YOU to have been with your previous employer at least two years. This suggests you'll stay with them a while, too.

'Take This Job And Shove It' – okay, so it was a stupid song – but is there anyone out there in the workforce that hasn't longed to use those exact words at some time or another? Take heart, lads – even in this time of desperate economic rationalism, there are still times when a man's gotta do what a man's gotta do. Everybody should quit at least one job in their life, if only to treasure the experience for the remainder of their days. Here's how you tell when to throw in the towel.

- **WHEN YOU GET A BETTER OFFER.** This is the obvious case, and while it may not happen as often as we'd like, you're mad if you don't take the chance. Be careful, though. As always, anything that looks too good to be true probably is. A job isn't just about money. There's job satisfaction, security, work environment, duty statement and loyalty to consider. Unless you're completely jack of your old job, it's a good idea to give them a chance to make a counter-offer. Who knows? You may have underestimated your value to your current employer.

- **WHEN THE SHIP IS SINKING, JOIN THE RATS.** If you can see that your current employer is definitely going under, for whatever reason, it's time to ask politely for a reference and get while the getting is good. This is a pretty ruthless and opportunistic view of things – but it assumes that you're not the man in charge. Only captains have to go down with the ship. If you ease yourself out of your job with a decent reference and severance pay before the whole organisation folds, you'll be in a much better position than everyone else to find your next pay-cheque.

- **BEFORE THAT NERVOUS BREAKDOWN HAPPENS.** Your job is *not* your life. Don't let anyone tell you otherwise. If you know for certain you're reaching the end of your tether, take a walk before something snaps. Granted, we all get overloaded from time to time. Likewise, a good long holiday may refresh and re-fire you. Assuming you've considered these things, if you can still feel the icy touch of dread every time you contemplate returning to your job, the writing is on the wall. Explain the matter to your boss, ask for a reference, and hit the road. You're doing the employer a favour too; there's nothing worse than an employee who cracks up on the job.

- **WHEN PERSONAL ETHICS WON'T BE COMPROMISED.** You're a bank flunky. The boss sends you round to foreclose on an orphanage. Can you live with yourself afterwards? Go and read *x*, and contemplate the prospect of a life without any form of self-respect or integrity.

- **WHEN THE BRASS RING ROLLS AROUND.** If you have ambitions and ideas of your own, one day you're going to have to either put up or shut up. The workforce is full to bursting with sad, decaying would-be entrepreneurs, artists, writers, inventors, travellers and leaders. The only real difference between these pathetic wannabes and the genuine article is that at some stage, the true performers made the decision to back themselves, and went after the dream for all they were worth. If it's in you – if the strength and desire and ambition is there – then one day, when the books are fairly well balanced and you haven't bogged yourself down with debts and responsibilities, you're going to have to go for it. Even if you don't ultimately turn into a big success, even if you eventually return, a chastened, wiser man to the ranks of the proles, you'll have to give it a try. If you don't, we guarantee you'll regret it all your living days.

WHEN NOT TO QUIT

§

SEIZE THE DAY

You can't wait for somebody to do something for you. You've got to decide what's important for you. Get your order of priorities sorted out and go live your life. Otherwise you'll sit back and it will pass you by.

You'll need a bit of curiosity and initiative. You must travel widely in your own country and then the world. People are wonderful everywhere. You must meet people and listen to them and enjoy their company. – *Roger Woodward*

§

• **YOU HAD A FIGHT WITH THE BOSS.** If it was bad enough, the boss will fire you. If not, you've still got a job, and things may yet improve. Never quit in the heat of the moment. It should always be a considered decision.

• **YOUR JOB IS GOING NOWHERE.** It's stupid to quit one job just to go looking for another. Look for another position while you're still in your old one. Then, when you've got a better offer in hand ...

• **YOU'RE NOT BEING PAID ENOUGH.** At least it's a pay-cheque, right? Again, go looking for a new job while you've still got the income from the current one.

• **YOUR FRIENDS TELL YOU YOU'RE TOO GOOD FOR THE JOB.** What the hell would they know about it anyway?

• **THINGS ARE TOUGH AT HOME.** If they're tough there now, chances are they'll get a lot worse with you unemployed. If you really must, take some time off, or try to negotiate a part-time work arrangement.

---

§

FANTASY JOB #3: WHAT WOMEN WANT IN A MALE STRIPPER.

They want a good body, good looks and an outgoing personality. They don't really care about dancing ability. Some ask for short hair, some for long. But the two main questions are always do they look good, do they have a great bod. The guys themselves come from different backgrounds. They're there for the dollar. The younger studs might be there for a bit of fame and glory but us older blokes, we want the cash.

Anybody who thinks they could be a male stripper should understand that women are a lot wilder than men in strip shows. Men tend to be a little bit reserved. Maybe because they don't tend to let themselves go under any circumstances, but more particularly because there's always a lot of heavy security at their shows. Quite frankly we wouldn't want men behaving as badly as women. They're bigger and stronger and things could get out of hand. I think the guys themselves know that. They know the potential for disaster when a lot of them get together in a confined space with alcohol and naked women. So they will sit quietly and maybe talk about it later over a few beers. The women, on the other hand get very excited. They go wild, jumping around, screaming and yelling obscenities. The male strippers love it. The more the women lose control the more energy the guys will put into their show. They like to be liked. My opinion about this is that until recently women have had their sexuality repressed and inhibited by society. They have only just started to unleash and express their sexual selves as our values change. – *Steve Darcy*, Frisky Business.

§

CHAPTER THREE

Women, Sex, And All That Stuff.

PECS VS PERSONALITY: WHAT WOMEN LIKE ABOUT MEN.

- **SELF-CONFIDENCE.** One thing is clear. The most attractive thing any man can possess is self-confidence. Not a swaggering, hairy-chested, king-o'-the-world machismo, nor smug, preening narcissism, but a genuine sense of self-worth – a bloke's belief in himself, that he is *basically* interesting and worthwhile.

Being physically well-built (this doesn't mean the same thing as 'well-hung') is certainly no handicap. But personality and confidence are capable of transcending the physical. When we asked relatively sane and normal women to identify 'sexy' public figures, some of the damnedest results kept coming up – Robbie Coltrane was a big fat spunk. Jean Claude Van Damme was a big fat joke.

- **A SENSE OF HUMOUR.** A couple of other mental and emotional characteristics score well in excess of any physical gifts. Being able to make women laugh – without seeming to work at it, mind you – rates very highly with them. Wit, charm and intelligence will get you a lot further than being hung like a horse.

- **INTEREST.** Somewhat more subtly, a man's attitude to women will play a large role in whether he gets to make out like a bandit or spend most Saturday nights beating off to thoughts of Xena and Gabriel. Gentlemen, we know of no way to put this gently: if you don't know how to simply *like* women, you're in deep, deep trouble. You need to enjoy their company. Pay attention to them when they're talking. Appreciate their sense of humour. Enjoy their stories. Give them their half of the conversation. Be interested in their opinions and their experiences. Share the remote.

- **LEARN TO LOOK PAST THE TITS.** This last one is really important. Women are just not impressed by men who talk to their breasts. If you can't stop staring at her tits, at least pretend you have a congenital deformation of the neck or something. And get used to the fact that it's going to be you and Xena and a packet of Kleenex again this weekend.

BITS OF MEN THAT WOMEN LIKE

- **YOUR NUMBER ONE SEXY FEATURE IS YOUR EYES.** Unfortunately, women aren't too specific on what exactly it is about the eyes that does it for them.They just have this vague idea that eyes are really sexy, and that they can 'read' a man from them. Which takes us back to self-confidence.

- **NUMBER TWO IS ARSES.** A nice, tight, well-rounded arse is definitely an advantage! We're sorry, but gratuitous objectification cuts both ways.

- **NUMBER THREE, AS OFTEN AS NOT, APPEARS TO BE HANDS.** You can do *a lot more* to pleasure a woman with your hands than you can with your dick. If you're in the habit of regular exercise think about throwing twenty or thirty finger push-ups into your routine to add to your digital strength. Keep your finger nails clean and well trimmed. When you use those hands on a babe be strong and yet sensitive to her reactions. We're telling you, you'll have them on all fours baying at the moon in no time.

- **A LOT OF WOMEN LIKE HARD, FLAT STOMACHS.** But strangely enough a lot more confess to being attracted by a small pot belly. Go figure. None seem to mention rippling pecs or monster biceps as a turn-on. And mention of an elephant dick produces reactions ranging from puzzled stares through rueful smiles to outright laughter. Let's put this one to rest as permanently as we can. Chaps, a really big dick can be a handicap. It can hurt a woman. Really, really tiny tadgers (down at the 6cm fully erect mark and below) do represent a minor disappointment, but remember that lesbians don't even have that and they never seem to go short of pussy.

- **TWO MORE THINGS ARE PROBABLY WORTH MENTIONING** Tone of voice, and overall grooming. Keep yourself relatively neat and tidy – or at least, rakishly unkempt – and cultivate a decent speaking voice. They don't rank particularly high on the list, but if you're a short, scrawny, deeply uninteresting guy with bad acne, crossed eyes and a micro-penis you can at least work on those.

HOW TO PICK WOMEN UP

Actually, Modern Man doesn't 'pick women up'. He *meets* them. If a constant stream of casual bonkings suits you, work out how to do it for yourself. There are perfectly good places to go to meet women who feel the same – crowded pubs and nightclubs spring to mind. Nightclubs are probably the better of the two: if you like the way she looks, and you think she might be on for a night of lubricious athletics, why not just try dancing with her?

CONFIDENCE IS HALF THE BATTLE

I have a friend with two strangely contradictory reputations. First is as a guy with a very small dick. A teeny weeny peenie. Second is as a guy who scores with the babes. He not only admits to both, he boasts about it. Reckons he can have any woman he chooses. He just won't shut up about it. So I put him to the test. We're out at this pub and he's crapping on as usual and I finally just point at this frighteningly pretty woman and say, 'Right, ten minutes, go for it'. They leave together about twenty minutes later. I can't believe it. I've got to know what happens. He tells me the next day. He buys her dinner, takes her dancing, gets her home and they work themselves into a frenzy on the shag pile. He's taken her dress off and then he's stripped naked himself. That's when she sits bolt upright, points at his micro dick and says, 'Who the fuck do you think you're going to satisfy with that?' And it doesn't faze him at all, he looks back at her, grins and says, 'Me'. – *Magyver*

Don't make it complicated. Nothing is more obvious and embarrassing than a pickup line – unless you're clever enough to deliver a clichéd pickup line and make it look like a joke. Just ask her onto the floor, and be prepared to smile and move on if she refuses. Make eye contact on the dance floor, put your heart (and your hips) into your dancing, try her out on a little casual physical contact (try dancing with your hands on her hips or shoulders) and see if you can't read the signals. Hell, she knows what you're there for as clearly as you do. If she's interested, cool. If she's not, she'll wind up dancing with someone else, or disappearing at the first opportunity.

Meeting women is a much more subtle and elegant art than picking them up. In the 'pickup', at a nightclub or wherever, you may select and discard or be rebuffed by more than a dozen women in short order. It has all the style and dignity of … well, drunkenly hitting on every woman you meet until you find one desperate or stupid enough to have sex with a loser like you.

Meeting women, however, requires the ability to deal with women as people. You have to listen, and respond, and genuinely get to know the person before you even consider moving to the next stage – and by then, you should know intuitively whether or not you want to move on. If you've got any instinct at all, you should also know whether or not *she* wants to move on.

WHERE TO MEET WOMEN

- **AT WORK OR THROUGH WORK.** This is the biggie, isn't it? It's easy. The two of you are already trapped in the same building. With only the slightest amount of effort, you can arrange to have lunch with her, bitch about the same things, or go to after-work drinks with the other drones down at the local. Meeting women at work is about as tricky as getting shot in Beirut.
- **AT UNIVERSITY.** Just a little trickier than 'at work'. On the plus side, the place is a hotbed of sex. Anybody who isn't getting some usually figures that they ought to be – and that includes the women. On the minus side, university is the place where a lot of young women are first exposed to academic feminism. Avoid anyone majoring in 'Wymyn's Studies' or 'Marxist Philosophy' until they've come back to Planet Earth.
- **ON PUBLIC TRANSPORT.** Quite tricky. Can be done in one of two ways. There's the repeat approach, whereby the two of you take the same bus, train or ferry day in, day out. At first, you ignore each other. Eventually, you smile and nod. Maybe say a terse, 'Good morning.' Gradually, you

§

SPECIAL PEOPLE NEED LOVE TOO

My cousin went to Melbourne on some road trip with two or three mates. They all went out to the pub together but his mates took off home an hour or two before him. They were sleeping downstairs in the lounge room when they were awoken by this really weird clomping and banging around upstairs. Like he was moving furniture or playing hockey. It would get faster and kind of irregular and they'd yell at him to shut up. It'd calm down for a bit then get worse again. It finally died away. They could not for the life of them figure out what he was doing. All was explained the next morning when the girl he had snuck into the house for the evening turned up to breakfast on her wooden leg. – *Scot*

§

progress to neutral subjects like the weather, and the weekend news. From there, it's just a matter of turning it into a real conversation, wherein you can actually have an opinion, and wield that famous charm and wit. Sometimes it works. Sometimes it's known as stalking.

More difficult is the 'bolt from the blue' approach. This technique is necessary if one of the two of you isn't a regular commuter. If she's in conversation with someone else, see if you can't find something useful to add at a clever moment – a quote, or a joke. Smile. Be the Bored Commuter Seeking Entertainment. If she's not in conversation, you might try the wide-eyed Lost Traveller approach: 'Excuse me, but could you tell me the best stop for the Arthouse Movie Theatre? I'm afraid I don't know this bus service very well.' The thing is, you're going to look as obvious as Hell. If she's not interested pull out and leave the poor woman alone, you groper.

- **AT THE LIBRARY.** Advantage: you might get a good conversation as well as a good fuck. Disadvantage: she's probably too smart to fall for your bullshit. Watch carefully to see what books she's carrying or studying. Then approach her and ask whether or not she intends to borrow the book, as you were just looking for it a moment ago. If she doesn't scream for a security guard try asking whether she's read anything else by the author, or whether she can recommend something else on the same topic … maybe you can discuss it over a cup of coffee? Put this last question with your most disgracefully boyish grin. Almost any sort of bad behaviour can be excused by a boyish grin.
- **AT THE SHOPPING MALL.** Definitely not an easy one. However, you might make the hapless male approach. Women are suckers for hapless males in search of advice and guidance. Perhaps because we so rarely ask for it when we so often need it.

GETTING PAST THE FIRST FIVE MINUTES

This is not easy. Much depends on the mood of the woman you've just fronted. If she's busy, in a hurry, or just plain uninterested, you're going to get nowhere. If the conversation curls up and dies in the first sixty seconds or so, just smile and say, 'Nice meeting you.' Then leave.

Look for signs of feedback from her. Eye contact is good. Smiles are excellent. Outright laughter – with you, not at you – is even better still, definitely something to aim for. If she gently touches her hair or face during the conversation, that too is good. Arms folded is neutral, but a little defensive – don't give up, but don't make any sudden moves, either. Hands on hips are definitely not good. Hips tilted towards you is good, likewise if she points her feet towards you, or leans in during conversation or rubs her pubic mound against your leg.

Obviously, if these signs are there to be read in her, you should be able to 'broadcast' something in reply. And of course, pretty much the same things go – tilt of the hips, touching the hair or face, feet pointed towards her, and all the rest. A much easier and sneakier tactic to use is 'mirroring'. Psychologists have long known that feeding back someone else's posture and body language to them is a sign of respect and interest. Try not to make it too obvious, but see if you can't copy the way she sits, the way she holds herself, the way she lifts her drink, and any other mannerisms you can identify.

Another excellent idea is to take advantage of the lighting. Don't stand with a bright light in your eyes. Dilated pupils are one of the strongest subconscious signs of arousal and interest, and equally subconsciously, both males and females respond to the pupils of others. If you can arrange to meet in dim light, so much the better: your big, black pupils will make it look as though you find her the most fascinating thing on the planet.

Women and men both find it encouraging and rewarding if the person whom they are with focuses in upon them. So don't be shy – focus solely on her and what she is saying. Stop thinking about the time, how much this is all costing you, and when your parking fee runs out. Lean towards her and make plenty of eye contact. Don't interrupt what she is telling you, but do make appropriate noises of interest at the right times. If you've got a killer joke to tell, wait until she pauses or runs out of breath, and make sure it's relevant to the topic she was just discussing. Really, we can't stress this one enough: WOMEN WANT YOU TO BE INTERESTED IN THEM.

THE ART OF CONVERSATION

Dancing is nice. Shared interests are great. The thing that will engage a woman most, though, is conversation. Not telling stories. Not amusing a crowd. Not whooping it up with a bunch of beer buddies, but *conversing*. Your rat cunning will get you that initial meeting. Your confidence and charm will tide you over the difficulties of the first five minutes or so, but if you want her to find you interesting you'll need to be able to *talk* with her.

Here we come back to that business of liking women. Personally, we like women a lot. On the whole, they're better to talk things over with than men. They have interesting opinions and oddly-skewed views which make for long and fascinating chats. Plus they smell good and they feel nice, all soft and squishy, but that's not the point, is it? See, when you like women, you can spend a long time in their company and not get bored. Also, you can maintain a conversation without drifting off and wondering what they'd look like bouncing around on the end of your love pump.

§

How to Pick Up Women

1. The first rule is, wherever you are, smile. Not like a geek. Make eye contact. Then, in no particular order, do the following.
2. Remember that conversation comes before sex. It's not, as most men believe, the other way around.
3. At first, leave some space between you. Don't fence her in or intimidate her physically.
4. Talk about her. Don't talk about your mates or your mother. You can mention ex-girlfriends or wives but only briefly, to show that you are capable of having a relationship.
5. Never say you've never had a girlfriend.
6. When she's talking, don't interrupt. Be a good listener.
7. Tease her about her obvious strengths. Don't make her feel self-conscious about any weaknesses. No thigh jokes.
8. Touch her lightly (more seductive than being grabbed or gripped).
9. Be considerate and kind. Remember, women are subconsciously thinking about the long-term. If you get this part right, it won't matter if you don't have a cent in the bank.
10. If you ask her on a date, don't be vague; have a specific plan.

Size does matter, sort of. Well-below average is definitely a cause of mirth. Sorry. – *Kathy Bail*, editor of *HQ*.

§

The most important thing about being a good talker is being a good listener. If you just make the right noises at the right times and keep up the appearance of interest, most people won't notice if you let them run off at the mouth for hours at a time without yourself adding a word. It's called 'positive listening': nod, or say 'yes', when she seems to want confirmation. Ask leading questions: things like 'What's your opinion of ...' or 'What did you do about ...'. Find out early what version of her name she prefers – full-length, shortened, nickname or whatever – and be careful to use that version to other people in her presence. Always, always keep track of the matter under discussion, even if it's as boring as batshit. If you do lose track, don't say something like: 'Sorry, I missed that.' Try something more subtle – ask a clarifying question about the last point in the conversation you can actually recall. Worst comes to worst, ask for a pause to get a drink, or go to the toilet, and see if you can't get her to recap when you get back.

Initially, you should keep your own input limited. Anecdotes and observations should be short and to the point. Keep an eye out for signs of boredom, and bring the conversation back around to her if they occur. Remember she may be interested in you, but like all human beings, she's much more fascinated by herself. If she's got a hard-on for something about which you know little or nothing, don't try to fake it. Ask her to explain it to you. You may learn something in the process, and you'll make her feel good. If she's talking about something you know more about, don't seize the opportunity to show off. Never contradict her outright. If you must be a fucking know-it-all let her defend her opinions, and *gently* unfold your own knowledge of the subject. Unlike men, women do not use conversation as a sort of sublimated unarmed combat. (Mr Flinthart begs to differ with Mr Birmingham about this last, and has some very impressive ego bruises with which to back up his case.)

GETTING HER INTO THE BEDROOM

'So, what about a root?' If you've ever said that, or anything like that, with a straight face, put this book down and go back to your cave. It's not going to do you any good. Granted, these days a lot of women (Praise be to Allah!) are taking the initiative and expressing their desires directly. Even so, there are many who want to be gently nudged, cuddled and teased into the bedroom. And even the most self-assured and personally empowered of modern women is likely to baulk, however briefly, at a blunt and ugly carnal proposition. But if you're short on time and you're absolutely determined to give it a try, at the very least – pitch it with a sense of humour, will you? You're giving the rest of us a bad name.

Despite the crassness of the blunt approach, it's necessary

to make this clear: the old system of 'dating' a woman was nothing more than a politely managed system of mutual face-saving. Making formal arrangements for dinner, or a film is just as good as saying 'I think I want to screw you,' except that it's more polite and expensive. Far, far better to get to know the woman first than to plunge straight into the quagmire of dating. Don't get too personal too fast. Arrange a few jaunts with mutual friends. See if you can't manage to get invited to a party with her. Let her get used to your presence before you drop your pants and swing from the light fittings.

A subtle way of escalating things is with gifts. Again, don't start out with stuffed animals, chocolates, flowers or jewellery. You might as well walk up and say, 'Hello, I am a prat'. Does she like to cook? Pick up a new and interesting spice or herb. Tell her you saw it at the local markets and thought of her. It's no big deal. You're just being thoughtful. (This is untrue of course. Getting into her pants is a big fucking deal indeed. But it's the *effect* you want to create.) Is she big on reading? Try to find a second-hand copy of one of her favourite authors – or give her a well-thumbed copy of one of yours. Keep your initial gifts small, simple, and not too frequent. It's less suspicious if you're in the habit of doing the same sort of things with your other friends, too.

Before getting into the dating scene, look for seemingly innocent ways of spending time with her on her own. Is she going to the corner shop? Don't let the conversation die away; mention casually that you need something, get up and go for a walk with her. Does she work alongside you? Maybe you can give her a lift one day. Going to a party at her house? Get there a little early (not *too* early) and offer to help with the preparations. Don't be pathetic and needy about it. Just helpful. Again, all you're doing is getting her used to your presence.

If you work slowly and gently in this fashion, and avoid looking like the desperate no-hoper you actually are, there's a good chance she'll begin to help you out – if she's interested. Keep an eye out for unexpected invitations, over-lengthy telephone calls from her, or a tendency for her to send her flatmate out for cigarettes when you come visiting. Once you start getting positive feedback – once she starts letting you know that she likes having you around, then you might try something more formal and 'serious'.

When you've cultivated the right degree of intimacy you can start playing the romance angle. And 'romance' is the key word. Again, restaurants, chocolates and flowers may be functional – even expected – but if you can demonstrate a bit of flair, if you can surprise her even once with your poetic streak, it'll work wonders. Know any good rooftops? Pack a picnic basket, a couple of bottles of good wine, and hold your very own inner-city rooftop sunrise picnic. Or sunset. Or moonrise. Check out the section in this book on 'cooking for sex'; you could do a lot worse than to prepare her a meal with your own hands.

Summer proving to be long and hot? Meet her late at night with a fresh rose. Pack a couple of towels in the boot, and head to any beach you know that will be deserted by midnight. Even if you don't manage to convince her that a nude midnight swim is the height of romance, a long walk on a cool, starlit beach will help your cause immensely.

YES, BUT WHEN DO WE GET TO THE BONKING?

Patience, grasshopper. Making love with a woman is not dissimilar to getting a social worker to change a lightbulb: first, the lightbulb's got to *want* to change.

To be honest, modern women are much more clued into sex than you

§

SELF-CONTROL IS THE KEY

Normally bucks parties are for everyone but the groom. It's like they're showing him what he's leaving behind, and most guys are probably happy enough to see the last of that bullshit. That's why most grooms look like they're being tortured on their bucks night. They can't wait for it to be over. But this guy I know really got into it. The stripper came out and tied him to a chair with her fishnets, did the thing with the carrot and the ping pong balls, we all cheered, and she figured that's it. She can collect her hundred dollars now. But this guy's not finished, not by a long shot. He went berko trying to get to her. He's still tied up in the chair but he starts sort of shuffle-hopping and chasing her around the nightclub. He just would not leave her alone. Bang bang bang around the club until the bouncers finally had to come and throw him out, chair and all. They just couldn't risk untying him. – Sam

§

might imagine. As ever, the trick is simply to listen to what she's telling you. If you start getting lots of little sideways glances and stray body contact, put on a clean pair of underpants at once. Conversations with vague double meanings should light up your radar. Likewise, invitations to visit wherein you discover her flatmates have mysteriously vanished for the evening. If you suspect you're getting the green light, wait for one of those carefully planned moments of spontaneous romance, and see how she responds to a kiss.

Kissing is a damned good way of opening the proceedings, actually. In fact, we don't know of any better. Don't immediately try to establish base camp on her tonsils with your tongue – kissing is definitely a creative, expressive art. Nibble things – earlobes are good. So are throats and collarbones … yum! Soft, fluttery kisses on the eyelids work nicely, too. Gently bite her lower lip. Kiss the palm of her hand, and bite softly into the muscle at the base of her thumb.

If you've made it this far, chances are that you're well on your way to big night in. However, there's an important point to make – and much as we don't want to come on like some Neo-Brutalist bull-dyke, we have to say: 'No Means No'.

Interestingly enough, most women won't agree completely with that statement. Apparently, there are times in most every woman's life when she wants you to demonstrate just how much you want her, when you are supposed to ardently, gently pursue and woo, when the whispers of 'no' are likely to give way under your burning kisses to a throaty 'oohh …'

Well, tough luck. It's a great idea – but its day has passed. If she expresses any reservations about the matter, tuck your johnson into your boxers and think of Bronwyn Bishop. To any women who may be reading this: welcome to the post-Feminist world. If you want that night of passion, be prepared to ensure that your chosen partner knows exactly what you've got in mind.

Of course, if she does seem reluctant, the thing to do is not instantly to straighten your clothing, look at your watch, and say: 'My, look at the time! Must be going. Thanks for a lovely evening'. You may not have made the grade this time, but acting as though the sole goal of your efforts lay in getting her underpants to half-mast is the best way to ensure you won't get another chance. Keep up the nibbling, kissing, caressing and cuddling. At the very least, it's fun. It also shows that you're interested, that you're prepared for the long haul, and that you're not utterly single-minded. At best, she might even decide to change her own mind on the matter.

Back-rubs and foot-rubs are another commonplace and effective way of getting into a hands-on situation. As Vincent Vega rightly observed, there's a certain communication involved here. It's not sex, sure, but you won't be offering a foot-rub to your mates on the cricket team any time soon will you? Go with the flow. Create an intimate, physical situation, and see what arises.

Anyhow, the point of all this kissing and cuddling – aside from the fact that it's fun – is that it's a mood establisher. Women, unlike men, don't just click into sex-mode with a snap of their trouser-pleats. A whole bunch of things need to be working in unison, all of which add up to the 'right moment'. If you've decided the relationship looks ripe for a physical encounter, you need to pay considerable attention to ensuring sufficient time, space, and privacy are readily available. Sure, you may have encountered a female fire-cracker who is slavering to knock knees in a stalled elevator – but most women, for that first occasion at least, rather appreciate the idea of being the absolute centre of your attention. And that means no worries about audiences, discoveries, schedules, appointments, cramped conditions, sand, burrs, or anything else.

THE DEED!

So, okay – you've set up a nice back-rub in a quiet bedroom. Tenderly, carefully, with appropriate words and sounds of appreciation, you've assisted her in the removal of her clothing – and your own has found its way to the floor. Surreptitiously, you've taken the phone off the hook. Your flatmates are under instruction not to be back until tomorrow. The lights are down, the music and the massage oil have done their work. Thunderbirds are go!

'I don't believe it!'

Go where?

Well, the first thing to know is that practically the entire body is an erogenous zone if licked, nibbled and tickled appropriately. The next thing to consider, however, is this joke: what's the difference between a set of car keys, and a clitoris?

Apparently, most men can find the car keys if they look long enough.

Let us not name names, nor point fingers. Let's just flatly admit that most of us, when we're getting started, not only know very little about what a clitoris does or where it hangs out. Therefore, take note of the drawing which accompanies this page. See that thing marked 'clitoris'? You really, really need to know where it is and what it does.

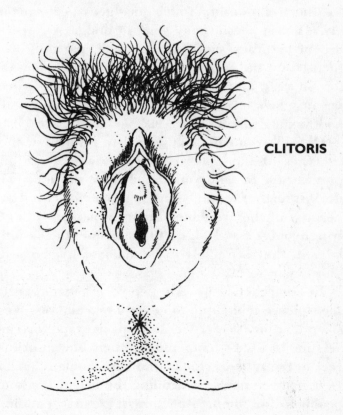

CLITORIS

The clitoris is a relatively small organ, composed of highly sensitive erectile tissue (not dissimilar to a small penis in that sense) usually protected by a hood of delicate skin. When a woman is sufficiently aroused, the clitoris hardens and fills with blood, and will usually partially emerge from the hood. It is an extremely sensitive organ, and is pretty much central to the process of orgasm in women. Get to know it well ...

§

How to deal with premature ejaculation

At least ninety percent of premature ejaculation problems relate to emotional and psychological difficulties. Even when that's recognised it's just not going to go away and therefore there's a need to seek professional help. PE is often related to unfinished business from past relationships. It could be because of stress and conflict in the existing relationship which produces performance anxiety. Then a person may start to dodge sex because they are afraid they can't please their partner. PE can be focused on the fact that the guy wants to please his partner so very much and therefore he tries too hard. And because he's trying so hard there is a build-up of tension and anxiety which causes PE.

Old folk remedies like trying to remember the batting averages of the Australian test cricket team and other ploys to try to take your mind off it do not help a great deal. It might for some but for the majority it won't. Also, because of the avoidance factor, a person with PE is likely to avoid sex and so, on the infrequent occasion they do have it, they are likely to be abnormally aroused leading once again to PE.

In our practice we give people practical exercises like the squeeze technique to control ejaculation. We also use sleep learning tapes. We do a special tape for each client relating to what's happening in their life, in order to correct in the subconscious mind this problem leading to PE. PE is just the penis controlling the brain. It's long been a problem for men. But honest sexual communication between partners can really help. Remember that PE is 'our' problem not 'his' problem. – *Graham Ascough*, Secretary of the Australian Sexual Therapists and Researchers Association.

§

Your first move is *not* for her clitoris, though. For starters, you'll probably scare the bejeezus out of her if you plunge straight for that delicate spot. More importantly, until they're properly and fully aroused, most women aren't fond of direct stimulation. In other words, sorry pard', but you got a little more moseying around the ol' foreplay corral before you get to climb aboard this wild filly.

There's a time and a place for the fast and furious fuck. Sometimes, everybody likes a little quick, jungle sex – but when you're establishing a *relationship*, that first impression is the one that counts. Don't just take your time; take *her* time. It's a lot more important. On the whole, women take a lot longer to come to the boil than men, so before you move to the intense stuff, use everything you've got to make sure she's every bit as interested and excited as you are.

Explore. Nibble things. Ears, eyelids, lips, toes, fingers – it's all good stuff. Gentle raking of fingernails along the sides of her body, over her ribs and across her belly will often bring expressions of appreciation (or squeals of laughter, in which case, knock it off). Long, slow, sucking kisses to the small of the back – at the top of the cleft of her buttocks – work well. Slow stroking of inner thighs is nice. Hands are very sensitive; try passionately kissing her palms. Be gentle with her breasts. They're not sporting implements. Caress them smoothly, and brush your lips lightly across those nipples. When they stiffen up, gently caress them circularwise with the palm of a cupped hand. Lick them. Flutter your tongue over them. Suckle them gently. Nibble lightly. See if you can't make eye-contact with her while you're doing it. Even at this point it's better not to just stare at her tits muttering, 'Wow! Goddamn! I mean really!'

Run your fingers through her hair, over her scalp. Don't pluck at individual strands – but gently gather and releas handfuls. Kiss her some more – long, slow, passionate kisses. Stroke her belly. Lightly trail your fingers over her mons veneris. Gently rake your nails over her inner thighs. Cup her sex in the palm of your hand, and delicately, lightly, ever-so-slightly part her labia with your fingertips.

What you're working to produce is excitement, which should show itself as any of a number of physical signs, which in turn tell you when to proceed further. Ragged breathing, closed eyes, gasps, and movements of her pelvis against you or your hand are all excellent indicators. Likewise, the presence of abundant, slick moisture in the genital area. (It's natural lubricant, which makes penetration pleasurable as well as possible, stupid.) If you're getting a lot of these kinds of things, *now* you might consider gently working your way to her clitoris.

Again, don't just seize the poor thing and begin frotting. You might start by gently rubbing the whole genital region with your cupped hand. Lightly tickle the labia. Delicately, carefully circle the clitoris with your fingertips. Use a little saliva if there isn't yet sufficient moisture to make the skin slick in that area. Watch her closely as you stimulate the clitoris and clitoral hood; this is a very sensitive organ, and you should be prepared to lighten your touch and backpedal, or change direction and focus at a moment's notice.

Right about now, you should be giving serious consideration to the fine art of cunnilingus. It is a sad truth, my friends, that according to the Hite Report among others, only 30–40% of women are capable of achieving orgasm through simple intercourse. When you consider that only a tiny fraction of women are in fact clinically frigid – incapable of reaching orgasm – this should tell you a great deal about how to proceed with your love-making.

Blunt language time: everybody likes a blow-job, right? Women too. And just as for men, it's a lot more fun if the partner seems to enjoy being part of the process. Dining at the 'Y' is without doubt the most widely-practised and reliable method of helping a woman reach an orgasm. There's no point in backing away from it, in being squeamish or visibly reluctant. Pussy is like your veggies. If you plan to live a long and rich life you're going to be eating plenty of it. Not only do you need to go down there, but you need to do it with verve, gusto and every sign of enjoyment. If you're really worried about sexual scents and tastes, arrange for a nice erotic shower or bath beforehand. Then get stuck in. Your sex life will be far the better for it, we guarantee you.

Enthusiasm is probably the most desirable feature in a practitioner of cunnilingus. Women often take far longer than men, even under this most direct form of stimulus, to get off. You should be prepared for a stint of ten, fifteen, twenty minutes – even half an hour or more. Hell, if she's enjoying it, and you are as well, there's no very good reason to stop, is there?

Technique is important, though. If you've got any good lesso friends, get

> §
>
> I REGRET TO SAY THAT we of the FBI are power-less to act in cases of oral-genital intimacy, unless it has in some way obstructed interstate commerce. – *J Edgar Hoover*
>
> §

drunk with them and ask for a few pointers. Those babes know what they're doing. Appeal to their public spirit.

Failing that, though, things come back once more to the clitoris. Again, don't start in on the poor thing straight off. Nibble, lick, and explore your way around the region. Circle the clitoris with your tongue. Use the broad surface of your tongue to caress from bottom to top of the vulva. Use the very tip to probe and tickle the clitoris itself. Settle into a steady, firm lapping motion only when your partner seems comfortable with the sensation. Seal your lips around the clitoris and hood, and suck gently, teasing the clitoris with your tongue as it emerges. Let it go. Blow *gently* on the area. Don't inflate her like a balloon. Don't try and jam your whole head up there. You're not bobbing for apples you know. Nibble and lick some more, and start all over again.

Don't neglect your hands in the meantime. You can caress thighs, hips and buttocks – even reach up for a nipple if you've got appropriately long arms. Sliding a gentle finger or two into her vagina works well for some women. Trace out the alphabet with the tip of your tongue, and make note of her favourite letters. Eventually, you should detect an overall increase in her total body tensions. She may grab your head with her hands, or squeeze tightly with her thighs, or begin to thrust against your face with her hips. Her breathing may become ragged, or she may begin to moan. Whatever; you'll get to know the signs. At this point, you should continue what you're doing, gently intensifying the stimulation until she enters orgasm – usually, but not always, characterised by vaginal spasms, gasping, and a certain loss of co-ordination. (Frequently, there is also a strong blush to the upper body, between breasts and collarbone. However, what with ambient light-levels and general distraction, this can be quite hard to spot.) For a very intense orgasm, repeatedly suck as much of her flesh into your mouth as hard and as fast as you can.

Let her finish what she's doing before you stop altogether – but you'll certainly want to throttle back a touch as she starts to come down. The clitoris becomes mighty sensitive immediately after a good orgasm, and even in women who are routinely multi-orgasmic, there's usually at least a short period where they like the level of direct clitoral stimulus to be reduced and altered. Still, while you're down there ... studies indicate that with time and practice, most women are capable of popping off several times in relatively quick succession. Give her a few moments to catch her breath, while maintaining light but definite contact with her genitals, then see whether or not she's amenable to a return of light, delicate tonguework. If she doesn't twitch away, or otherwise complain of sensitivity, you might just see if you can't work her up all over again. If she's a talkative gal you'll soon start getting some *very* admiring looks from her girlfriends.

Penetration proper – penis in vagina – can be achieved in lots of different positions. Take care with the initial entry. Be slow and gentle until you're certain she's properly lubricated and ready to go. The actual position you take depends on the preferences of the pair of you. They all work pretty well, though some have advantages over others. Feel free to suggest experimentation – but be prepared to back off if it doesn't work out very well. Don't neglect kissing, nibbling, whispering encouragement, and manual stimulation just because you've finally managed to 'get your end in'.

And for pity's sake, once you've had an orgasm, don't just grunt, 'Thanks mate,' and reach for a beer, or even worse, crash into a coma. Few things are more certain to disappoint a woman than hearing her man snore the moment he's stopped ejaculating. The word you're looking for is 'Afterplay', gentlemen.

There's some sort of Latin quote which, translated, means roughly that 'All animals are sad after a good shag'. Humans are no exception. When the passion levels spiral back to normal, make certain you're there for her – if you want a repeat performance at some time in the future, that is. Cuddle her. Talk to her – *not* a post-mortem on your mutual performance, although the occasional politely enthusiastic compliment won't go astray.

Continue kissing her, and stroking any part of her that comes into reach. Scratch her back, slowly and sensuously. Massage her scalp, or if you happen to be down the other end, her feet. **MAINTAIN THE INTIMACY!** If you've held up your side of the bargain, gradually she will herself subside into a purring mass of boneless contentment. *Now* you can get up and go to the fridge, or grab a joint, or just roll over and flake out.

HOW TO NOT HAVE BABIES

Don't stuff up on this one, or the two of you may find yourselves with a real problem. The law requires both parents to contribute to the support of a child. Your only intended contact with mother might have been a quick five minute face plant on the kitchen bench. But the government has this sneaky branch of the tax office which simply deducts a large chunk of your income from your pay-cheque and deposits it with mum – if she's the one caring for the kid, that is.

The most effective form of contraception is abstinence. It's also a write off. Vasectomies work very nicely, and they don't cost much – but the reversability of the operation is open to debate, and the legality varies from place to place too. Anyway, when you come right down to it, nobody wants some stranger messing around with a sharp knife down there, so we'll rule out the Big Snip as well.

Next most efficient means of contraception is the female contraceptive pill. It's supposed to be about 99% effective against even the most super-humanly determined sperm (actually, it's the descent of the ova to the fer-tilisation zone which is affected, but that's not quite such a nice visual metaphor) which makes it a pretty safe bet. Unfortunately, the pill has a few medical side effects that crop up with some women, and may or may not be linked to all kinds of dubious female conditions later in life.

That leaves us with the condom. While its efficiency is slightly less (about 97%), it has an added attraction: it acts as a barrier against the interchange of body fluids, which goes a long, long way towards prevent-ing the spread of sexually transmittable diseases.

Condoms are a major part of modern sexual etiquette. Essentially, in any short-term or non-monogamous relationship, a condom should be con-sidered mandatory for safety and peace of mind. The decision to stop using condoms and move on to something less expensive and more effective, like the pill, should be taken only after careful mutual discussion, and should be made only when both partners have decided the relationship is going to last for a while. It's not unreasonable to arrange for a mutual test for the whole range of STDs before you take that step. Not very romantic, admit-tedly, but sensible.

Use of condoms also has a very specific etiquette of its own. It's not a good idea to carry one or two in your wallet; it suggests to your chosen part-ner that you're the sort of man who thinks he might need one at any time of the day. Over a long time the rubber tends to break down from body heat too. Leaving a nice, new box, prominently by the side of the bed is also not a great idea. Sex is tricky enough without the added pressure of expecta-tions. Best bet is to have them stashed somewhere near the most likely site – close at hand, but not in direct view. And as for the physics of putting them on and using them ... read the instructions on the packet, you prawn. Do we have to tell you everything?

THE BIG CRASH

IT'S A PITY THAT RELATIONSHIPS don't come with a use-by date stamped on them. It'd save such a lot of trouble. Often, there's no more than a couple of weeks worth of frantic sex before both of you come to your senses. Sometimes, though, it can be quite difficult to detect The End and leaving a relationship can be just as tricky as getting into one. After all, she's got *friends*, among whom there are probably half a dozen candidates for your next carnal commando raid. Therefore, you want to make as good an impression as possible, so that your future chances remain high. In order to do that, you need to know about the three differing kinds of break-up.

BOTH PARTIES WANT OUT

This is the best kind. Usually, it's characterised by an increasing disinterest from both of you. She goes out with her friends and forgets to mention it beforehand. You take the opportunity to catch a Steven Seagal video at home. You forget her birthday. She doesn't kill you. A week or two of this kind of thing, and both of you will know, although neither of you will have said a word.

When this happens, it is not a cause for gloom, but celebration. Both of you are going to get out of the relationship alive, and with all your goods and chattels intact! All you have to do is hold a single decent heart-to-heart talk with her. Come under a white flag – bring a bottle of good wine. She'll be terrified that you're trying desperately to rekindle things, and worrying about how to let you down easily – so when you explain that you've seen the writing on the wall, she'll be so relieved you'll probably wind up having an evening of absolutely wicked last-minute sex. (This, by the way, is your opportunity to try out all those kinky things you were too wussy to spring on her before. Go for it! What have you got to lose?)

Now hold a large, drunken party, and declare your mutual singleness to the waiting world.

SHE WANTS OUT. YOU DON'T.

Firstly, you need to wake up to yourself. Don't fuck around. When she's spending all her time with other people, not answering your phone calls, and finding reasons to avoid your parties, you're dead meat on a hook.

- **JUST DEAL WITH IT.** Desperate attempts to inject new life into a dead relationship, invariably produce painful, crippled, doomed and embarrassing results which you will regret for the rest of your life, or at least the next three months. Over is over. Have a talk with her – to get it in writing, as it were. And while you're at it, you might try to find out what went wrong and pick up some handy tips for your next bite at the cherry.

    Most important is this: *never* promise to make a bunch of changes to your life. *Never* promise to become a better human being. *Never* beg for another shot. Firstly, you won't be able to keep your promises. Secondly, whatever she tells you was the problem is almost certainly only part of the problem. The heart of the matter is that she's decided she's had enough. If she doesn't like you the way you are, she probably won't like you a whole lot better once you've tried to change. And nobody likes a groveller, anyhow.

- **DON'T MAKE IT ANY HARDER FOR HER THAN YOU HAVE TO.** Don't follow her around. Don't loom threateningly at her next boyfriend. Don't lurk outside her house. Don't phone her five times a day and hang up without saying anything. Go out, get blind staggering drunk with a bunch of mates. Talk about what a bitch she really was. Say a bunch of stupid stuff, and bruise your knuckles on a wall or two. Then go home and sleep it off. Once the hangover has cleared, you can get on with your life happy in the knowledge that you haven't had your last feed at the sexual smorgasbord. Somewhere out there is another hot babe. Perhaps with bigger hooters.

- **DON'T BE MANIPULATED.** If she ends things before you'd like it, and then comes back to bed when it starts to look like you've got an interest in someone else, tell her politely but firmly to piss off. She didn't want you last time. Chances are, if you dump the new prospect and get back together with her, it won't be long before she realises all over again why she wanted out in the first place. If you're *really* stupid, this sort of thing can go on through two or three potential new lovers.

YOU WANT OUT. SHE DOESN'T.

This is where things get really tricky. First, you need to be absolutely certain that it's over for you. Lots of relationships go through temporary lows. The decision to end things must occur while you are clear-headed and completely sober.

How do you know when you're over her? Lots of things, really. You're not afraid of her parents any more. Sex is more trouble than its worth. The blonde on the 8.05 train is starting to look really, really good. You begin to realise that it's a very long time since you went out and got blind with the

§

HOW TO JOIN THE FRENCH FOREIGN LEGION

Notice we specify 'French', rather than simply 'Foreign Legion'. You see, the Spanish have a Foreign Legion too, and it's a lot easier to get into. On the other hand, it's also an awful lot nastier, by all accounts, so if you really feel you've made all the errors you can make in a civilised country, definitely try the French first.

The place you're looking for is called *Fort de Nogent*, which is the major recruiting office for *Le Légion Étrangère*. It's in Paris. Borrow the money for a ticket to Paris from someone you don't like very much. Buy the ticket. Make it a first class ticket, because you might as well enjoy what life remains to you.

Throw a large party. Get savagely drunk. Dispose of everything you own in an orgy of gambling and excess. Offer your real opinions to everyone you've ever despised. Make serious, unmistakeable attempts to bed every woman who's ever caught your eye.

In the morning, you should have created enough havoc

boys. The funny whistling noise her nose makes when she's asleep is driving you insane. That cute, baby-talk thing she does – it's like an ice pick in the head.

Here's the rule: it's over when you're not enjoying it any more. When that happens, there's no point in prolonging it for her sake. You're not doing her any favours by staying. In fact you're being unfair. If she's got half the qualities you thought she had when you got together in the first place, she wouldn't want it that way anyhow, right?

Having made the decision to split, what you do next is surreptitiously put your CD collection, your guitar, your car, your best clothes and your cat into safe storage. This is known as 'taking precautions.'

Once these preparations are made, the time has come for The Talk. There's no right way to do this - you'll need to figure out your own, inimitable style of dumping her without our help. However, there are a large number of wrong ways to do it, techniques of dumping which are much more likely to provoke the Fatal Attraction response you are desperately trying to avoid.

---

and damage that there will be no choice for you but to get aboard that Paris-bound flight. Get drunk again on the flight. You can do that for free in First Class.

In Paris, book yourself into one of those totally decadent hotels with a price tag like the GNP of a small African nation. You're not going to pay the bill, so why worry about it? Try the Ritz. Take in a night of uttermost indulgence. If you can find a firm which supplies ... *dancing partners* and is prepared to bill your hotel room, so much the better.

Next day, you front at *Fort de Nogent*. Enlist under an assumed name. It's perfectly legit from their viewpoint, and it's enormous fun. One tip: don't go with 'Beau Geste'.

And that's it. Your life is now in someone else's hands. Brutal, vicious hands. Hands which will gladly hunt you down like a dog and kill you if you so much as attempt to desert. But look on the bright side: if you make it through your stint, you wind up with French citizenship, complete with rights to be rude to everyone in sight, live on wine, cheese, bread and garlic, and to bomb Greenpeace back into the stone age.

§

- **DON'T DO IT BY PHONE, FAX OR EMAIL.** It's cowardly, and she knows it, which gives her lots of ammunition to fling back at you. Tell her face to face, or not at all.
- **DON'T GET SOMEBODY ELSE TO DO IT.** Same as above and two people will think you're pathetic.
- **DON'T FORGET TO TELL HER.** Having her arrive in the middle of your next seduction is a guaranteed Total Melt-down. From both women.
- **DON'T TRY TO CUSHION THE BLOW WITH GIFTS, FLOWERS AND ROMANTIC SETTINGS.** That's for beginnings, not endings. She'll be expecting something entirely different from you if you've arranged a special occasion, and boy, will she be cranky.

> §
>
> **YOU SHOULD MAKE A POINT** of trying every experience once, excepting incest and folk-dancing. – *Anonymous*
>
> §

- **DON'T JUST AVOID HER AND HOPE SHE GETS THE MESSAGE.** She probably will, but you'll feel like a scumbag, and she'll think of you in pretty much the same way. And so will her friends who you might want to knock off next.
- **DON'T WIMP OUT.** No matter what she promises – and this means no matter *what*, okay? Put the baby oil and the vibrator away, you swine. If you know inside you that it's over, no amount of effort on her part is going to change anything. Make it clean and final.
- **DON'T TELL HER AND THEN DO A RUNNER.** Real men are prepared to face the bad stuff. She probably needs to get it out of her system anyhow. Right up to this point, you've been the best friend she's got, so who the hell is better qualified to be there for her?

That doesn't seem to leave a lot of leeway, does it? Tell you what: if you're really terrified by the whole idea, or if she's got a gigantic family full of brothers with extensive criminal records, this is probably the time to go on that long backpacking trip you've been thinking about. Tell her that you've just come into a little money, and if you don't go right now you never will. Say that you'll think of yourself as a coward forever if you don't go out there and try yourself against the world, and she wouldn't want to spend her life with a coward, would she? Now run, don't walk, to the nearest exit, and get on the next plane to Uzbekistan.

Stay overseas until you're certain she's given up. If all else fails, get someone to send her a message saying you've been killed in Rwanda, and move to another city when you get back home. If you ever see her again, you can always claim the authorities in Rwanda got it wrong. How reliable are they, anyway?

FEMININE EPHEMERA

• **PRESENTS ARE GOOD.** Crucial things to remember are her birthday, and the anniversary of the day you officially got together. These are 'occasions.' Chocolates, flowers, and cute bath-oil drops are for any old time you want to remind her of your romantic streak and should be programmed into your calendar on a semi-regular basis if you want her to keep wearing those thigh-high leather boots to bed. 'Occasions' require real presents. Buying a present for a woman is easy. Not only do they all want things, but they talk about their insatiable material desires in a way that men almost never do. Listen and take note. Then, when the next 'occasion' arises, buy her one of those things. Only crank it up a little: make it a version slightly more deluxe and expensive than she was thinking about.

• **TELEPHONE BEHAVIOUR IS TRICKY.** Early in the relationship, you'll probably find yourself inventing excuses to telephone her. Don't do it more than twice a week for any reason other than making arrangements to see one another. Sure, initially it's nice that you're phoning her, but eventually, she's going to get tired of having the receiver clamped to the side of her head. Also, you're wasting good conversational material which could be put to better use face to face.

Never, never get involved in one of those 'whoever puts the phone down last wins' games. It's boring. And tacky. Just hang up when you've said good-bye. Most importantly, *never* carry on a telephone relationship with someone on another continent. We know a guy who racked up a $2000+ phone bill yacking to a woman in New Zealand. Worse still, when he finally imported her, she turned out to be mad as a cut snake. Chased him round the house with a cleaver. Actually needed to be exorcised. You can do the maths for yourself.

• **THE G-SPOT.** The jury's still out as to the reality of a 'G-spot', or area of erogenous sensitivity inside the vagina. (Actually, the upper two thirds of the vagina don't feel a whole lot at all. Minor surgical procedures up there are routinely carried out without anaesthetic.) However, it can be fun trying to find it – so here's what you do: first, gently and carefully insert a finger into her vagina. She should be on her back, and your palm should face upward. Now curl that finger back towards you until it encounters the vaginal wall. At this point, if you have fingers of normal size, a firm but gentle 'beckoning' action should effectively stimulate the area where the 'G-spot' is supposed to be. Don't be surprised if not a whole lot happens, but on some women, the results are ... very interesting.

• **FEMALE EJACULATION.** Tales of female ejaculation – emission of fluid by women at the point of orgasm – are largely apocryphal. The medical fraternity (or 'brotherhood' – there's a giveaway for you as to how much they'd know about the topic!) holds that there's no structure down there which can produce the sudden surge of liquids necessary, other than the bladder, of course.

This particular medical opinion is crap. Some women do indeed produce a sudden, distinct rush of fluid, especially during a particularly powerful orgasm. Don't be put off by this. It's definitely not urine, which doesn't have the same slick, lubricious texture – nor the same flavour, for that matter. Unfortunately, due to lack of public information on this matter, few women are aware of the phenomenon, and those who do 'ejaculate' may be embarrassed, thinking they've accidentally urinated in the throes of passion.

Your job is not to worsen her embarrassment. Don't come up coughing and gargling if you happen to have caught a mouthful; chances are she's put up with a lot more from you, after all. Take it as a compliment to your technique, reassure her, and then get on with the fun and games.

• **JUST DO IT** If you think that reading one slightly flippant chapter in a very flippant book is going to make you an expert on dealing with the most complicated and exasperating organisms in the universe, you're mad. Take it from us: all the reading in the world is no substitute for hands-on, practical experience. And even that is no guarantee.

CHAPTER FOUR

Drinking: The Hair of Our Dogma.

DON'T KID YOURSELF THAT YOU already know everything there is to know on this topic. Booze has been around as long as civilisation – possibly longer. You may indeed have a natural flair and talent for the consumption of alcohol, but it's a fair bet you don't know nearly as much as a 21st Century Man should know.

Alcohol – ethyl alcohol, or ethanol – is a depressant which works on your central nervous system. It is detoxified by your hard-working liver, which can handle one standard drink (a glass of wine, a shot of scotch, or a pot of beer) per hour. Drink any faster than that, and you will become drunk.

Being drunk can be fun. It disinhibits the drinker, leading to behaviour which one might ordinarily shy away from – but for most people, this is kind of fun. It gives rise to loud singing, frenzied dancing, thoughtless propositions, bizarre urges to jump off the roof, and a host of other really interesting stuff. However, being drunk also impairs judgement and co-ordination. In high dosages, alcohol causes nausea, unconsciousness, and even death. Also, there are some nasty long-term problems associated with heavy alcohol use, not least of which are addiction, brain damage and liver dysfunction. If you find yourself with an alcohol problem go and see a professional counsellor at once. (Don't worry. Your friends will tell you, if you don't work it out for yourself by your lack of employment, declining bank balance, shattered memory, poor health, over-riding need for booze, and occasional bouts of screaming hallucinations.)

BEER, GLORIOUS BEER

SORRY, FRIENDS: BEER IS *NOT* a food group. Nor does it legitimately count as a cereal, even if it is made out of barley, or wheat, or malt. Beer is booze. Carbohydrates, water, and of course, ethanol.

Now personally, we really don't recommend the kind of in-depth research and dedication to the amber fluid which is necessary to become a genuine Beer-Wanker, able to identify scores of different brews by taste and fizz alone, but we do suggest that you learn a little bit about the stuff. Why? So that when someone accuses you of being a tasteless, beer-swilling yobbo, you can draw yourself up to your full height, look down your nose, and sneeringly deliver a very brief summary of the intricacies and wonders of the World of Beer. Pretend – if only momentarily – that you

§

ACTUALLY, TWENTY-THREE BEERS WILL *NOT* IMPROVE YOUR JUDGEMENT.

When I was about sixteen or seventeen my friends and I were known as mad drinkers and I once turned up for this very civilised birthday party about four hours before it officially started. I was lugging a carton of beer under one arm and had crammed my shirt pockets full of those dangerous little bottles of spirits you get in hotel room bar fridges. I've never liked to be tardy about these things. By the time most of the other guests had arrived I'd knocked off that carton and most of the mini-bar and had devolved into a horrible, drooling grease spot in the corner which everyone, particularly the women folk, were keen to avoid.

I passed out for a bit and came to with the other party-goers having circled the wagons in the backyard. They were all sitting around chatting politely and attempting to balance soggy paper plates full of chops and snags and home-made coleslaw on their knees. I slowly blinked and licked my lips and dragged my stinking carcass from the floor and out into the light. There was a moment, which I infer rather than remember, when everyone saw me and went into a panic attack, all praying I wouldn't collapse next to them. Or on top of them. I fished about in an esky for someone else's beer to drink, cursing and muttering darkly to myself about the shards of broken mini-bar bottles digging into my chest. I shambled unsteadily over to the barbecue to scoop up the

actually *care* about the difference between a Pilsener and a Vienna. Suggest that anyone who doesn't know why Cooper's Ale, brewed in open-top fermenters, is a wonderful and special substance is a contemptible boor.

Beer is an ancient drink. Its origins are lost in the depths of pre-history, but there is solid evidence that the Sumerians enjoyed a drop some five thousand years ago. It is also a very widespread drink. Practically every culture in the world, barring the Aborigines and a few obvious ones like the Inuit and the Lapp, has its own indigenous alcoholic drink made from fermented grains.

scraps of burned onion and meat refuse. I slowly turned to examine this group, started shovelling this garbage into my face, and tried to wash it down with an icy cold beer, most of which I just poured all over myself like the action guy from the old Solo commercials.

When people realised I'd probably be content to leave them alone the conversation slowly restarted and climbed back up from a murmur to a noisy buzz. They spoke too soon though. My targeting radar had settled on some poor med student called Karen, a fresh-faced little babe with curly cute bangs which, sadly for her, set lights a-flashing and sirens a-wailing inside my head. I narrowed my eyes and stared at her, trying to nut out an approach which would be certain to move her, with all dispatch, from an uncomfortable perch on a kiddie-sized folding stool into the arms of a stinking drunk with a whole lotta lovin' to give. I knew that she knew I was scoping her out because she studiously avoided looking anywhere even vaguely in my direction. I figured, 'Fantastic!', she knows I'm interested. Then my moment came. From way across that backyard, through a haze of twenty-three cans of full strength lager, I spied, with my little eye, something beginning with 'S'.

A spider. A spider crawling across the top of Karen's shoe. A spider which might soon make a dash up her lovely leg. A spider which had to die that I might love.

A momentary shiver passed over my body, a physical intimation of the knowledge of what I was to page 82 >

Beer is made through the fermenting action of yeast on sugar. Most commonly, the sugar is provided by malt. Malt is grain which has been germinated, then dried and powdered. The most frequently used grain is barley, but wheat beers are also well known. The brewer takes the malt and cooks it in hot water to dissolve the sugars. The sugary liquid produced is called a wort, and is then boiled up with hops, (dried flowers of a plant related to the cannabis species) which give the beer its distinctive, bitter flavour.

When the wort has been hopped, and allowed to cool to something like room temperature, the yeast is added. Yeast is a living organism, lads. It is one of those microbiological miracles which suggests that God may not be

< from page 81 about to do. I closed my mind to any doubts. Took one last swig of fortifying ale, stiffened the sinews, summoned up the blood and launched myself through the thin circle of garden chairs, into the air, across the expanse and onto the foot of the girl I intended to make mine forever.

Unfortunately Karen didn't see herself as the life mate of a drunken baboon with a half-chewed daddy long legs sticking out of his mouth, and nothing ever came of it. Except that three or four other guys beat the crap out of me and threw me into the back of somebody's ute where I landed on top of some old bricks and farming machinery.
I could have made her so happy.

§

Seizing the moment, John leapt over the startled partygoers and upon the spider before it could threaten the lovely Karen. He was unable, after sobering up, to recall how he had come to be dressed only in his underpants.

dead after all, because yeast has the truly heaven-sent ability to transform plain, ordinary sugar into sacred ethanol. Absolute magic. Anyway, when the yeast is added to the cooled wort and left to its own devices, the eventual outcome is ... *beer*.

Beer is produced in a number of distinctive styles. Unfortunately, here in Australia, emphasis on hygiene and consistency of product has produced a certain uniformity. Only a very few truly individual beers are available on the domestic market, and by far the greatest consumption is of lager-style beers, usually lightened and strengthened with added cane sugar. For the record, though, here's a brief summary of beer types and styles:

- **LAGER.** Comes from the German word for 'to store', or 'to put away', referring to the old Bavarian practice of putting their beer away to mature in Alpine caves. Usually a pale-gold, sparkling beer of about 5% alcohol, not too bitter, and served chilled. These days, *Lagers* are usually distinguished by the fermentation process – when the yeast has done its work, it stays in the bottom of the vat and the lager is poured off the top. *Pilsener* is a style of pale-gold lager originating in the town of Pilsen, in the Czech Republic. Well-known pilseners include Heineken, Carlsberg, Tuborg, Singha, Bintang, Anchor, Tiger, Tsingtao, Asahi and Kirin. In Australia, Fosters and Fourex both are nominally lagers.
- **ALE.** A very old word, now used mostly to describe beers made in the old traditional style, wherein the yeast floats on top of the vat and is drained off, leaving the drinkables behind. Belgium and Britain are the great strongholds of ales, but despite the fact that most of the world has turned to lagers, there are actually a number of very interesting ales still in existence. *English Bitter* is probably the best known of these, and still does very well on its home ground. *Pale Ale* isn't actually very pale, tending to be a lovely rich amber colour, but it is usually fairly bitter, and reasonably strong. Coopers' Sparkling Ale is a lovely example here in Australia, and notable for the fact that it's fermented in open-top vats ... which, under Australian temperatures, is quite an achievement. *Mild Ale*, which is now not particularly popular, is a low-fizz dark tan brew with limited bitterness, and a lowish alcohol content. *Brown Ale* is a little less dark in colour than *Mild*, and has a higher alcohol content. Newcastle Brown is probably the best-known and most widely available of these. *Stout* is a dark, almost black, rich creamy ale usually made with black malt or roasted barley. Australia cranks out some very nice stouts, particularly from Coopers and Cascade.
- **OTHERS.** *Wheat beers* are beers made from malted wheat, rather than malted barley. Redback, from Western Australia, used to be one such. It produces a very distinctive taste which may not initially be palatable to the barley drinker. *Dry beers* are little different from a normal lager, saving that they've been designed to ferment out a bit further, reducing the body of the beer and producing an odd 'dry' sensation on the tongue. *Light beers* in Australia are simply low-alcohol beers, made by reducing the sugar content of the wort. Beware, though, of American light beers. American beers are generally as weak as a politician's excuse; to an American, 'light' beer is actually a carbohydrate-modified low-kilojoule beer.

There's a lot more that could be said on the topic of beer – the grand range of *Belgian ales*, for example, including their strange, spontaneously fermented Lambics. Or the hideously potent Doppelbocks of Germany, including Terminator and Kulminator. However, if you really want to be a genuine Beer-Wanker, you're better off getting out amongst the pubs and learning on the road. The only other thing this book can offer you with regards to Beer is a short, simple guide to Doing It Yourself ...

MAKING YOUR OWN: HOW AND WHY

Brewing your own beer is a very popular pastime amongst Men, and there are a number of excellent reasons for this. The most obvious is expense: a cold slab of fairly generic beer will set you back about $25.00. On the other hand, a starter's kit which will eventually turn into twenty-five litres of the stuff will cost you less than $10.00. Even if you factor in the expenses of non-renewable equipment, like bottle tops, sterilising solution, and a great big fermentation vat, you're still only looking at $50 or so. With prices like that, you can drink yourself silly pretty much any time you want and not damage the budget.

There's a lot that can be said on the topic of drinking beer.

Another good reason to brew your own is quality. Most Australian beers are generic these days. Sure, there's minor differences between Fourex, VB, Tooheys and Fosters, but on the whole, they're much of a muchness. And the really nice ones are brutally expensive. Once you get the hang of brewing your own, though, there are all kinds of things you can do to personalise and improve the product. Add more sugar, get more alcohol. Add more hops, get more bitterness. Use a different kind of hops, get a different flavour. Use a better grade of water – save your rainwater – and make a truly marvellous beer. When you've managed to brew an interesting, flavourful and potent brew out of bananas and malt and rainwater, then not only have you got something cool with which to oil the throat, but something deeply impressive to talk about with other Men in the process.

The 'How' of brewing your own beer is a little more complex. You can, of course, simply go down to the local home-brew outfitters, buy the basic kit and a tin of commercial beer-stuff, and follow the instructions – or you can do a little reading, find out what's going on, and enter more fully into the world of biochemical black magic wherein yeast turns sugar into heaven on earth.

In the simplest terms, to brew your own beer you will need the following things:

1) Water.
2) Something to ferment, containing sugars.
3) Live yeast.
4) A large vat to carry out fermentation.
5) A lot of bottles to put the beer into for purposes of maturing and carbonating.
6) A quiet, out-of-the-way place protected from the sun and extremes of weather.

Water's easy. Tap water will do. (Rainwater and springwater are better, though.) It's best if you can put it aside in a container to stand for a day or two before you use it, but it will work straight from the faucet. Getting something to ferment is a little more tricky. Eventually, you could probably get around to boiling your own grains into a sugary mash, straining off the liquid wort, and then steeping the wort with hops – but for starters, you're better off buying a commercial beer mix. They don't cost much, and they're pretty reliable. Also, they usually come with their own yeast, which is very helpful.

The vat and the bottles represent your major equipment outlay. Fortunately, you can acquire the bottles through the not particularly arduous process of buying commercial beer and drinking it. You'll need to buy some bottle caps and a crown seal, but the home-brew store will have them, and they're cheap too. One thing worth noting is that plastic soda bottles also work well for maturing and carbonating your beer, and if they explode – as sometimes happens with glass bottles too – at least there won't be a savage rain of glass shrapnel to worry about.

Once you've got all the equipment, you can go to work. Firstly, use a simple bleach solution to sterilise both your fermenter and some kind of stirring rod. Rinse both thoroughly. Then open the beer-mix, and stir it into

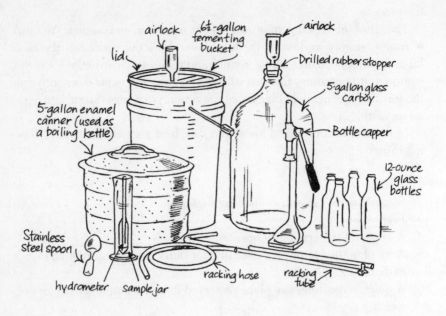

a pot of boiling water. Pour all of this mixture into your fermentation vat, and bring the vat up to the 22 litre mark with clean water, and add about a kilo of granulated sugar. Be careful not to touch the sterilised fermenter with your unsterile hands, or with anything else which hasn't been thoroughly cleaned and disinfected. Yeast is good. Bacteria are not.

When the wort has been diluted to fill the fermenter, toss in the yeast and give it a good stir. Then put the lid on, and stand the fermenter in your dark, out-of-the-way place for a few days. Leave it there until you stop seeing bubbles coming through the water-trap on the lid.

Now use the bleach to sterilise your bottles. Add a heaped teaspoon of sugar to each bottle of 750ml or larger, and a level teaspoon to each 375ml stubby. Decant your beer from the fermenter into the bottles, and seal them thoroughly. The bottles will now need to stand quietly for a minimum of a month or so. During this time, the remaining sugar will be fermented, producing a little more alcohol, and some carbon dioxide. As a result, when you take the lid off a month or so later, the dissolved carbon dioxide will immediately begin to bubble forth, just like it does in commercial beer. Cheers!

IMPORTANT NOTES

- **YEAST IS TRICKY STUFF.** Try to keep all fermentation between 20 and 30 degrees C. Cooling the process will slow it dramatically, and if you put half-fermented beer into bottles, you run a *serious* risk of explosion. On the other hand, if it gets too warm, the yeast may die, and you'll be left with a nasty, sugary solution which hardly resembles beer at all.
- **EXPLODING BOTTLES CAN HAPPEN EVEN TO THE EXPERTS.** Put your bottles in a safe, sheltered, out-of-the-way position, and check them regularly. If you can, don't stack them all together, as one exploding bottle in the midst of its brethren can create a tragic chain reaction.
- **STERILISE, STERILISE, STERILISE.** Probably the single greatest hazard to home-brewing is bacterial contamination. Wash everything you use promptly after use, and sterilise everything before using it with a solution of bleach, or commercial sterilising agent. If at any stage, your beer begins to smell funny, grow nasty jelly-like masses, turn an unexpected colour, or behave in a manner unlike beer, abandon the exercise. Dispose of the product, sterilise everything in sight, and try again. *Never* try to salvage spoiled beer.
- **FINALLY,** if you do decide to get deeply into the brewer's realm, remember that you're not alone. There are associations of home brewers all over the place, and any number of excellent books to inspire you towards a more perfect product. Even the simplest search of the Internet will show that Men all over the world are fascinated by this pastime, as well they ought to be. A deep and abiding interest in all things Beer-like is a very reasonable trait for the ideal 21st century Man.

WINE

THIS IS THE GOOD STUFF. Wine is the fermented product of the grape – although technically, it's possible to make wine from other fruits as well. We say 'technically', because to date, every non-grape wine we have imbibed has borne an uneasy resemblance in flavour to such unlikely things as smoked oysters, pastrami, and yoghurt. Our heartfelt recommendation is definitely to stick with the grape.

Wine is the great Wanker's Drink. Europeans – especially the bloody French – have been swilling the stuff for centuries, and there's a gigantic system of naming, controlling, pricing and etiquette which surrounds it.

There's rules about what temperature to drink it at, how long to let it stand after opening, how to raise or lower its temperature, how to store it, how to taste it, what order to drink different wines in, what kind of glasses to drink it out of, how to open the bottles, what kind of food to eat with it — it's a bloody nightmare.

At least, it looks that way on the surface. We'll let you in on a secret, though. It's pretty simple: *good wine tastes good*. Beyond that, Sturgeon's Law applies. (Sturgeon's Law: 90% of everything is crap.)

Most of the mystique, most of the hyper-complicated system of rules around drinking wine — these are all bullshit. Invented by the French to confuse the rest of the world into thinking the French actually knew something important the rest of us didn't. Even the French don't pay it a lot of attention, though. Do you suppose that Pierre the cab-driver really worries whether the chardonnay he's having with his garlic snails is oaked or un-oaked? As if. Pierre is concerned about a few limited things: how much it costs and how it tastes.

That being the case, we're going to discuss just a few simple guidelines, and we guarantee they'll work like a charm with any bottle of wine you can buy for $50 or less. Once you get past that range, though, you're buying something which looks less like a nice way to get pissed, and more like an investment portfolio. If you really want to get into the good stuff, go do a course. There's a million of them out there.

HOW TO ENJOY A BOTTLE OF WINE

- **CHECK THE PRICE.** It's hard to find a decent drinking wine for under $10 any more, though they're still out there. You need to know what you're looking for, if you're chasing that kind of thing. In Australia, most of the wines between $10 and $20 are reasonably palatable. Quite a few of them represent real bargains, when compared with their European counterparts. And if you buy a bottle over $20 and get a dud, you're definitely entitled to complain.
- **THINK TEMPERATURE.** When are you going to drink it? White wines come off better a bit (but not too) chilled. If you're going to drink it straight away, get it from the refrigerated section of the bottle-o. Reds, on the other hand, are better at room temperature, so long as you're not up in the tropics. If you *are* planning to drink a big red up above Brisbane, a quick visit to the fridge is probably in order. Just so that it doesn't feel like you're drinking blood.
- **WHEN YOU OPEN IT, CHECK THE CORK.** Slowly, gradually, pain-fully, the winemakers of the world are moving towards artificial corks — which is a good thing. The single most common reason for wine

becoming undrinkable is that the corks dry out and shrink, permitting air and possibly bacteria through to the product. When you remove the cork, check to see that the bottom part is still damp, and preferably stained with wine, and that the seal is good. (That's why the snooty waiter waves the cork under your nose at an expensive restaurant: you're supposed to be checking that the wine was properly stored and sealed. And by the way: if the cork *doesn't* look sound, don't hesitate to send the bottle back. At the near-criminal mark-ups used by most restaurants, they don't dare kick up a fuss and the sneaky fuckers will probably foist it on the next poor bastard anyway.)

- **LET REDS BREATHE.** Red wines usually have a lot of dissolved carbon dioxide in them. If you drink them straight away, this stuff stays in solution as carbonic acid. All acids taste sour. Therefore, when you're going to drink a decent red, it pays to let it 'breathe' first, to let the carbon dioxide escape into the air. You can do this one of two ways: take the

§

BE NOT AFRAID OF WINE

Wine is a drink and must never be regarded or feared as anything more than a drink. It's something to be enjoyed with food and that's the end of it. There's much too much nonsense and snobbery about wine and it really is nothing more than a lovely drink to enjoy with good food and friends.

James Braid, the great Scottish golfer who won the Open five times at the beginning of the century, was once approached by a young man who said, 'Could you give me three tips on how to play golf better?' Braid said, 'Yes, by playing golf, playing golf and playing golf.' And the paraphrase is entirely apt for wine. Honestly, the only advice I can give a young man on approaching wine is to drink it. He shouldn't be concerned about vintages and all that. He should just drink it. Really that is the only advice. By drinking, he will enjoy, by enjoying he will want to understand. And if he doesn't want any of those things it doesn't matter what you do—he'd be a bloody dead loss anyway. – *Len Evans*

§

cork out and let the bottle stand somewhere for about half an hour, or gently pour the wine into a decanter, and let it sit for five or ten minutes. This is definitely not part of the bullshit surrounding wine; it makes a very big difference to the way your wine will taste.

- **MAKE AN EFFORT TO REALLY TASTE YOUR WINE.** Good wines are complex things, generally – although there are some fresh, young wines which make outstanding quaffers. Smell your wine first. Don't be embarrassed – put your nose in the glass, take a deep sniff, and slowly breathe out through both your nose and mouth. Then take a decent mouthful, and roll it around on your tongue before you swallow it. Finally, exhale slowly, tasting the flavours and odours on the back of your palate too. With a bit of imagination, you'll be able to identify hints of all kinds of different things – berry, lemon, spice, oak, and toast are the sorts of things you hear Wine-Wankers rabbiting on about at length.

- **TRY TO SUIT YOUR WINE TO YOUR FOOD.** Food and wine go together in a big, big way, and it pays to try and match them up. In general, the big reds go well with dishes of red meat, strong sauces, and nice sharp cheeses. Cool, crisp white wines suit salads and fruits, and lighter dishes of chicken and fish. Heavy, sweet wines like gewurz-traminers and sauternes make for a nice dessert on their own, especially if accompanied with a little fruit and cheese. Reinforced brutes like the ports and sherries are probably best in small quantities after a meal. And remember: nothing on earth goes well with Fruity Lexia.

It was my Uncle George who discovered that alcohol was a food well in advance of medical thought. – P.G. Wodehouse.

- **DRINK THE LOT.** If you've opened a genuinely good bottle of wine, don't mess around. Unless you have one of a couple of different special devices to help with re-corking and storage, that last third of a bottle won't survive the night. Even if you keep it in the refrigerator, it will still taste like crap the next day. It's the action of oxygen on the complicated molecules in the wine, you see – it breaks them down and destroys the subtle flavours. Reds are worse than whites for this, but on the whole, it's a waste of time storing any leftovers.

- **RED WINES AGE BETTER THAN WHITES, AS A RULE.** When you're buying wine to drink within a day or so, reds over three years old are usually more drinkable than the younger ones. On the other hand, few Australian whites are made to cellar, so you needn't worry if you're knocking off a white that's only a year or two old.

Well, that's it. That's all you really need to know to enjoy drinking wine. Our advice to you right now is stop reading here, go out, get yourself a bottle, and practice. However, for those of you who want to look like Wine Wankers, there follows a basic wine primer. In general, we've stuck to using Australian terms of reference, and wherever a variety of wine is discussed, we've tried to recommend one or two of the better Australian examples. If you feel short-changed, and you deeply feel the need to take up Wine-Wanking in the manner of a true Euroweenie go and buy another book.

WINE-WANKING: A BRIEF GLOSSARY

- **BAROSSA VALLEY.** Spot about an hour's drive north of Adelaide which produces an uncanny number of really excellent wines, especially from the Shiraz, Cabernet Sauvignon, and Sauvignon Blanc varieties.
- **BOUQUET.** Wine-wanker talk for 'the way the wine smells'.
- **CHAMPAGNE.** A region in France. Only bubbly wines made in this particular region are actually permitted to be called 'Champagne', after the decision of the international courts some five years ago. Anybody else in the entire world who wants to make wine of that sort has to call it 'Methode Champagnoise'. This is not simply because the French are bastards, but because they weren't enjoying the competition provided by Australian wines, amongst others. If you're still smarting at those bastards over nuclear testing drink Petersons or Hungerford Hill from the Hunter Valley. They're great fucking drops and it'll piss off the frogs.
- **CABERNET SAUVIGNON.** Variety of grape grown for premium red wines. Small quantities also used in rosé, and in vintage port. The French regard Cabernet Sauvignon as the best of the five(!) varieties which can be legally used to make wine with the name 'Bordeaux'. Cabernet wines are characterised by strong fruit flavour and a bouquet which is supposedly like freshly crushed young gum leaves. Fully $3/4$ of Australian Cabernet grapes are grown in South Australia. The Coonawarra region is famous for its rich, powerful Cabernet wines.

- **CELLARING.** Storage of wine in the bottle. The better and more complex varieties of wine continue to change and mature in the bottle, and some big reds are best drunk only after ten years of gathering dust. Stored wine should be kept at a cool, even temperature, and left on its side, so the cork stays moist and keeps the seal intact. Keep the wine out of the sunlight, as well.

- **CHABLIS.** Famous French white wine. Here in Australia, however, a Chablis is basically whatever the winemaker says it is. It's a good way to label a white which otherwise might have to be called something like 'Vin Blanc'.

- **CHARDONNAY.** The premium white-wine grape grown in Australia. Can be mixed in with Pinot Noir to make Champagne-style wines. It also makes an excellent, robust white in itself – dry, with good fruit flavours and a full finish. These days it is becoming fashionable to drink Chardonnay which has not been aged in oak casks (un-oaked Chardonnay). This is, of course, rankest heresy. If you want a white without that distinctive oak flavour, go and suck on a Chablis. In the meantime, don't interfere with one of the few white wines that actually benefits from a couple of years in the cellar. Look for Chardonnay out of the Hunter Valley, and Northern Victoria.

- **CLARET.** Bit of a meaningless term when applied to Australian wines. Originally from older English, meaning 'Light red', or 'Clear red'. A bit like a red wine version of 'Chablis'.

- **DRY.** Having little leftover sugar or sweetness in the wine. Not to be confused with 'acid'. Few Antipodean white wines are dry by European standards, but Tasmania and New Zealand are heading in this direction.

- **FRONTIGNAN.** The grape responsible for muscat dessert wines – a group of very sweet, very rich red wines indeed. Best are the produce of Rutherglen and surrounding districts in North-Eastern Victoria. Also known as Brown Muscat, or Frontignac.

- **FRUITY LEXIA.** Don't do it. Just don't. Okay?
- **GRENACHE.** Wines of the grenache grape mature early. It makes excellent rosés, and light, dry red wines which should be drunk young for full enjoyment.
- **HUNTER VALLEY.** Area inland from Newcastle, along the Hunter River, a noted wine-producing region since the middle of the 19th century. Now produces some fine Pinot Noir, Merlot, Semillon, and Chardonnay grapes.
- **MERLOT.** Another 'Bordeaux' variety. Produces soft, velvety, red wines. Usually seen mixed with Cabernet Sauvignon, to produce 'Cabernet Merlot'. This combination brings together the body and fullness of the Cabernet Sauvignon grape with the softness of the Merlot, and is becoming a very popular table wine in Australia. Straight Merlot is also beginning to take off, though it lacks something of the power of similar red wines.
- **MOSELLE.** Supposedly a fresh, light, young, fruity white wine. Generally made from Rhine Riesling or Semillon grapes. Also, generally cheap, disgustingly sweet, and quite, quite nasty.
- **PINOT NOIR.** A dark, almost black grape (hence the name) which is very important in making Champagne-style wines. While there are few really good straight Pinot Noir wines yet in Australia, some of the Hunter Valley styles are very good indeed, with the classic floral bouquet and flavour for which this wine is noted.
- **PORT.** Sweet, fortified (extra alcohol!) red wines. Australian varieties are styled after the Portuguese. Vintage ports are made from grapes that are all of the same year, and need to be left alone for a long time before they become drinkable. **AVOID CHEAP VINTAGE PORT AT ALL COSTS.** Tawny ports are made from blends of old stuff and new stuff, so you've got a better chance of getting something you can drink straight away. Good stuff now coming from Northern Victoria, especially Rutherglen, including the Morris ports.
- **RHINE RIESLING.** A variety of grape noted for its full, fruity flavour, and high acid content. Buying a Riesling in Australia is a dangerous business, as you are apt to get a nasty, cloyingly sweet monstrosity suitable only for poisoning feral cats. Good Rhine Riesling is a real treat, though, with strong flavour, just a hint of sweetness, a little acid, and a wonderful, fresh, crisp finish. Try some of the older, more expensive vintages of Leo Buring.
- **SAUTERNE.** Thick, sticky dessert white wines, usually made from

Semillon grapes. Only to be taken in small doses. Try the better de Bortoli products. Sauterne has largely replaced port as an after dinner wine.

- **SAUVIGNON BLANC.** Grape which produces a nice, full, fruit-flavoured but dry white wine. It is also a relatively soft wine to drink without the acid apparent in many whites. Some very decent Sauvignon Blanc wines now come from the Barossa Valley.
- **SEMILLON.** White wine grape which produces some of the finest of the Hunter Valley table whites. It's the grape behind the sticky-sweet Sauternes, but also stands as a soft, mild drinking white in and of itself. A good Semillon has complexity, however, and withstands cellaring nicely. Leave them alone for at least three years before you drink them.
- **SHIRAZ.** Also known as 'Hermitage', this is the grape which produces Australia's finest reds, including the legendary Penfolds Grange Hermitage. At its best, Shiraz produces a big, bold, swaggering kick-arse red wine with lots of fullness and body, and a powerful, heady finish. If you can't afford the Grange, go for some of the other Barossa region greats: try Henschke's 'Hill of Grace' Shiraz – or at least, St Hallett's 'Old Block' Shiraz.
- **TRAMINER.** White grape variety, producing wines with lots of fruit and spice. Sometimes called 'Gewurztraminer.' Again, cheap Traminers tend to be disgustingly sweet, but a really good Traminer is an excellent dessert wine, often with marked flavours of citrus and spice.
- **VERDELHO.** A white wine grape which makes a fairly undistinguished, but drinkable, dry wine. Used in Western Australia to make fortified wines.

> §
>
> **CLARET IS THE LIQUOR FOR boys; port, for men; but he who aspires to be a hero (smiling) must drink brandy.** – *Samuel Johnson*
>
> §

THE HARD STUFF: SPIRITS & LIQUEURS

SPIRITS ARE MADE BY DISTILLATION, which is the process of boiling off and re-condensing the alcohol from a fermented mash of some sort. The end result depends on what your original fermented mash was – vodka comes from potatoes, rum comes from molasses and sugar, whiskey comes from barley. Most spirits come in at the 35%-40% alcohol range, so treat them with respect. (Beer is usually less than 5%, wine 10-12%.)

The easiest way to tell good quality spirits is by the price. Anything over $50 a bottle is pretty good. Spirits tend to vary in quality and flavour rather less than wines and beers. The only place you really need to start taking care is with good malt whiskies and good brandies.

A liqueur is a drink based on a distilled spirit, heavily flavoured with other exciting substances. Usually, liqueurs are quite sweet, and the only time you'd even consider drinking them on their own is after dinner, as a kind of liquid dessert. Most liqueurs should not be iced or chilled – though there are exceptions – because it sharply alters the texture and flavour of the drink. Of course, that rule goes right out the window when you start mixing up the cocktails.

For drinking purposes, you need know only the five classic liqueurs: Drambuie, which tastes like top-grade scotch as touched by God himself; Cointreau, which is orange juice and lightning; Pernod, which is liquorice and a sledge-hammer; Grand Marnier, which tastes of oranges and moonlight; and Benedictine, which is sweet and deeply strange. These five you may drink on their own. All other liqueurs exist solely for the purpose of mixing into cocktails. And as for the spirits …

SPIRIT OF THE WORLD, UNITE!

- **ARRACK.** Generic name for any one of a number of fiendish white spirits. In the Middle East, arrack will usually be strongly anise (liquorice) flavoured. In Indonesia, it's just plain old white spirit, distilled from rice. Be careful with any arrack. As often as not, it's home-brewed, brutally powerful, and may have exciting secondary ingredients from careless distillation, such as methanol, or even lead. Mix your arrack with water.

- **BOURBON.** American corn-mash whisky. Jack Daniels is pretty much the industry standard. Tastes vaguely like methylated spirits strained through pencil shavings. Wild Turkey is a lot more expensive, and much smoother and more drinkable. Mixes with soft drinks, especially Coke.

- **BRANDY.** Also 'Cognac', and 'Armagnac'. This is a dark spirit distilled from fermented grapes, and without a doubt, the French make the finest brandies in the world. The terms 'Cognac' and 'Armagnac' refer to the different areas where the grapes are grown, and where the stuff is made. Good brandy should never be mixed with anything. It should be drunk slowly from a balloon glass, without ice. Cheap brandy can be mixed with lemonade and poured straight down the sink.

- **GIN.** Clear spirit flavoured with juniper berries. Gin and tonic water over ice is one of the few great contributions of the British to world culture.

- **Ouzo** Savage Greek clear spirit which tastes inexorably of liquorice. There is no such thing as a good ouzo. Mix it with lemonade if you must.
- **Rum.** Can be had as both a clear spirit (white rum, such as Bacardi) and a dark spirit (e.g. Bundaberg). Both are distilled from sugar cane. Neither is particularly nice, having an ugly, medicinal sort of taste. Clueless high schoolers prefer to swill it down with Coke and a slice of orange. White rum goes very well in a number of cocktails.
- **Tequila.** Mexican spirit, of dubious and variable colour, distilled (apparently) from cactus fermentings. Sometimes has a worm in the bottom, which in times past was usually full to the gills with mescaline, which made eating the worm a very entertaining pastime. These days, the little bastard is just there for colour, and we recommend slipping it into the salad and seeing if you can get the restaurant to give you a free dinner. If you must drink tequila, do it straight up. Knock off a shot of tequila, lick a little salt from the back of your hand, and bite straight into a wedge of lime. Centennial is a decent tequila.
- **Vodka.** Russian/Central European spirit distilled from potatoes. Strong, clear, and relatively tasteless. Mixes well with orange juice, or can be drunk straight, very very cold, after the fashion of the Russians. The brand you want is Stolichnaya.
- **Whisky/whiskey** This is a dark spirit distilled from fermented barley mash. If it's spelled with an 'e', it's from Ireland. The Irish stuff – Jamesons and Bushmills – is pretty smooth and drinkable. If there's no 'e', it's supposed to be scotch. This is kind of tricky. Blended scotch will have all sorts of age-claims on the label, but you should remember that even with the most expensive blends, only a little of the whisky has been aged like this. The rest is last year's barley-distillate, thrown in for cost's sake. Two rules: better to buy the cheapest of single malt scotch whiskies than to buy the most expensive blends. And never mix good whisk(e)y with anything, even water, or ice. If water you must have, take it in a glass, on the side. If you're a bit of a nancy boy cheap scotch goes just fine with soft drinks – especially dry ginger ale.

COCKTAILS

EVERY 21ST CENTURY MAN NEEDS to know how to make a basic half-dozen or so cocktails. Why? Because they're slower to mix and it takes you longer to get drunk. Because they look so groovy in their little glasses. Because if you mix them *extra strong* you can maybe get her drunk before she notices. Because of the air of worldliness and sophistication you can put on while you're mixing them. Because you can use cheap rum and pretend you've run out of the good stuff. Because the ones with fruit in ensure that you're getting at least some of your daily vitamin requirement – but most of all, because women like them. (Actually, men like them too, but it's mostly women who are prepared to admit it.)

It's far better to know half a dozen classics off by heart than it is to have an entire encyclopedia of all the cocktails ever created. For starters, who the hell can afford to keep a bar stocked with the kind of crap that goes into a B-52? Stick to the classics. Your bar bill will be more acceptable, and you won't be in danger of succumbing to those weird, midnight urges to drink yourself stupid on amaretto and crème de menthe when there's nothing else left in the house.

One important note: stay away from cocktails with stupid and suggestive names. If she comes out and asks you for an 'Orgasm', or a 'Slow Comfortable Screw' or even a 'Slippery Nipple', you can lift your eyebrow in the manner of a young Roger Moore and say something vaguely witty and suggestive – but only if she asks you first. Anybody who really drinks these stupid things deserves all the bad karma they get.

The six cocktails you really ought to know, in no particular order, are: the Martini, the Margarita, the Daiquiri, the Pina Colada, the Bloody Mary, and the Tequila Sunrise. Before we get down to the business of how to make them, though, you'll need to know one or two things ...

THE BASICS:

- A **JIGGER** is one and a half ounces. (Sorry. They're not metric in Drinkieland yet.)
- A **SHOT** is one ounce. With most liquors, this is One Standard Drink.
- A **DASH** or **SPLASH** is seven to ten drops.
- **SIMPLE SYRUP** is made by adding 200g of granulated sugar to a cup of

boiling water. Simple syrup can be substituted one for one for any measurement of granulated sugar. Takes a lot of trouble out of the mixing.

- **COCONUT CREAM/MILK.** This ain't what you get out of the middle of a coconut. It's thicker, sweeter, and altogether heavier. You get it in tins from your local supermarket, or any Asian grocery.
- **CRUSHED ICE.** This is not snow. It's ice that's been pounded down to a fine gravel. Easiest to do in a blender, but bulk fun to do with a mallet.
- **SHAKING AND STIRRING.** Don't mess around. Do what the recipe says, and James Bond be damned. As a rule, you shake fruit juices, and gently stir carbonated drinks to keep the fizz intact.
- **TWIST.** This is not a wedge. This is a chunk of fruit, twisted over the drink to add the juice. For a garnish use a wedge at least half a centimetre wide.

THE MARTINI

There may never have been a drink anywhere with such mystique as the martini. In its little triangular glass, with that single olive eye looking out at you, it positively reeks of sophistication and worldly elegance. Problem is, everyone knows that, and ever since James Bond hit the big screen, ordering a Martini has become an exercise in embarrassment. Not to worry. If you learn how to mix them yourself, you'll never again have to put up with snide comments from your drinking companions. Plus, you'll have the perfect excuse for lounging around your residence in a bathrobe …

Classically, the martini consists of:

Four parts gin

One part dry vermouth

A twist of lemon

One large olive.

Served in a conical, long-stemmed glass. The alcohol itself should be cold, since if you're working with the classic conical cocktail glass, ice is not really an option. (Makes the drink quite hard to control.)

Ignoring any comments from anyone, you can stir or shake this as you see fit. There are endless variations on the martini. Our favourite is actually the vodka martini, which is almost as classic a recipe as the original. Personally, we also favour a 6:1 mix of vodka to vermouth, and we prefer to serve it in a standard highball glass, with ice. We also rarely drink the things, as they have a kick like Bruce Lee on veterinary steroids. Best served just before dinner, in the infamous 'cocktail hour'.

IMPORTANT NOTE: the olive is *not* optional. If there's no olive, it isn't a Martini.

THE MARGARITA

Possibly the finest excuse for drinking tequila ever invented. Margaritas conjure up images of sunny days in Baja or Cancun (wherever the hell those places actually are), and for a great many people, their first Margarita is like that first step on the road to hell – there's no turning back.

Half-fill your blender with smashed ice. (Note: if you can't afford a blender – which you should have, because you can do lots of other things with them too – then you're positively going to have to buy a cheap cocktail shaker from any bar or kitchen supplier.)

Add: a jigger of white rum

Half-shot of Triple Sec

Two shots lime juice

(Optional) half-cup simple sugar syrup

Zap hell out of the mixture in the blender (or shake like a bastard) for about thirty seconds. Add a twist of fresh lime juice. Now, grab the glasses. Margaritas are usually served in those conical jobs, just like martinis. Run the lime peel round the rim of the glass (outside, not inside!) and roll the damp rim in ordinary table salt, so you get a nice crusting of salt around the rim. Pour out the margarita mixture, and serve. Fantastic on a hot day. Mr Birmingham, who will have no truck with sugar syrup, adds a dash of Cointreau to his mixture before blending, at which point Mr Flinthart slaps his forehead in theatrical dismay.

DAIQUIRIS OF ALL KINDS

A daiquiri is a fruit and rum cocktail which has long been considered a bit 'girlie' here in Oz. Tough shit. Actually, a decent daiquiri is a kick-arse drink, especially if you make them as iced daiquiries. Nothing better on a hot Queensland summer day than to settle back with a tray of new strawberries, a bottle of rum, and a bag of ice, and get yourself (and anyone around) seriously bent on iced Strawberry Daiquiries.

Your basic one-drink daiquiri is:

A jigger of rum

two tablespoons sugar syrup

two tablespoons fresh lime juice

Run the lot through the blender, and serve over ice. Nobody drinks basic daiquiries, though. What you do is, take your basic daiquiri, throw in an equal measure of your favourite fruit (kiwifruit are excellent, strawberries are great, bananas are so-so, mangoes are wonderful, but mulberries are really disgusting. Take it from Mr Flinthart. It was a very bad day.)

Even better than this is to add the fruit to the blender, and also a cup of smashed ice. The resulting drink is a bit like an alcoholic fruit slurpee.

PINA COLADA

We don't much like this one, but it's a big favourite with some people. And it looks spectacular, with the different fruit juices. If you happen to have a bunch of those pointless paper cocktail parasols, or even some unoccupied pointy toothpicks, now is the time to start skewering bits of fruit both as decoration and in an effort to improve your diet.

$\frac{1}{2}$ shot each of dark rum and light rum

About a shot apiece of lime juice, orange juice, and pineapple juice.

A splash of grenadine.

Serve it over ice in a tall glass, and top it up with coconut cream. Don't stir it. Leave it in layers for the aesthetic effect.

TEQUILA SUNRISE

A jigger of tequila (try not to get the worm into the glass).

2 jiggers of orange juice

Shot of grenadine

Mix the tequila and the juice in a tall glass, with ice, and pour the grenadine over the top so it makes a nice splash of red. Don't mix it in. This one is often served up as a sort of 'hair of the dog' hangover cure, and if you just make sure there's plenty of orange juice, we suppose it might just do the job.

BLOODY MARY

This classic has the advantage of being a vegetable based cocktail, so you can get some dietary fibre and a bit of iron into you along with your ethanol intake.

Jigger of vodka

Two jiggers tomato juice

large splash of Tabasco pepper sauce

Pour the liquid ingredients over ice into a cocktail glass. Stir with a celery stick – and leave the stick in the glass for food value. Top with a sprinkle of fresh-ground black pepper.

KAMI-KAZE

Actually, you don't need to know this one. It just happens to be a personal favourite of ours. It's kind of like a stripped-down, cranked-up version of a Bloody Mary, with a strong suicidal streak.

One shot of white spirit – preferably something like grappa or
    slivovitz, at 80% alcohol.

One level teaspoon Tabasco pepper sauce

Chill your rocket fuel in the freezer until the bottle is frosty cold. Quickly pour a shot, and add your teaspoon of Tabasco. Toss it back in a single gulp. Then spiral in to the deck of the enemy ship and explode in flames ...

HANGOVERS: A USER'S GUIDE

A HANGOVER OCCURS AS THE result of excessive alcohol intake. A really, really good hangover involves intense nausea and vomiting, blinding headaches, photophobia, extreme sensitivity to sound, severe vertigo, and temporary loss of a good portion of the senses of smell and taste. In other words, you'd probably prefer being pack-raped by a herd of drug-enraged gila monsters.

The bad news is this: the only real way to avoid getting a hangover is to avoid getting drunk in the first place – and none of us are really interested in trying that out are we? However, there are some things which can be done to ameliorate the severity of your hangover, once you've decided to have one.

- **THE HEADACHE.** Perhaps the single nastiest symptom of a savage hangover is the headache. A high-grade hangover headache matches all but the most brutal of migraines; it's a pulsing, pounding, grinding monster that fills your head and prevents any form of rational thought. Aspirin, paracetamol and ibuprofen will all work on it to some extent, and should not be neglected (take all three!), but there's a slightly better method of dealing with it.

  The hangover headache is caused largely by water loss, it seems. Alcohol, for those of you who may not know, is a diuretic: it makes you urinate frequently and copiously. As a result, you dehydrate. Considering that your brain is mostly made of water, it's no wonder the poor thing shrivels up and goes nasty.

  One of the best ways to avoid a serious hangover headache is to get a lot of water into yourself – preferably, the night before. In other words, as soon as you're done with your booze-up, (or better still, in between alcoholic drinks) you should be sucking back the Perrier like a bastard. Litres of the stuff, if you can stomach it. Trust JB and your Uncle Dirk. If you can get it in you, and keep it down, you'll feel an awful lot better about yourself the next day.

- **THE NAUSEOUS BITS.** Another of cause of Hangover Doom is the evil mix of chemicals other than ethanol in your average alcoholic drink. These side-chemicals are called congeners, and can include an absolutely eye-popping range of complex organic compounds and insidious toxins. As a rule, the cheaper and nastier the booze you've chosen to drink, the less care has been taken about the manufacture of the stuff. Unlikely as it may seem, it's better to be hung over on a bottle of Glenfiddich (single malt scotch whisky) than it is on a bottle of Glenfucker. Apparently, there's a better grade of congener involved.

Another way you can reduce your intake of evil congeners is to take your ethanol in a purer form. Brain-shatteringly strong white spirits, such as akvavit, grappa, slivovitz, arrack, and Polish vodka are less dangerous in chemical terms than the more drinkable things like rum, tequila, and whisky. Speaking from experience, if you can stick to drinking one of these things with, say, orange juice, and take a decent glass of water between drinks, you'll wake up in the morning feeling rather better off than you have any right to do.

- **THE VITAMIN B THING.** Another possible culprit in the Hangover Horde, is vitamin B loss. This is pretty much hearsay; there's no solid medical evidence to suggest that short-term B-group vitamin deficiency can cause hangovers, but it's definite that alcohol abuse temporarily reduces your body's ability to take up and utilise the B-group vitamins. That being the case, it follows that it might be worthwhile knocking back a few strong B-complex vitamin tablets while you're drinking all that water to prevent your hangover.

PREVENTION IS BETTER THAN SOBRIETY

As a matter of fact, there is at least one product on the market which goes a long way – in the experience of ourselves and a host of other dedicated drinkers – towards cutting down the damage if you use it correctly. Dissolve a couple of Beroccas in a litre or so of water, and swill it down about an hour before the drinking session starts. If you do this, and keep up your intake of water through the course of the booze-up, chances are you'll be able to get up in the morning and pretend that nothing much happened the night before.

You'll note that all of these are preventative measures, not cures. Personally, we have yet to encounter anything that will pull you together once you're firmly in the clutches of the Black Hangover Beast, with the exception of time, water, and rest. We're told that if you can arrange for a medical friend to supply you with a litre or so of IV saline, plus a quick injection of a powerful nausea-suppressant drug, it can be very helpful. Coca-Cola is a reasonable bet as well – it's full of water, sugar and caffeine, all of which are useful. 'Hair of the Dog' remedies (taking another drink) only work on mild hangovers; anyone who's had a genuine case of the Morning After will tell you that there is no possible way you could stomach yet another drink while the room is spinning, your stomach is heaving, your brain is pounding, and purple lights are flashing at the edges of your vision.

Another important thing to note is that hangovers get worse as you get older. When you're young, your liver thinks it's immortal, your brain knows no better, and you bounce back with an unfeasibly stupid eagerness. Age makes it a lot more painful. The trick is to learn to pace yourself, and be cagey about the way you drink. Most importantly, you need to cultivate the right attitude towards your occasional hangover. It'll only last 24 hours, or so. Don't moan and complain unnecessarily; nobody likes a whinger, and after all, if you've got a hangover, you probably earned the bloody thing, right?

§

Booze. A cautionary tale.

I've done a lot of dumb things trying to impress girls. And the level of dumbness has tended to correlate closely with my state of drunkenness. It's like the porter says in *Macbeth*, strong drink both awakens and discourages lechery. It provokes the desire, but it takes away the performance. If only I'd paid more attention in school. The teachers were only trying to help. They knew a lot of useful things. Things like, It provokes the desire, but it takes away the performance.

But I did not pay attention to my teachers and consequently my girl-chasing adventures were always a little ... unbalanced. I was either driving them mad with blank-eyed, emotional flatness or running these weird Mission Impossible sex scams on them, with three or four conflicting storylines and sub-plots and a host of improbable props and devices. I once helped organise a ball, a formal black tie affair, because I had fallen in lust with one of the other organisers – this girl called Lauren – and I was looking to spend lots of time with her. And of course, there's something about a guy in a dinner suit which drives the babes wild. But it didn't happen for me, not with Lauren anyway. You see she was a very popular girl. There must have been about thirty other guys trailing along in her wake, and compared with most of them I had nothing going for me. I had no job, no money, no future, no nothing. The other guys were these impossibly glamorous, totally connected, well-heeled types. Guys who could afford to hire limos to pick her up and take her to restaurants where they didn't ask if you wanted fries with your main course. I didn't even drive, still don't, and as for fries? Well, I used to dream about having fries with my meal.

I tried all sorts of desperate ploys with this woman. Even cultivated alliances with all her girl friends. Had them running interference for me on the football jocks and junior captains of industry. And they did look after me, those girls. Even took up a collection so I could invite Lauren out to an actual restaurant. The Black Duck, in Toowong. Man, this place was classy with a capital 'K'. It had all the trappings of synthetic French snottiness: a maitre'd, lotsa candles, no beer list, and scary waiters with napkins draped over their forearms. Of course I couldn't just ask her out. She might have knocked me back and then I would have had to have curled up into a tight little ball and sat in a corner for two or three years. No, I had to be certain of getting her into that restaurant. So I used one of my faves. An oldie but a goodie: told her my best friend had just been killed in a horrible service station explosion on the Nullarbor Plain and I just couldn't be alone that night.

Whether she fell for it and took pity on me because of my recently immolated best buddy, or whether she took pity on me because it was just about the lamest, most pathetic pick-up line she'd ever heard in her life, fact was she took pity on something and agreed to come out. Went pretty well too. The food was way too rich for me, after living on rice and fish fingers for so long, and I was nearly sick a couple of times. But by the end of the meal I was cruising. I'd figured out the cutlery and the wine ordering business and as the sticky, syrupy golden dessert stuff was slipped in front of us I relaxed for the first time that night. Leaned back in my chair. Crossed my legs. Got a cramp. And knee-jerked the table and everything on it all over my date.

I guess I was her date from Hell. Yet all this was still in the future when we got to this Ball, which was crawling with smarmy dudes looking to snack down on the girl of my dreams. I decided I wasn't going to make a fool of myself moping around her all night. I'd put so much work into this bash I figured I might as well enjoy myself at it. So I started putting away jugs of beer and schooies of whisky and lots of joints in the toilets and more beers and more joints and more whiskies and so on until I was this totally fucked-up drooling excuse for a boy.

When I got to that point where one more scotch would have pushed me over the line into a long term vegetative state, this woman came up, stone cold sober, and introduced herself to me. Her name was Sondra *to page 108 >*

< from page 107   Johannson, or Villalobos, or something. I forgot it about a half a million times on the night too. I vaguely recognised her from somewhere but she seemed to know all about me. So we talked for a bit. Or rather she talked and I sort of swayed about and bumped into the furniture a lot, until I got bored and wandered off to have another joint in the toilets. I vaguely recall maybe another jug of beer, and I definitely remember sucking a half a litre of warm champagne out of some drunken trollop's filthy stiletto before turning around to find this sober woman at my elbow again.

Oh yes, they called me Mr Smooth in those days.

This went on all night. Now, my threat detectors hadn't shut down completely and somewhere through the fug of alcohol and marijuana a little red warning light kept blinking frantically at me. I dimly remembered seeing this Sondra woman turn up with some huge bearded guy, about seven foot tall and two axe handles across the shoulders. I'd said something about this guy and she'd gone, 'Oh, he's my lover'. So you can see I had good reason to be running away and hiding in the toilets all the time. Trouble was, whenever I came back she was waiting for me. Finally, she asked if I wanted to dance. I'm thinking fuck, I can hardly stand up, let alone dance, and there is the issue of this gigantic jealous man lurking around somewhere. Old Redbeard looked as if he could have snapped my spine like a paddlepop stick. On the other hand, she's a pretty good-looking babe, and I'm horribly drunk, and there is the bitter frustration of the unreachable Lauren O'Brien to deal with, so yeah, okay we'll have a dance.

A big mistake.

We got out on that dance floor and I got that pneumatic body pressed up against my filthy, beer-stained dinner jacket and my little red warning light blinked out forever, swallowed up by this hot, sludgy lust which welled up from my groin and smothered whatever was left of my rational mind. I'm thinking, Yeah, this is good, I'm gonna put the Move on her, that's right the Move. And the thing is she's cool for the

Move. She likes the Move. She *wants* the Move. And even now, years later, all I can think is, why? What did she see in me? I was sweating, I was drunk, I was stoned, I was just about the worst catch in the world. And it got worse. Friends kept coming over, wanting to know who she was. Wanting to be introduced. And I kept forgetting her name. I must have done that about six times in a row. And she just patiently introduced herself to this procession of drunken yahoos.

The Ball started to wind down about two in the morning. Redbeard was gone, disappeared without trace, leaving me with his girl friend. Even then though, hanging off this girl's arm like some drunken retard, I was still scanning the room for Lauren, still trying to track the thirty competitors who were also after her. Most of all I was wondering what Lauren was going to make of this overly forward and completely sober woman leading me into the night. Wondering if maybe I shouldn't just give this woman the Flick right now. Because the Flick was coming, we all knew that I guess. So why not just jump to the Flick? Save us all a shitload of hassles. In the end it would have been better if I had.

Sondra knew I had a room at the Sheraton. Each of the ball organisers got a complimentary room. And she suggested we go back there. But by now I had the Fear. I was so confused by this woman's interest in me, and by what I was going to do about Lauren, and by the location of the big spine-snapping jealous dude with the red beard, I was so unbalanced by all of these things and by the massive amounts of alcohol and marijuana in my bloodstream, that the Fear took over. We were walking back to the hotel room because I couldn't think of anything else to do. I was probably calm enough on the outside, or so wasted you couldn't tell, but inside I was freaking. Luckily we got to the room and it was full of people, maybe twenty or thirty had turned up there for drinks and it was like a reprieve from the gallows. I'm thinking, 'Whew!' I had enough drinks and cones to finish me off and I passed out on the floor.

When I woke up the next morning my friends had cleared out and I was alone. In a hotel room. *to page 110 >*

< *from page 109*   With Her. The scenario quickly degenerated into one of those really bad fifties British comedies. Sondra lay on the bed, slowly drawing her ball gown up over her legs while I was tearing around the room in a frenzy, *Oh gee check out's soon and this room's a fucking pigsty I think I'd better clean this room d'you think they've got a vacuum cleaner here I bet room service does I'll call down and get a vacuum cleaner from them that's the trick!* But the ball gown kept whispering and creeping up and revealing ever more leg as Sondra crooked a finger and motioned for me to come hither. I felt like a dead man as I trod over to her and climbed onto the bed. I just didn't want to be there. I couldn't believe this was happening. I'd started to go through the motions when the phone rang. It was Lauren, the other girl, the girl I'd actually wanted to go out with. She asked if I wanted to have breakfast with her, and inside me this little cartoon guy jumped about about ten feet in the air, punched the sky and went 'Yes!'

I clambered off Sondra and told her we had to go to breakfast. I think that was the first time I really upset her. But I just got changed and dragged her to breakfast and pretty much behaved as though we'd bumped into each other on the way down. She kept giving me this strange look as if to say, you know, what the fuck's wrong with you, I've just spent the last eight hours throwing myself at you, I could have thrown myself at any of two hundred worthless, drunken bastards and I picked you, you sick joke. Like, what part of the word 'Yes' don't you understand! I didn't know how to cope with it. All my reproductive urges were still locked in on this other girl and I just couldn't come at the idea of abandoning that hopeless quest. So I did a bad thing. I ignored Sondra from then on.

Cut her dead for the next three days until she eventually pissed off. I look back now and I think, what a shameful fucking episode that was. And a real waste too. As I said, I never went out with Lauren O'Brien and as far as I know she married a druid.

§

CHAPTER FIVE

Culture and the 21st Century Man

MANY'S THE TIME WE'VE HEARD otherwise sane men bewailing the loss of some semi-mythic culture in the anonymity of the modern world. As though thousands of years of accumulated knowledge and tradition can just vanish overnight. These pantywaists almost always become very enthusiastic about dopey 'wildman' seminars, where otherwise normal grown-ups paint themselves with mud and beat drums, in the mistaken belief that they're getting in touch with some sort of primal manbeast within?

What a bunch of crap. The Beast Within is only a six-pack away. If you really need the Primitive Man experience, grab some drinking buddies, a couple of slabs, and go to the cricket. Leave the drumming and the dancing and the howling to people who still go in for that kind of thing – like House Music freaks, for example.

None of that stuff is culture, so far as you're concerned. Your culture put men on the moon, and sent a message to the stars. Your culture has learned to harness the lightning, and to liberate the power of the sun from the heart of the atom. Your culture has thwarted disease, healed the sick and lame, and is working hard on raising the dead. Your culture, the Western Culture, has been kicking arse for thousands of years and if some shitpot little third world tyrant like Dr Mahatir thinks that's gonna change any time soon then he's one sorry, self-deluded motherfucker. That being the case, the next time some tosspot waffles on about the superior spirituality of the Red Indian give them a swift clout to the head and point out that boxing is a part of your culture which goes back to the Ancient Greeks. And it has highly spiritual overtones, too, as pugilistic combats were dedicated to the Gods of Olympus ...

The thing is, Western culture is so gigantic, so vital, so aggressive and overwhelming that many people have lost sight of the fact that it is a culture in the first place. And yet, a culture it most certainly is, replete with myths and stories, makers of art and music, and thinkers of the first water. Just because your culture has left behind the need to paint itself blue and huddle round the fire to keep the evil spirits at bay doesn't make it any less valid. Don't get Stone-Age retro on us; just learn the following names instead, and you'll be more than a match for any pissant Confucians or quasi-barbaric towelheads on the planet!

About The One Hundred

THE BASIS OF DECISION FOR including people on this list, or turfing them, wasn't entirely arbitrary. However, you will notice there are no great generals or statesmen here. Government is not an art, nor a form of culture. Government, to date, is a system of thinly-veiled threats designed to preserve the status quo at the cost of the people. That being the case, the only leader of any note included here is Mohandas Gandhi, who was so deeply opposed to the idea of government-by-violence that it would have been a crime to leave him out.

If your favourite writers and artists aren't represented here – well, tough. Paring the list of names down to one hundred, out of all the myriads who have shaped the Western world – that was a very, very demanding task. Thanks to everyone who offered assistance and suggestions. And if we left your suggestions off the list, please don't phone us up to tell us about it!

ART
We're afraid there are no contemporary or Australian or female artists on this list for the sad but incontestable reason that they don't deserve a guernsey.

BRUEGHEL, PIETER (1525-1569) The last step in the Flemish version of the Renaissance in art, which began with Van Eyck. Brueghel kicked the Italian habit of muscular nudes, idealised scenery, and mythological subjects, moving slowly and gradually towards some kind of contemporary realism. He's famous for complex, intricate scenes of village life – feasts, dances, harvests and the like. His characters aren't gorgeous demi-gods; they're notably ugly, grubby peasant sorts engaged in grubby peasant occupations, observed with a fine eye for detail and a wonderful sense of humour. See his *Peasant Kermis* and *Peasant Wedding Feast*.

BUONAROTTI, MICHELANGELO (1475-1564) Florentine painter, sculptor, and architect. One of the prime forces in the Italian High Renaissance, and arguably one of the most inspired artists of all time. His marble statuary is breathtakingly exquisite, and shows true mastery of form, proportion, and perspective. See his *Pieta*, and the all-too-famous *David*, and of course, the murals on the Sistine Chapel ceiling in Rome, where he also designed St. Peter's Cathedral.

DALI, SALVADOR (1904-1989) Spanish-born King of the Surrealists. Basically, the idea behind Surrealism was to try and create a kind of mystical symbolic message/meaning through art, especially by incorporating dream-like images. Dali's works, notoriously featuring limp clocks, flaming giraffes, and melting heads, have become the best-known icons of the Surrealist movement. Dali was a real weird-arse, heavily into auto-eroticism and exceptionally bad moustachios. However his works have a certain merit, characterised by careful draftsmanship, sharp detail, and strong, vivid colours. We kind of like some of them ... *The Persistence of Memory* and *Slumber* in particular.

DA VINCI, LEONARDO (1452-1519) Florentine artist and all-round winner who provided the basic model of the Renaissance Man. He painted, he sculpted, he wrote, he designed machinery, he built war engines, he scored big with the babes ... trouble is, he didn't finish most of what he started. You can see the *Mona Lisa* (La Gioconda) in the Louvre, though. And that drawing of his, of the man with six arms and four legs – that's been on more T-shirts than Bart Simpson. Honestly, though, Leonardo was a sharp bastard. Most of his scientific work was never disseminated within his lifetime because he liked to write in crazed mirror script – but the things he discovered about anatomy, geology, hydraulics, aerodynamics and meteorology anticipated the rest of the world by a couple of hundred years. Definitely a heavy dude well out of his time.

---

§

ART IS VICE. YOU DON'T **marry it legitimately, you rape it.** – *Edgar Degas*

§

DEGAS, (HILAIRE GERMAINE) EDGAR (1834-1917) French painter of the Impressionist period. Painted with great insight, especially when painting women, which he did a lot of. His various paintings – especially his dancers – are often breath-takingly beautiful pieces, capturing true moments of vulnerability and strength in his subjects.

GOGH, VINCENT WILLEM VAN (1853-1890) (That's pronounced van Gockkkhhh, by the way.) Mad but brilliant Dutch Post-Impressionist painter, famous for having lopped off a piece of his ear to send to a hooker of whom he was particularly fond. And really, we've all been there, right? His most famous works, done late in his life, are characterised by intense colour, and thick, swirling strokes of paint. See his *Sunflowers*, *Starry Night*, and the series of *Irises*. Van Gogh shot himself which made him a sort of tortured artist to many people, but a bit of a loser to us.

MATISSE, HENRI EMILE BENOIT (1869-1954) French painter, leader of the Fauvist movement, who excelled in his ability to use colour and form to convey emotional expression. Matisse's work represents one of the great influences on the development of 20th century art. Check his *Portrait With A Green Stripe*, *Odalisque With Magnolias*, and *Pink Nude*.

> §
>
> **WHAT I DREAM OF IS an art of balance, of purity and serenity devoid of troubling or depressing subject matter ... a soothing, calming influence on the mind, rather like a good armchair which provides relaxation from physical fatigue.** – *Henri Matisse*
>
> **[GOD] INVENTED THE GIRAFFE, THE elephant, and the cat. He has no real style, He just goes on trying other things.** – *Pablo Picasso*
>
> §

PICASSO, PABLO RUIZ Y (1881-1973) Spanish painter and sculptor, sometimes regarded as the greatest artist of the 20th century. He was sure as hell one of the most prolific of all time, leaving behind him over 20,000 works. Picasso was a massive innovator. He messed with form, colour, medium and style with complete aplomb and utter disregard for artistic convention. As a result, he practically founded the Cubist movement, which followed on from Surrealism and Dadaism. No matter how you approach his stuff, Picasso's work is characterised by an inescapable strength and vividness which shines through even his weirdest moments of hallucinatory cubism. See his *Guernica* and die.

ROSSETTI, DANTE GABRIEL. (1828-1882) Born Gabriel Charles Dante Rossetti, he was an English poet and painter who didn't like the times into which he was born – all grubby and steam-powered and Victorian. Rossetti gathered together a bunch of other wet blankets and formed the Pre-Raphaelite movement, which was dedicated to drawing inspiration from medieval ... err, stuff. Rossetti and his Pre-Raphaelite Mafia are an excellent early example of the sort of crap we still have to put up with today – they felt that modern times were characterised by crass commerciality and ugliness, and that the human spirit had been somehow nobler back when nobody knew about dental hygiene, and you could tell the King because he didn't have shit all over him. These days, he'd probably be painting dung pictures of buffalo on hand-woven weasel-hair blankets, and running 'wildman' seminars. And he wasn't half the poet his sister Christina was, either.

TITIAN (1477-1576) Born Tiziano Vecellio, Titian was the greatest of the 16th Century Venetian painters, and major shaper of the Venetian school. He is noted for the sensuality of his colours, and for his technique of painting realistic events within wild, almost impressionistic settings. Titian was a major talent, who fully understood his own place within the Renaissance art world, and his work had huge and lasting effect on Western art. Check out his *Three Ages of Man, Annunciation, Crowning With Thorns*, and *Battle of Cadore*.

TURNER, JOSEPH MALLORD WILLIAM (1775-1851) Greatest of the English landscape painters, whose flair for the portrayal of natural light on landscapes and seascapes has also made him one of the most imitated painters of all time. In fact, he was so good, he practically paralysed English painting for the better part of a hundred years. See his *Bay of Baiae, Rain, Steam and Speed*, and the wildly famous *Approach to Venice*.

VAN EYCK, JAN (1390-1441) Flemish painter who helped found the 'Ars Nova' (new art) school which pretty much dragged Northern Europe kicking and screaming into the Renaissance. Instead of flat, depthless depictions of saints and other religious topics, Van Eyck got into perspective and natural colours, and even did some portrait work too. All of this was a bit of a revelation for the times, and Van Eyck's reputation as the Godfather of Oils hung around well into the 16th century.

van Rijn, Rembrandt Harmenszoon (1606-1669) Dutch Baroque painter who ranks amongst the greatest masters of the Western artistic tradition. His strongest feature was a truly amazing ability to depict light and shadow, but he had an eye for detail and an ability to convey genuine images from life which was extremely unusual for the times. See his *Portrait of the Painter in Old Age*, *Return of the Prodigal Son*, and the complex and interesting *Night Watch*.

SCIENCE

Archimedes (287-212 BC) Greek mathematician who wrote a lot about geometry, arithmetic and mathematics. Defined the principle of the lever, and invented the compound pulley. Also discovered the law of hydrostatics, supposedly while in the bath.

'Eureka!' (Shit, this bath is hot!)

Aristotle (384-322 BC) Actually, putting this bloke in with the scientists is not unlike calling Godzilla an Urban Planner. Aristotle – who tutored Alexander the Great – was probably the single greatest scientific disaster of all time. Other than some decent work in the principles of logic, he seems to have carefully avoided writing anything factual throughout his career. And yet it was his works on natural history, astronomy and physics which became the absolute truth of 'science' for the next fifteen centuries, or thereabouts. Aristotle is the swine who brought us the Flat Earth in the Centre of the Universe model. He is also the twat who insisted that heavy objects fall faster than light ones. And that all the universe is composed of four elements – fire, earth, air and water – a notion which is still propping

§

Give me but one firm spot on which to stand, and I will move the Earth. – *Archimedes*

The roots of education are bitter, but the fruit is sweet. – *Aristotle*

There is no excellent beauty that hath not some strangeness in the proportion. – *Francis Bacon*

§

up bullshit new-age spirituality to this day. Essentially, he was a second-rate rival to Plato, who was himself a self-described shadow of Socrates. Don't read anything he wrote – except maybe his work on Rhetoric.

BACON, ROGER (1214-1294) English philosopher and proto-scientist. He did some work in optics, and messed around with gunpowder, but most of that stuff he seems to have borrowed from the Arabs. What was important was that he was one of the earliest and most tenacious proponents of the Scientific Method: Observe, Theorise, Test – and if your theory fails the test, start all over again. Prior to Bacon, science consisted pretty much of agreeing with whatever Aristotle had written.

COPERNICUS, NICOLAUS (1473-1543) Polish astronomer who theorised that everything revolved around the Sun, rather than the Earth. Since the Earth-centric idea was the one held by that prat Aristotle, and enthusiastically championed by that giant collection of corrupt angry monsters, the Catholic Church, this theory got Copernicus and a lot of other people into a great deal of trouble.

CURIE, MARIE (1867-1934) Polish-born scientist who married a Frenchman, and became the first female recipient of the Nobel Prize in 1903, when she shared the honour with her husband Pierre, and with Antoine Henri Becquerel, for the discovery of radioactive elements. Marie Curie was the person who coined the term 'radioactive', and despite the fact that women of her time were supposed to be basically doorstops and baby-factories, she did the hard yards in a very difficult field of science. She and Pierre processed a couple of tonnes of Uranium ore to discover Polonium and Radium. When Pierre was run over by a horse-cart and killed in 1906, she stepped in and took over all his teaching duties at France's top university as well as continuing her own research, and in 1911, scored her very own Nobel prize in chemistry – still on radium. In the end, all the playing with radioactive elements put the zap on her, and she died of pernicious anaemia. One of her daughters also later shared a Nobel prize for radio-chemistry. Hell of a family, when you consider it.

DARWIN, CHARLES ROBERT (1809-1882) British naturalist who became one of the most misunderstood and misquoted men of all time with his Theory of Natural Selection. Prior to Darwin's work, there were a lot of weird ideas as to where all the different species of animals and plants came from. Mostly, the Christians held the floor with the theory that God just spat 'em all out on day three. This didn't account for the fossil record, though, and the idea that God threw the fossils in to confuse scientists didn't really wash. Darwin suggested, in his book *On The Origin of Species* (1859) that species gradually changed over many generations as a result of selective survival of individuals who best suited their environment. The Christians have hated him ever since. Point to note: Darwin did not say humanity is descended from the apes. He stated that we may share a common ancestor with modern apes.

> §
>
> A HAIRY QUADRUPED, FURNISHED WITH a tail and pointed ears, probably arboreal in its habits. [On man's probable ancestors] – *Charles Darwin*
>
> IF *a* IS SUCCESS IN life, then *a* equals *x* plus *y* plus *z*. Work is *x*; play is *y*; and *z* is keeping your mouth shut. – *Albert Einstein*
>
> §

DAVY, SIR HUMPHRY (1778-1829) Heavy-duty British chemist who built the world's biggest battery, discovering potassium, sodium and boron in the process. He also discovered how much fun you could have with nitrous oxide (rather a lot), and invented a safety lamp for coal miners.

EINSTEIN, ALBERT (1879-1955) German born physicist, who became an American citizen noted for his Theories of Special and General Relativity, and for his amazingly bad hair. School – high school in particular – bored him senseless and he did not do well. However, working as a patent clerk, he postulated the particle theory of light, and explained the photo-electric effect, then went on to produce Special Relativity in 1905. It was the first real change in the way the universe had been described by science since Isaac Newton, two and a half centuries prior. Einstein's most famous work is the simple formula which shows that matter and energy are basically the same thing: $E=mc^2$. It is this idea which led directly to the conception of the atomic bomb.

EUCLID (300 BC?) Greek mathematician behind all of that plane geometry stuff that made your life so miserable in high school.

FARADAY, MICHAEL (1791-1867) British physicist and chemist who did a lot of the underlying work in electromagnetics and electrochemistry. Boring, but really, really important.

FLOREY, SIR HOWARD WALTER (1898-1968) Australian scientist who isolated penicillin from the antibacterial mould discovered by Sir Alexander Fleming. In doing so, this pair have probably saved more lives than anybody else in the history of the world. Aussie! Aussie! Aussie! Oy! Oy! Oy!

FREUD, SIGMUND (1856-1939) Austrian physician, neurologist, and founder of psychoanalysis. The history of treatment of mental disorder is quite disturbing. When Freud happened on the scene, it consisted mostly of locking up anyone who behaved in what was regarded by the public as an irrational manner. Freud, despite being one of the most neurotic individuals in history, at least made a stab at bringing some sort of method to the treatment of madness. His major contribution to the field lay in demonstrating that at least some mental disorders had discernible, treatable mental causes, rather than purely physiological ones. The influence of his ideas on dream analysis, symbolism, and the unconscious has continued to assert itself, long after many of his more scientific notions have been shot down in flames.

> §
>
> **THE GREAT QUESTION THAT HAS** never been answered and which I have not yet been able to answer, despite my thirty years of research into the feminine soul, is, 'What does a woman want?' – *Freud*
>
> §

GALILEI, GALILEO (1564-1642) Italian mathematician and astronomer who ran afoul of Aristotle and the Church by arguing that Copernicus was right – the Earth went around the Sun. Discovered four of Jupiter's moons, demonstrated that Aristotle was a butt-weasel by showing that objects of differing weights do not fall at different speeds. The Catholics threatened to charge him with heresy, so he wimped out and publicly agreed that the

Sun went around the Earth. And Hell, who wouldn't if the alternative was to be turned into a one-man weenie-roast?

GUTENBERG, JOHANNES (1400-1468) Shall we call him a scientist? Why not? He was a German born goldsmith, who turned his hand to printing. The thing which makes him memorable is that he brought his goldsmith's precision to the art of creating printer's type – and more importantly, he invented movable metal type. Prior to Gutenberg, printing was done by etching a chunk of stone or metal, or carving from a block of wood. Gutenberg cleverly made a whole bunch of high-quality metal letters which could be set, line by line, as type, and re-set for each new page of print. Gutenberg's invention had consequences which really are beyond the limits of this book. Essentially, it was the movable-type printing press which brought literacy out of the hands of the aristocracy, and created the society in which we live. Nothing today remains of Gutenberg's printing work, except a few fabulously valuable copies of a bible he printed, in a vain effort to pay off his debts.

KOCH, ROBERT (1843-1910) German bacteriologist – the first one, really – awarded the Nobel Prize in 1905. Koch was the man who demonstrated beyond a doubt that diseases were caused by specific micro-organisms, and not evil spirits, noxious fluxes, or frumenty.

MENDEL, GREGOR JOHANN (1822-1884) An Austrian monk who grew sweet-peas. Observing the flowers, he formulated a set of ideas about heredity which led to the eventual development of genetic science. Gardening to Jurassic Park, in one easy step!

MENDELEYEV, DMITRY IVANOVICH (1834-1907) Russian chemist who devised the periodic table of chemical elements. This was a very clever move, because it allowed scientists to look for elements that should exist but weren't known as yet, and to predict the characteristics of as yet unknown elements.

NEWTON, SIR ISAAC (1643-1727) Extremely smart cookie. Invented calculus in 1666 – although to be fair, a couple of other people were working in the same field at the time. Codified the Three Laws of Motion, which led to his Theory of Gravitation which was expounded in his *Principia Mathematica* of 1687. Newton's work was so good that his picture of the universe wasn't really re-drawn until Einstein came along with the Theory of Relativity.

NIGHTINGALE, FLORENCE (1820-1910) Florentine-born British nurse and hospital reformer. When Florence Nightingale arrived on the nursing scene, about the time of the Crimean War, nursing was a menial job carried out by largely untrained personnel. She busted her arse in the Crimea, raising the quality of hospital care and hygiene, and then later, turning nursing into a respected part of the medical profession. Her work in the war saved countless lives, and her later work, in literally creating the role of the modern nurse, has gone on to save countless more.

§

IF I HAVE SEEN FURTHER, it is by standing on the shoulders of giants. – *Isaac Newton*

NO MAN, NOT EVEN A doctor, ever gives any other definition of what a nurse should be than this – 'devoted and obedient.' This definition would do just as well for a porter. It might even do for a horse. It would not do for a policeman. – *Florence Nightingale*

§

NOBEL, ALFRED BERNHARD (1833-1896) Swedish chemist and inventor who invented dynamite. This made him a fortune, but his work in explosives and fire-arms also made him feel guilty. To assuage his conscience, he set up the Nobel Prize fund, which yearly gives a lot of money and recognition to people working in physics, chemistry, medicine, physiology, literature, and world peace. (And since 1969, economics. For God's sake!)

PASTEUR, LOUIS (1822-1895) French chemist and microbiologist, who did a large number of very clever things, including devising vaccinations for anthrax and for rabies, demonstrating that micro-organisms caused the fermentation process which is vital to BEER, and invented the process of pasteurisation to preserve milk and wine. Most importantly, though, he proved finally that micro-organisms don't just spontaneously spring into existence, but must be introduced to whatever it is they're going to grow on – thus destroying the best excuse Man ever had for the state of his fridge.

PYTHAGORAS (550 BC, or thereabouts.) Greek mathematician and philosopher who ran a school of weird fundamentalist philosopher-mystics. Noted for the pythagorean theorem of right-angle triangles, and for being the first known in history to propose that the earth revolved around a central fire with the other planets.

RUTHERFORD, ERNEST (1871-1937) New Zealand chemist, awarded the Nobel Prize in 1908. First person to suggest the nuclear structure of the atom, after messing around with Beta particles a lot. And didn't that lead to a great big mess of trouble! Shame New Zealand! Shame!

TESLA, NIKOLAI (1856-1943) Croatian born American engineer and inventor, who came up with the basics for practically everything electrical or electronic in the world. Over the objections of Thomas Edison, for whom he worked briefly, he developed and marketed the generation and transmission of Alternating Current (AC) electricity, which powers a world full of vibrating dildos today. He also managed radio well before Marconi; the patent was eventually awarded to Tesla by the international courts, but he was dead by then. Tesla was a deeply weird individual who really, really liked pigeons, enjoyed playing with lightning, and was afraid of women wearing pearl earrings ... but at least he didn't publicly electrocute dogs to demonstrate the evils of AC current, the way Edison did. He also invented those neat spark-throwing gadgets which appear in the lab sequences of all the best *Frankenstein* films.

TURING, ALAN MATHISON (1912-1954) British mathematician and cryptographer who put together a lot of the basic ideas behind computing. Perhaps best known for his theoretical 'Turing Test' to determine whether or not an artificial intelligence is 'sentient' ... basically, if you can have a conversation with it and not realise it's artificial, then it's 'sentient'. Of course, the Turing Test falls on its face because it assumes that the person administering the test in the first place has to be sentient, a condition which does not apply to the greater mass of the human race.

MUSIC

ARMSTRONG, LOUIS DANIEL (1900-1971) He wasn't the only jazz virtuoso soloist, but he was the first of the real big ones. Jazz had been around a while before the black American trumpeter known as 'Satchmo' burst onto the scene, but it was Armstrong's style, alongside his bands 'The Hot Five' and 'The Hot Seven' which really made Jazz into the international phenomenon it became. Armstrong practically invented 'scat' singing (you know – all that 'doobie-doobie-doo' stuff) Armstrong made the soloist – and the jazz solo – the focus of the music, and established jazz improvisation by working new melodies around the notes of the chords in the original piece, while in the process of performing. Listen to his 'Dipper Mouth' Blues', 'Sister Kate', 'Gutbucket Blues', and of course, the anthemic (wildly overplayed) 'What a Wonderful World'.

§

ALL MUSIC IS FOLK MUSIC, I ain't never heard no horse sing a song. – *Louis Armstrong*

MUSIC IS A HIGHER REVELATION than all wisdom and philosophy. – *Beethoven*

§

BACH, JOHANN SEBASTIAN (1685-1750) German organist and composer of the Baroque period. He was a totally amazing musician, with an enormous output of carefully structured music, most of it composed for the church. He handled counterpoint melodies like nobody before or since, and despite the highly structured and mathematical nature of music at his time, produced pieces with depth, texture and powerful emotional content. Listen to his famous 'Toccata and Fugue in D Minor', his 'Well-Tempered Clavier' series, and his gorgeous 'Brandenburg Concertos'.

BEETHOVEN, LUDWIG VAN (1770-1827) A German-born composer of the Romantic period, whose music is characterised by an unparalleled emotional power and intensity. Unfortunately, he was a temperamental and uptight man, never very tolerant of lesser mortals – which made him a tad unpopular amongst those around him. Sadly for him, Beethoven eventually went stone deaf. His letters speak of a 'terrible whistling and roaring' in his head, suggesting some sort of tinnitus. By the time he died, he could no longer hear the sound of a standing ovation in a concert hall. Didn't affect the quality of his music, though: his final symphony, the Ninth, remains one of the greatest musical works of all time. Try to hear the fourth, fifth, seventh and ninth symphonies, and as many of his piano sonatas as you can get hold of.

BRAHMS, JOHANNES (1833-1897) German composer of great note, combining the Classical and Romantic styles in his work. Brahms was especially interesting because he kept on writing in the older styles of music – and doing it very well, thank you – when all around him, everybody was jumping on the Berlioz bandwagon and producing strange, discordant chunks of wildly evocative, but not very coherent (and frequently not very enjoyable) pieces of music. Try out his first four symphonies for a real taste of Brahms.

HANDEL, GEORGE FREDERIC (1685-1759) One of the real monster composers of the Baroque period. Handel was born in Germany, and unlike most of the other composers in this list, his family had bugger-all to do with music. Young George, however, was such an obvious talent that by his tenth birthday the local organists insisted on giving him lessons. Handel really got around. In Italy, he wrote opera and cantatas. In Germany, he was court composer and conductor to the Hanover kings. Then he shot through to London, where he had a fine old time until the British royal family went kaput, and they had to bring in George I as king. Coincidentally, this same George was the Elector of Hanover, Handel's previous employer, from whom the composer had absconded. No matter. Handel put together a big suite of music and smarmed his way back into George's good graces. For listening purposes, check out the 'Water Music', the 'Music for the Royal Fireworks', and of course, the unforgettable oratorio 'Messiah'.

§

HOW TO LIKE CLASSICAL MUSIC

Listen to Tchaikovsky's Sixth Symphony and Beethoven's Seventh twice each. If you don't like them after that, forget classical music for a while. – *Anon*

§

HANDY, WILLIAM CHRISTOPHER (1873-1958) American composer, cornet-player and bandmaster. His great claim to fame lies with being the first man to publish 'Blues Music' (starting with his 'Memphis Blues' in 1912), thus beginning the process of assimilating the essentially oral tradition of Black American blues into the mainstream of western music.

JOPLIN, SCOTT (1868-1917) American composer and pianist, who pretty much created the ragtime music movement. Joplin had a great life, learning to play piano in sleazy bars and brothels while he was still in his teens. He had an enormous respect for Black American music, and published an opera – *Treemonisha* – at his own expense which was supposed to transcend ragtime to create an inherently 'Black' opera. The work crashed and burned, and pretty much took Joplin with it. You will have heard some of his work though – nobody since the 1973 movie *The Sting* has managed to avoid his rag, 'The Entertainer'. Ragtime in general, and Joplin in particular, had an enormous effect on the later development of jazz and blues for the piano.

MENDELSSOHN-BARTHOLDY, JAKOB LUDWIG FELIX (1809-1847) German composer who became one of the leading lights of the Romantic period. Not only did he, in his regrettably short life, produce such beautifully melodic works as the incidental music to *A Midsummer Night's Dream* and his fourth and fifth symphonies, Mendelssohn was also responsible for the return of the music of Bach to the centre stage. In 1829, after having found part of the score wrapped around his fish'n'chips, Mendelssohn conducted the first performance of *The Passion of St Matthew* since the death of Bach nearly eighty years before. While he could never be regarded as a musical revolutionary, certainly his music reflects the absolute best of the Romantic ideas.

MOZART, WOLFGANG AMADEUS (1756-1791) Austrian born composer central to the Classical period of Western music. Mozart moved sharply away from the formal, relatively simple and mathematical Baroque style of music characterised by Bach and Handel. He was a child prodigy, an accomplished performer on violin, clavier and organ by the time he was six. His lifelong output was phenomenal – more than 600 works, including opera, concertos, oratorios, sonatas, and full symphonies. Catch 'Don Giovanni', 'The Marriage of Figaro', and 'The Magic Flute' as well as 'Cosi Fan Tutte'. Also, see the film Amadeus to get a nice précis of his life and doings.

PAGANINI, NICOLO (1782-1840) The violin hasn't always been the show-pig of the orchestra. Once upon a time, Mr Piano was the one with the big brass balls. Then along came this bloke Paganini, from Italy. His playing was so totally amazing that rival violinists started a rumour which said: 'Paganini has sold his soul to the Devil. His violin sounds so much like the voice of a woman because he has killed his wife and strung the violin with strands of her gut. He is evil incarnate. Do not go to his concerts, or you will certainly be damned.' As far as we're concerned, this makes Paganini the ancestor of modern Heavy Metal. Whatever else may be said, he was hell on mag wheels when it came to the fiddle, and if you can get hold of any of his 'Caprices', or of his violin sonatas, they're well worth an ear. There's also a fairly funny old B&W film which puts Stewart Grainger into the role of the great violinist. Grab a six-pack, rent the film, and get some cultcha into you.

PRESLEY, ELVIS ARON (1935-1977) Although most of his gold records came for his gospel singing, Elvis is remembered as the King of Rock and Roll. A good, Southern White Boy, Elvis borrowed from Black American blues and gospel singing to create his own signature brand of hip-pumping, guitar-backed music. Alongside such luminaries as Chuck Berry and Buddy Holly, Elvis must be acknowledged as one of the true fathers of Rock, even if he was a fat bastard who died on the toilet while scarfing down gigantic greaseburgers. See just one of his movies – say, *Blue Hawaii* – to get an idea of the man as a performer, and listen to 'Blue Suede Shoes', 'All Shook Up', 'Heartbreak Hotel' and 'Hound Dog' to identify his musical style. Then you can join the rest of the civilised world in

§

YOU AIN'T NOTHIN' BUT A **houn' dog**
Cryin' all the time.
You ain't nothin' but a houn' dog
An' you ain't no friend of mine!
                                    – *Elvis Presley*

MY MUSIC IS BEST UNDERSTOOD by children and animals. – *Igor Stravinsky*

§

quietly celebrating the fact that he died before becoming fat enough and Republican enough to run for the US presidency.

STRAVINSKY, IGOR FYODOROVICH (1882-1971) Russian-born composer who led the way from the stuffy conventionality of 19th century formal music into the atonal, disorganised nastiness of 20th century orchestral music. Stravinsky's best works are from his earliest period of composing, back around 1910, when he was putting together ballet music for Sergei Diaghilev. Back then, his music represented an interesting and refreshing break away from a tradition which was becoming increasingly moribund. Sadly, as his own work became more the model for the mainstream, Stravinsky continued to incorporate more and more 20th Century Art-Wanker Crap into his music. It was fine while he was ripping off ragtime, but once he got into the weird, twelve-tonal Serialist stuff, his compositions became impenetrable to the regular listener. However, that didn't stop every other composer of the time trying to out-Stravinsky Stravinsky ... Listen to 'Petrushka', 'The Rite of Spring', and 'The Firebird Suite'.

TCHAIKOVSKY, PYOTR ILLYICH (1840-1893) Russian composer, perhaps the foremost of the 19th century. Unfortunately for him, he was a screaming bender, in a time and place which didn't tolerate the idea, so he lead a distinctly troubled life. Listen to his incidental music for the ballets 'Swan Lake', 'Sleeping Beauty', and 'The Nutcracker'. His fifth and sixth symphonies are particularly good, and his '1812 Overture', which describes in music Napoleon's attack on and subsequent retreat from Russia is one of the best known and most stirring pieces of music in Western history.

WAGNER, RICHARD (1813-1883) If your idea of opera involves fat blonde women in metal bikinis shrieking at the top of their lungs, you've been a victim of Wagner. Wagner got heavily into Teutonic mythology, and the 'ubermensch' ideals of Nietzsche (although he misunderstood them, of course) and his big, bold, brassy music made him a real pin-up boy for the right-wingers of the day. To be fair, Wagner did return the concept of 'story' and 'drama' to opera, which had pretty much lost that thread by his time. On the other hand, since Wagner's most famous operatic effort is a four-parter which relates the tortuously complicated story of the Ring of the Nibelung from German mythology, maybe he was taking things a bit far. And when you consider that each of the four operas in the Ring cycle is three to four hours long, you have to suspect that maybe he was a little unbalanced. Grab a couple 'best of Wagner' compilations, read a treatment of the Ring cycle, and you'll know everything you need to.

PHILOSOPHY

BEAUVOIR, SIMONE BERTRAND DE (1908-1986) Perhaps because she undeservedly spent so long playing second fiddle to Jean-Paul Sartre, this French novelist and heavyweight philosopher played a very profound part in illuminating the role of women in the modern world. Check out 'The Second Sex' on that topic. She also made some heavy observations on aging, and the way society treats the aged in 'The Coming of Age'.

> §
>
> **ONE IS NOT BORN A woman; one becomes one.**
> *– Simone de Beauvoir*
>
> §

DESCARTES, RENE (1596-1650) Tough to decide whether he should be a philosopher or a scientist – but Monty Python put him in 'The Philosophy Song', so who are we to disagree? As a scientist Descartes (pronounced Day-cart, you ignorant goon!) did some of the first known work in optics, invented the notation of mathematical indices, and did good work on the curves. As a philosopher, he was the first bloke to come out and suggest that we should stick to philosophising about things we can actually prove, instead of just quoting Aristotle a lot. Unfortunately, Descartes couldn't actually prove a whole lot; he started with 'I think, therefore I am', and pretty much gave up after that. Still, it was a fair start.

GANDHI, MOHANDAS KARAMCHAND (1869-1948) Indian leader and exemplar of civil disobedience, who founded the world's largest democracy. Gandhi is the only national ruler who gets a guernsey in these pages; he remains the only one who got to the top while remaining unshakeably committed to non-violence and pacifism. Indebted to Tolstoy and Thoreau

> §
>
> **IT IS DIFFICULT BUT NOT impossible to conduct strictly honest business ... What is true is that honesty is incompatible with the amassing of a large fortune.** – *Mohandas Gandhi*
>
> §

for his philosophies and techniques, Gandhi cut his political teeth in South Africa, trying to get Indian immigrants raised above the level of, say, a flatulent camel. Naturally, the white South Africans of the 19th century didn't think this was such a good idea, and Gandhi learned a great deal about how to get the shit kicked out of him on a regular basis.

He must have enjoyed it, though, because when he was done with the South Africans, he went back to India to take on the Brits. The tale of his battles with the English Colonial government of India is too long to be told here, and lasted well over twenty years. But for an old man whose major weapon was threatening to starve himself to death if his opponents didn't co-operate, Gandhi achieved amazing results. His policies of civil disobedience, boycott, and non-violent non-co-operation eventually so stymied and undermined the British rule of India that the modern Indian state was founded.

Gandhi's impact on the world can't be overstated. Though others had propounded his methods before, he was the man who demonstrated that they could be made to work. Sure, he was a bit of a fruit loop who drank his own urine, but you have to admire someone with that much determination and will, someone who actually walked the walk as well as he talked it. When you look around at the political leaders of the world at the moment, and think of this guy, it makes you want to cry.

HOBBES, THOMAS (1588-1679) English political philosopher and conservative turkey. Basically, he argued that all people fear each other, and must therefore submit absolutely to the judgement of the state in all matters, both secular and religious. Unfortunately, some of his ideas still influence modern political thinking, particularly amongst the One Nation crowd. Hobbes represents a knee-jerk conservative response to the Reformation, and the movement towards enlightenment and personal freedom it represented.

KANT, IMMANUEL (1724-1804) German mathematician and philosopher, and one of the most influential thinkers of recent history. Despite the fact that nobody has ever really understood what Kant was on about with his 'antinomies', his emphasis on logical reasoning over revelation, even in approaching religion, was a major influence on Hegel, Marx, and the entire empirical school of philosophy. Buy a copy of his *Critique of Pure Reason* for your shelves. Tell everyone you're just about to read it. Then hollow it out and keep your drugs in there. Nobody will ever look.

§

MORALITY IS NOT REALLY THE doctrine of how to make ourselves happy, but of how we are to be *worthy* of happiness. – *Immanuel Kant*

IT IS ONE THING TO show a man that he is in error, and another to put him in possession of truth. – *John Locke*

THE FIRST METHOD FOR ESTIMATING the intelligence of a ruler is to look at the men he has around him. – *Machiavelli*
(Kind of makes you worry about
John Howard, doesn't it.)

§

LOCKE, JOHN (1632-1704) English philosopher, founder of the school of Empiricism, which holds that truth needs to be derived from real, solid, experiential things, rather than from wafty intuitions and dubious deductions. Locke was one of the Good-guys. He argued against the Divine Right of Kings, and suggested that sovereignty lay not with the state, but with its people. Many of his ideas on civil and 'natural' law, such as personal rights, property rights, and the obligation of government to defend those rights went pretty much wholesale into the United States constitution. Locke championed religious freedom, and separation of church and state. He also defended the three-branch system of government, wherein legislative, judicial, and executive powers are given to different organisations. (That's the separation of powers, Sir Joh, you goon.) Best of all Locke stated that revolution was not only a right, but often an obligation. Read his *Essay Concerning Human Understanding*, and his *Two Treatises of Government*.

LUTHER, MARTIN (1483-1546) German theologian who initiated the Protestant Reformation of the Christian Church. He is popularly supposed to have nailed his famous Ninety-Five Theses to a church. (Thus demonstrating that the Catholic Church was largely comprised of evil old goats who'd probably gang fuck the Virgin Mary as soon as look at her.) Not long after that, he defended his views in front of Emperor Charles V, at the Diet of Worms, whatever that was. (God, we hope it wasn't what it sounds like.) Anyway, there was an extraordinary fuss. A lot of people decided Luther was onto a good thing, and the single greatest schism within the Christian faith was born.

MACHIAVELLI, NICCOLO (1469-1527) Florentine historian, statesman, political philosopher and all-round cunning ratbastard. He was an important mover and shaker in the time of the Italian city-states, and his most famous book is *The Prince*, probably the finest Western book on management practices of all time. You should read this, if only to work out the best way to pin the blame on someone else at every opportunity.

MARX, KARL HEINRICH (1818-1883) German philosopher who became the patron saint of Communism. Working alongside Friedrich Engels, Marx put together a monster volume called *Das Kapital*. He felt that history was a process – a dialectic, a struggle which was going somewhere. Marx figured that since the working class produced everything, and could therefore refuse to produce, they should control the state and the economy – and it was this non-capital-oriented, worker-controlled state which he envisioned and described. His dialectical materialism, or socialism, rapidly became the philosophical basis of Communism, which eventually spawned the Soviet Union, a lot of ugly wars, brutal dictatorships and some extra-ordinarily ugly architecture. Nobody did a very good job actually putting Marx's ideas into practice, and so Communism is practically dead as a form of government everywhere in the world.

NIETZSCHE, FRIEDRICH (1844-1900) German philosopher and poet whose writings on the concept of an 'overman' or 'superman' gave Adolph Hitler such a big stiffy, despite the fact that none of Nietzsche's ideas really supported that little creep's in any way. In essence, Nietszche said that traditional values – such as religion – were no longer particularly important in the modern world, and the 'overman' was a personally empowered and intellectually complete individual who would be able to define and pursue his own values in the face of any opposition. There's a lot more to it than that, but that's a start. Read *Man and Superman*, *Thus Spake Zarathustra*, and *Beyond Good and Evil*. Nietzsche eventually died of howling black syphilis, which is a pretty good way for any Man to go out, and certainly redeems him from his life of philosophy.

§

GOD IS DEAD; BUT CONSIDERING the state Man is in there will perhaps be caves, for ages yet, in which his shadow will be shown. – *Friedrich Nietzsche*

ONE SHOULD RESPECT PUBLIC OPINION in so far as is necessary to avoid starvation and keep out of prison, but anything that goes beyond this is voluntary submission to an unnecessary tyranny. – *Bertrand Russell*

§

PLATO (428 BC-347 BC) Greek philosopher. Socrates' number one student. Established the Academy in Athens in 387 – essentially, the first-ever 'university' which taught all kinds of stuff in the one place. His best and biggest work is the *Republic*, in which he outlines his idea of a perfect government. A lot of thought on the concept of 'ideal forms' which exist in the imagination, and of which all the world's elements are but crude representations. We also owe Plato a considerable debt for his preservation of many of his teacher Socrates' dialogues. Socrates wasn't big on writing things down, it seems. Like many modern 'philosophers' he preferred hanging around the markets and cafés knocking back the flat whites and working his jawbone instead of sitting at his desk to crank out the big ideas.

ROUSSEAU, JEAN-JACQUES (1712-1778) One the great French philosophers from a time when such things existed. He ran away as a sixteen-year-old to find adventure. Her name was Mme de Warens, a scandalous hussy who'd ripped off her husband and fled with the hired help to Savoy. Rousseau appeared at her door as a painfully shy, stammering boy and left as a champion philosopher, musician and pork swordsman. His central thesis was that progress had corrupted Man, rather than ennobling him and he set about the task of kicking six kinds of shit out of the Age of Reason. His *A Discourse on the Sciences and the Arts*, (1750) was one of the first steps on the road to the Romantic era, which of course came back to haunt us with a lot of bad bands and foppish haircuts in the 1980s. That's probably not Rousseau's fault though.

RUSSELL, BERTRAND ARTHUR WILLIAM, 3RD EARL RUSSELL (1872-1970) British philosopher, mathematician, Nobel laureate and dedicated pacifist. Russell was an extraordinarily smart cookie, whose insistence on logical analysis strongly influenced the course of the 20th Century. Russell was cited by Einstein as one of the dozen people in the world who genuinely understood Special and General Relativity – and Einstein did not include himself in that number. Despite the fact that he practically established the field of symbolic logic, and pretty much single-handedly refuted the reigning philosophy of 'Idealism', and went to prison for his pacifism and condemnation of both sides in World War I, the Nobel Prize was awarded to Russell for Literature(!), in 1950. Throughout his life, Russell fought and wrote against ignorance, tyranny, and destruction, to the point that at the age of 89, he was imprisoned after an anti-nuclear demonstration. The guy was a total hero. Read his *Unpopular Essays, The ABC of Relativity, Education and the Social Order, Our Knowledge of the External World*, and *Inquiry into Meaning and Truth*.

SARTRE, JEAN-PAUL (1905-1980) Bug-eyed French writer and philosopher, largely responsible for Existentialism and late twentieth-century teen angst. Sartre was an admirable enough figure, battling Nazis in WWII, fighting in the French Resistance, and doing lots of that black-beret wearing, Gauloise-smoking art stuff afterwards. Trouble is, his novels are boring. Come to think of it, so are his plays. And Existentialism, which swept the Western world in the fifties and still lurks in Universities, waiting to pounce on unsuspecting wannabe philosophers today, is also rather dull. His girl friend, Simone de Beauvoir, was soooo much cooler. In Existentialism, Sartre manages to restate the major theme of both Nietzsche and Zen Buddhism – that all people are absolutely responsible for their own actions. Nietszche thought this was grand. The Zen Buddhists think it's fun. Sartre finds it gloomy, depressing, and boring. Glance through *Being and Nothingness*, *Iron in the Soul*, and *Nausea*. Walk out at the intermission during a performance of *No Exit*. Burn your beret and your polo-neck skivvy, grab a sixpack and head down the beach to cruise for babes. You are, after all, absolutely responsible for what you do with your life ...

§

MY THOUGHT IS *ME*: THAT'S why I can't stop. I exist because I think ... and I can't stop myself from thinking. – *Jean-Paul Sartre*

THE UNEXAMINED LIFE IS NOT worth living. – *Socrates*

§

SMITH, ADAM (1723-1790) The Godfather of Capitalism, a kind of perfect Anti-Marx. This British philosopher and economist wrote a massive work in 1776 called *An Inquiry into the Nature and Causes of the Wealth of Nations*. In this treatise, Smith basically laid down the concepts of laissez-faire free-market Capitalism which have been the guiding principles of Western economics ever since. His basic argument was the 'invisible hand' – the idea that every individual, if left to themselves, will pursue their own best interests, and will as though by an 'invisible hand' be guided into doing good for all. While for the most part, Smith knew what he was talking about, this particular concept has proved to be a bunch of crap. Skasey, Bondy and all their mates did indeed pursue their own ends, but generally at the expense of everyone else.

SOCRATES (470-399 BC) Greek philosopher and total hero. Socrates did his time in the army, kicking lotsa Peloponnesian butt in the Peloponnesian War. He then took up what he considered to be his true calling – the pursuit of philosophy. Socrates didn't do a lot of writing. Nor did he establish any great schools. Instead, he appears to have wandered about the markets in Athens, arguing with anyone who would stand still long enough. Pretty much all we have of Socrates is what Plato preserved, plus a few notes from the odd historian of the time. Socrates was big on tolerance, justice, love, and self-knowledge. He taught that wisdom was virtue, and evil was only the result of ignorance. Eventually, the Athenian democracy decided he was too heretical to survive, and sentenced him to death. Rather than take the escape arranged for him by his followers, Socrates decided to obey the workings of the law, and calmly drank the cup of hemlock poison required. Definitely one of history's good-guys.

STANTON, ELIZABETH CADY (1815-1902) American social reformer who pretty much got the women's suffrage movement up and running, along with Susan B. Anthony. She cut her political teeth in the Temperance and Anti-slavery movements, and in 1840 organised the first-ever women's rights convention. A Declaration of Sentiments was drafted and passed at that convention, which declared that 'men and women are created equal'. History records that Cady was the ideas machine, the thinker, and Susan B. Anthony was the organiser and arse-kicker. It was their work which kicked off similar movements in England, and in Australia, which eventually became the first country in the world to give women the vote. One in the eye for fucking Germaine Greer.

§

REFORMERS WHO ARE ALWAYS COMPROMISING have not yet grasped that truth is the only safe ground to stand upon. – *Elizabeth Stanton*

I DETEST WHAT YOU WRITE, but I would give my life to make it possible for you to continue to write. – *Voltaire*

§

VOLTAIRE (1694-1778) The assumed name of Frenchman François-Marie Arouet, one of the leading figures of The Enlightenment. Best known as a satirist and professional witty bastard, Voltaire got into trouble for taking the piss out of all the things held sacred by French society of the time: the Church, the Government, the right of the Aristocracy to piss all over the peasants, and cheese. Interesting thing about Voltaire was that while he dumped heavily on religion as exemplified by the fat Catholic swineherd who ran the country, he was himself quite a devout Christian. In general, Voltaire stood up for freedom of thought and respect for all individuals, and rejected the irrational and incomprehensible. Read his book *Candide*, which manages to be funny two-and-a-half centuries later.

LITERATURE

AESCHYLUS (525-456 BC) Greek tragic dramatist. Be sure to pronounce it right – Esskeyluss. Otherwise you'll look like a prawn. Aeschylus was a Real Man, fighting for the Athenians against the Persians, and even taking part in the famous Battle of Marathon. He's supposed to be the bloke who really created the idea of action in drama, and drama in action. (Plays before Aeschylus were very dull.) Of his many plays – possibly as many as ninety – seven have survived, of which the Oresteia trilogy comprising Agamemnon, Choephoroe, and Eumenides are your essential reads.

---

§

EVERYONE'S QUICK TO BLAME the alien.
– *Aeschylus*

THE MAN WHO NEVER CHANGES his opinion is like standing water, and breeds reptiles of the mind. – *William Blake*

§

ALIGHIERI, DANTE (1265-1321) Italian poet, who ranks up there with the really big boys of literature on the grounds of his *Divine Comedy*, an epic poem about the poet's guided tour through Hell, Purgatory and Heaven. Dante was a very politically motivated and highly religious chap, as they all were at this time, and he took the opportunity when writing about the Inferno to stuff lots of his personal enemies into embarrassing roles. Really, you only need to read the *Inferno* to sound like you know Dante on a personal basis.

BECKETT, SAMUEL (1906-1989) Irish-born poet, novelist, and dramatist who was awarded the Nobel Prize in 1969. He is most notable for largely founding the Absurdist movement in theatre and literature, which finally acknowledged that the human condition is a hapless, hopeless, directionless absurdity, and not at all part of some vast, Godly plan for the betterment of the universe. Fortunately, Beckett had a strong sense of humour, which keeps his writing from being as boring and toxic as that French git Sartre ... See a performance of *Waiting for Godot* (or rent the Broadway version which starred Robin Williams and Steve Martin) and read *Whoroscope* and *Echo's Bones*.

BLAKE, WILLIAM (1757-1827) English poet, painter and engraver. Kind of an early romantic surrealist. Check out his *Songs of Innocence* and Experience for lyric, fantastic poetry, and *The Book of Urizen,* and *The Proverbs of Hell* for strange, unsettling images and ideas. Blake was a nice chap who wanted the best for people, and his poems and pictures are basically the result of a lifetime of not unsurprising disappointment.

BRECHT, BERTOLT (1898 -1956) German dramatist, director and poet who strongly influenced modern theatre with his strong social themes and willingness to depart from dramatic custom. He strongly condemned Capitalism throughout his career, and in pieces such as *The Threepenny Opera* and *The Caucasian Chalk Circle* he satirised Western society quite brutally. He was instrumental in getting away from the idea that theatre is supposed to be realistic – the old 'invisible fourth wall' concept, which had held sway for decades. In fact, he worked very hard to make sure his audiences were constantly reminded that they were observing art – a play, rather than reality. All of which makes his stuff hard to take at times.

BURTON, SIR RICHARD FRANCIS (1821-1890) Totally amazing dude. An excellent role-model for aspiring Dudes, Burton was a heavy-duty explorer, adventurer, and writer. He spoke and read a truly frightening number of Middle Eastern and Oriental languages, and was fluent enough in Arabic to make the pilgrimage to Mecca in disguise. Though he swashbuckled his way back and forth across Northern Africa in search of the source of the Nile, and wrote about a zillion words with regards to his travels, his greatest contributions to the course of English literature have been his translations. Burton was the first man to translate *The Thousand and One Nights* into English. On top of this brilliant piece of work, he also produced the first English translation of the *Kama Sutra*, and of the Arabic equivalent, *The Perfumed Garden.* Try to get hold of an unabridged translation of both of the Arabic pieces – excellent, salacious reading.

§

WHAT IS ROBBING A BANK compared with founding a bank? – *Bertolt Brecht*

§

BYRON, GEORGE GORDON (LORD BYRON) (1788-1824) The 6th Baron Byron was a relatively crap poet, but he knew instinctively how to buckle a swash. Byron was extremely important to the Romantic movement in literature. Alongside of his mate Percy Shelley, he created the 'Byronic' hero – the angst-ridden young man who wanders tragically about, avoiding humanity because of his naughty and regrettable past. Byron's poetry may have been sort of overblown and purple, but he certainly had one hell of a life. Swordsman, drinker, rakehell, avowed enemy of tyranny, warrior and infamous seducer, he twice swam a particularly dangerous stretch of water in Greece, called the Hellespont – a feat made famous in Greek legend from the tale of Hero and Leander. Of his writings, you need only know *Childe Harold's Pilgrimage* and *Don Juan* – but as a role model, you could hardly do better. In fact, don't mess around with his poetry: get yourself some big white floppy shirts, some tight black trousers, and a biography of Byron, and pretty soon you can set out to be your very own Byronic hero.

> §
>
> **PLEASURE'S A SIN, AND SOMETIME Sin's a pleasure. – *Lord Byron***
>
> §

CARROLL, LEWIS (1832-1898) English clergyman and mathematician – real name Charles Lutwidge Dodgson – responsible for writing *Alice's Adventures in Wonderland*, which may well be the best-loved children's book of all time. Carroll also wrote *The Hunting of the Snark*, which is a pretty cool poem that got made into a very ugly musical. He also did a lot of photography, including some very dodgy shots of small children which brought him a certain amount of criticism. Anyway, the 'Alice' books are fabulous stuff, and if you haven't read them already, you should correct that immediately.

DICKENS, CHARLES JOHN HUFFHAM (1812-1870) English writer, supposedly one of the most popular and brilliant novelists in the English language, with 'masterly storytelling, fantastic characterisation, exceptional observation, sharp social criticism, humour, and pathos'. In actual fact, one of the most boring men ever to blight the human race. Dickens got off to a bad start, being born in the early 19th century, and when his father quite rightly abandoned him (okay, so he was imprisoned for debt) the lad had to take up work in a blacking warehouse. Whatever the hell that is. Anyway, Dickens wrote interminable novels about children having a rotten time in industrialised England, and for some reason, people liked them. Titles include *David Copperfield*, *A Tale of Two Cities*, *Oliver Twist*, *Martin Chuzzlewit*, and *Great Expectations*. Don't read any of them. The BBC and a host of others have been making movies out of them for years, and it hurts a lot less when you can encapsulate it in a couple of hours, with a six-pack or two to lubricate the process.

DOSTOYEVSKY, FYODOR MIKHAYLOVICH (1821-1881) A brilliant Russian novelist who proved it was possible to write at the same time as Dickens and not be killingly dull. Oh, sure, he's a bit gloomy – but hey, he was Russian, right? His intellectual flirtations with socialism got him arrested and sent to Siberia for four years of hard labour, which brought on epilepsy which stayed with him the rest of his life. *Crime and Punishment* is as meaty and powerful a piece of psychological craftsmanship as ever you'll see, and should head your list. You must also read *Notes From the Underground*, and *The Idiot*, and at least consider *The Brothers Karamazov*.

DONNE, JOHN (1572-1631) English poet and clergyman, noted as the best of the Metaphysical poets. He may have been a cleric, but he was notable for his love poetry, and got himself into deep, deep trouble by

§

... IF THE DEVIL DOES NOT exist, and Man has therefore created him, he has created him in his own image and likeness. – *Fyodor Dostoyevsky*

NO MAN IS AN ISLAND, entire of itself; every man is a piece of the continent, a part of the main; if a clod be washed away by the sea, Europe is the less ... Any man's death diminishes me, because I am involved in mankind; and therefore never send to know for whom the bell tolls; it tolls for thee. – *John Donne*

§

secretly marrying Anne More, the niece of a powerful nobleman. Donne's sermons (he was Anglican. He could do that and still get married ...) were famous in his day, and he preached in front of the crowned heads of Europe, as they say. Check out his *Songs and Sonnets* and his *Divine Poems*.

ELIOT, THOMAS STEARNS (TS) (1888-1965) American-born poet, literary critic and dramatist, who had a major effect on the directions of 20th century writing, awarded the Nobel Prize for literature in 1948. Notable for unrhymed free verse poems on depressing, cramped themes of modern urban life. To be frank, other than his verses in *Old Possum's Book of Practical Cats* (which whimsical piece gave rise to the infamous *Cats* of Andrew Lloyd Webber) the most interesting thing about Eliot was how boring he could be. Big on symbolism, but very, very short of power and feeling. Read 'The Love Song of J Alfred Prufrock' and 'The Wasteland' to know Eliot, and the book of cat-poems to have at least a chance of enjoying his work. Dull, dull, dull – as you'd expect from anybody pompous enough to give up being a Yank to become a Pom.

FLAUBERT, GUSTAVE (1821-1880) Practically invented the soap-opera single-handed with his novel *Madame Bovary*, which chronicles the flaccid existence and petty love affairs of a small-town doctor's wife. Perceptive, definitely, and even readable – but was it necessary? Flaubert was pretty much the Main Man of the French Realist school of writing, and as such, everybody says he was a genius. Doesn't take much, does it?

---

§

THIS IS THE WAY THE world ends
Not with a bang but a whimper.

– TS Eliot

COWARDICE, AS DISTINGUISHED FROM PANIC, is almost always simply a lack of ability to suspend the functioning of the imagination.
– Ernest Hemingway

§

HEMINGWAY, ERNEST MILLER (1899-1961) American novelist and short-story writer awarded the Nobel Prize in 1954. Father of the two-fisted hairy-chested school of Real Man writing. He liked short sentences. Tight, punchy sentences. He was drunk a lot. He shot lions. He wanted to fight bulls. Served in the Italian Army as a volunteer in WWI, and opposed the Fascists along with everyone else during the Spanish Civil War. Hung around in Paris with people like F. Scott Fitzgerald and Henry Miller, Ezra Pound and Gertrude Stein. If you had to sum up his writing in a single word, it would have to be: 'Balls'. Great, big hairy ones. Check out *For Whom The Bell Tolls* (made into a very fine film), *The Old Man And The Sea* (not such a good film), and *A Farewell to Arms*. Big Ern blew his brains out with a shotgun eventually – a trendsetter to the end.

HOMER (Best guess is that he lived in the region of Greece around the 9th or 8th century BC) The grand-daddy of them all. Traditionally, he is supposed to have composed the epics of the *Iliad* and the *Odyssey*, which chronicle the events of the Trojan war, and of the later wanderings of the hero Odysseus (Ulysses). Some critics argue that the poems are probably composites, cobbled together from the works of many contemporary poets – but who cares? The epics are fantastic stories of blood, death, revenge, love, adventure and romance. Read them both, and see any of the countless 'Sword-and-Sandal' movies made on them by the Italians.

§

A MAN OF GENIUS MAKES no mistakes. His errors are volitional, and are the portals of discovery. – *James Joyce*

§

JOYCE, JAMES AUGUSTINE ALOYSIUS (1882-1941) Possibly the biggest name in twentieth century literature, despite a relatively modest output. Joyce changed the map with his book *Ulysses* (1922) which is outwardly about no more than a couple of blokes having a bit of a piss-up one summer day in Dublin. Though his earlier works were relatively sane and normal (*Dubliners, Portrait of the Artist as a Young Man*) he began to introduce things like stream-of-consciousness writing into *Ulysses* – which created an absolute storm and was banned all over the place. Then he wrote *Finnegan's Wake*, which nobody has ever understood, but is probably brilliant. You need to know *The Dubliners*, and *Ulysses*. It may also be helpful to know that Joyce married a woman named Barnacle, was nearly blind towards the end of his life, and that his secretary Samuel Beckett went on to be one of the biggest names in Absurdist literature.

MURRAY, LES (1938-) Grew up on a NSW dairy farm, dropped out of Sydney University, travelled the world and returned to become one of the world's greatest poets. He has sought to cock his ear to the voices and silences of the bush, and writes poems of indescribable beauty about all the things that Men should know about.

Read 'The Bulahdelah-Taree Song Cycle' and weep.

> §
>
> **We come from the Ice Age,**
> **poem makers, homemakers,**
> **how you know we are sacred:**
> **it's unlucky to pay us.**
>
> *– Les Murray*
>
> §

ORWELL, GEORGE (1903-1950) Was actually Mrs Blair's little boy, Eric Arthur. Despite a good middle-class English upbringing (he was educated at Eton), Orwell wanted to be a writer. It turned out to be a big ask, and as a result of living poor for a few years, Orwell decided he was a Socialist. This was a very fashionable decision amongst artists and writers of the time, with the result that a whole bunch of them went off and fought alongside the Commies in the Spanish Civil War. So did Orwell. Meanwhile, though, he was writing a lot of boring social-conscience stuff like *The Road to Wigan Pier* and *Down and Out in Paris and London*, which was a lot less interesting than the title might sound. Orwell is most famous for *Animal Farm*, his satire on the Soviet revolution (worth a read) and *1984*, which is probably *the* book on Totalitarianism. Bleak and scary – the origin of the phrase 'Big Brother Is Watching' – but definitely good to read.

SAPPHO (650-590 BC?) Greek poet, born on the island of Lesbos. She hung out with a bunch of babes, and composed very beautiful, very intense poetry for their weddings and the like. Sappho is widely supposed to have been distinctly queer, and aside from leaving behind her a lot of excellent poetry, she also gave us useful words like 'Lesbian' (from the isle of

Lesbos) and 'Sapphic'. That one's great – sapphic: referring to erotic love between women. Hot hot hot.

SHAKESPEARE, WILLIAM (1564-1616) Big Bill. The Man. The Dude. The original and the best. English poet and playwright, often regarded as the number one in literature. Born and bred in Stratford-On-Avon, he did most of his work in London. (As you would.) Especially remembered for his thirty-six known plays, a number of which have gone on to become household names – *Macbeth, Hamlet, Romeo and Juliet, Richard the Third, The Tempest, The Merchant of Venice*, and *A Midsummer Night's Dream*. He also wrote some very funky sonnets which imply he may have had a bit of a thing for the lads. At his death, he specifically left his 'second-best bed' to his wife. There is no record of who got the better one. For a quick fix, see the recent Kenneth Branagh productions of *Much Ado About Nothing*, *Hamlet*, and especially *Henry V* (one of the few movies in which grown Men are allowed to cry). Roman Polanski's *Macbeth* is also worth the effort.

SHELLEY, MARY WOLLSTONECRAFT (1797-1851) English-born woman who became the second wife of Romantic poet Percy Shelley, and

§

HOW TO WRITE GOOD ENGLISH

1. Never use a metaphor, simile or other figure of speech which you are used to seeing in print.
2. Never use a long word where a short one will do.
3. If it is possible to cut out a word, always cut it out.
4. Never use the passive where you can use the active.
5. Never use a foreign phrase, a scientific word or a jargon word if you can think of an everyday English equivalent.
6. Break any of these rules sooner than say anything outright barbarous. – *George Orwell*

§

in the end, considerably more influential than he. Mary Shelley wrote several novels, as well as travel sketches and books of verse and story, but in the final analysis, the one thing she did that really shook things up was her novel *Frankenstein, or the Modern Prometheus*. Not only did she manage to articulate one of the deepest human fears – that some day, we're going to lose control of all this technology and power – but the book itself was the grandmother of the entire genre of fantasy and science fiction. Read an abridged version, then go out and rent half-a-dozen different Frankenstein films on video. Make sure you get the original one, with Boris Karloff as The Monster. Note: Frankenstein isn't the monster. Frankenstein is actually the name of the mad doctor who builds the monster. The monster just gets called 'The Monster', or at best, 'Frankenstein's Monster'.

SWIFT, JONATHAN (1667-1745) Dublin-born Irish writer and famous satirist, whose best-known work is certainly *Gulliver's Travels* – a must-read. Make sure you get an unabridged edition, with all the dubious and risqué jokes which are usually cut out for the kiddies.

SUN T'ZU (Somewhere in the fifth century BC) Possibly apocryphal character, purportedly a Chinese general of phenomenal tactical insight,

§

I NEVER WONDER TO SEE men wicked, but I often wonder to see them not ashamed.
– *Jonathan Swift*

DO NOT GO GENTLE INTO that good night, Old age should burn and rave at close of day; Rage, rage against the dying of the light.
– *Dylan Thomas*

IF A MAN DOES NOT keep pace with his companions, perhaps it is because he hears a different drummer. Let him step to the music which he hears, however measured or far away.
– *Henry David Thoreau*

§

who wrote one of the most brilliant books of all time. The book is called *The Art of War*, and although it's short and simple, it remains mandatory reading for the world's military academies and business schools, some 2400 years after it was written. We're not going to even try to summarise the book; it's already short and succinct enough. However, we should point out that in the 19th century, a Prussian called von Clausewitz wrote in three volumes a highly regarded, but rather massive, book called *On War*. Well, Sun T'zu says everything that Clausewitz does, and a few things more, but he does it in the space of a short story. If you have never read *The Art Of War*, you are currently at an enormous disadvantage to everyone who has. Get it in Penguin classics.

THOMAS, DYLAN MARLAIS (1914-1953) Welsh poet. Though his language is often obscure, at his best, his works exploring themes of death, birth, and sex have a beauty and vigour and power that make them truly extraordinary. Read his *Collected Poems*, and the radio play *Under Milk Wood*. Dylan Thomas was more than fond of a drop, and eventually croaked in New York as a result of sucking back several crates of whisky.

THOREAU, HENRY DAVID (1817-1862) American writer, philosopher, and naturalist. Thoreau is one of those remarkable people who actually took the really great ideas and personally adopted them into his life. He was big on libertarianism and individualism, and tried to create for himself a way of life based on these ideals. His best-known work is *Walden*, in which he discusses in an alarmingly straightforward manner (for a philosopher, anyhow) why he lived as he did. He also wrote a very important essay called 'Civil Disobedience', reflecting some of what he learned from being imprisoned over failure to pay his poll tax in protest over the Mexican-American war. This essay went on to inspire people like Gandhi and Martin Luther King Jr, amongst others.

TOLKIEN, JOHN RONALD REUEL (1892-1973) South-African born British academic and writer of elaborate fantasies. Tolkien is a bit of a one-trick pony when you throw him in with this lot, but since *Lord of The Rings* was recently nominated as the most popular and influential English book of the twentieth century, what are we gonna do? To be fair, *Lord of The Rings* is a massive, scholarly work, grounded in the medieval myth-structures which Tolkien studied, and it's quite a reasonable example of writing in itself. It must have struck a chord, in any case – aside from becoming one of the all-time great best-sellers, it spawned an entire industry of imitators. Read *Lord of The Rings* – and that's about it. By the way: the imitators are, on the whole, absolute crap.

TOLSTOY, LEO (1828-1910) A Russian nobleman who led an early life of dissipation, and wrote two amazing novels – *War and Peace*, and *Anna Karenina*. However, Tolstoy had always felt a bit guilty about living high on the hog while his serfs ate mud, and sometime after 1876 he underwent a strange spiritual transformation, becoming a kind of Christian anarchist. After that, he wrote a great deal about morals and philosophy, and campaigned for the right of the serfs to be hit with sticks, but never wrote anything really interesting ever again. *War and Peace* is most notable because it's absolutely enormous. Humungous. Reading it is a great accomplishment – but once again, you're better off seeing a film version, and lying through your teeth if confronted. The book of *Anna Karenina*, however, is worth the effort.

TWAIN, MARK (1835-1910) This is the pseudonym of Samuel Langhorne Clemens, American satirist, novelist, and writer of short stories. At his best, his humour is brilliant – sharp, witty, and strongly satirical. The name Mark Twain comes from the cry of the depth-checker on a Mississippi steamboat. Despite being somewhat bitter and cynical towards the end, Mark Twain's material is still some of the best ever to come out of American literature. Read *The Adventures of Huckleberry Finn*, *A Connecticut Yankee in King Arthur's Court*, any of his short stories – and if you can find it, a terribly rare but blindingly funny satire on Queen Elizabeth's court, in which Sir Walter Raleigh, the Queen, and half-a-dozen other luminaries sit around discussing farts, sex, and booze. Mr Flinthart has only ever read it once, but was crying with laughter by the end.

§

LET US BE THANKFUL FOR fools. But for them, the rest of us could not succeed. – *Mark Twain*

§

WHITE, PATRICK (1912-1990) Grumpy, homosexual winner of the Nobel Prize for Impenetrable Literature in 1973. He fought the good fight with the RAAF in WWII and went on to write a lot of very heavy, myth-laden books about what a bunch of savages we are. David Marr's great bio of him is more readable than anything White himself wrote. See *The Tree of Man* (1955) and *The Twyborn Affair* (1979). If you finish *Voss* (1957) you'll be one of the few who has.

YEATS, WILLIAM BUTLER (1865-1939) Irish poet and dramatist, awarded the Nobel prize in Literature in 1923. Particularly fond of old Irish myths and legends. One of maybe a handful of poets whose work genuinely deserves to be called 'immortal'. Read 'Sailing to Byzantium,' and 'The Second Coming' in particular.

§

DIY LITERATURE: HOW TO WRITE
OBSCURELY BRILLIANT MODERN POETRY.

Once upon a time, writing poetry was a really tricky process, and poets were regarded with the kind of awe now reserved for Mel Gibson. Even today, writing poetry is still considered a worthy practice, which is kind of weird when you consider that even John Laws does it. Sort of, anyway.

The fact is that modern poetry is the easiest stuff in the world to write. Practically anybody can do it, once they know the Two Secret Things: Line Breaks and Obscurity.

That's it in a nutshell. Want to see how it works? We'll start with Line Breaks. What you do is take a simple prose paragraph – the kind of thing anybody can write – and just chop it up willy-nilly. Watch this:

Once upon a time writing poetry
Was a really tricky
Process.
And poets were regarded with the kind of awe
Now reserved for Mel
Gibson. Even
Today writing poetry is still
Considered a worthy practice
Which is kind of
Weird
When you consider ...

to page 150 >

< from page 149   See – easy, isn't it? And if you don't feel you can put together your own paragraph to work from, just borrow somebody else's. You can always claim it's Post-Modernism in action. Here's a paragraph stolen at random from Raymond Chandler (a genuine Real Man's writer) and chopped up into a really deep poem:

> *He shut the door and stood*
> *In the darkness*
> *Remembering*
> *Where the phone was.*
> *Then he*
> *Walked straight to it catlike*
> *In the dark room*
> *Sat in an easy chair*
> *And reached the phone up*
> *From the lower shelf of a*
> *Small*
> *Table. He*
> *Held the one-piece*
> *To his ear and said:*
> *'Hello'.*

So, that's Line Breaks. Now we need to consider Obscurity. Y'see, a poem which has a meaning which can readily be discerned is no good for our ends. What we're trying to do here is write poetry which will fool somebody into thinking we know what the buggery we're doing, right? So there's no value in writing a transparent piece of rubbish that anybody can tell used to be a paragraph of Raymond Chandler. What you need to do is Obscure the Matter.

The easiest way to do that is to insert a loaded word into the text at intervals. By 'loaded' I mean a word which has lots of meaning and power, like 'Death', 'Madness', 'Love,' 'Beer', or 'Mother'. Let's see what happens to our Post-

Modern Chandler Poem when we give it the Obscurifying
Treatment:

> *He shut the door and stood*
> *In the darkness (death)*
> *Remembering*
> *Where the phone was, mother.*
> *Then he*
> *Walked straight to it catlike*
> *Cancer in the dark room*
> *Death sat in an easy chair*
> *And reached the phone up*
> *From the lower shelf of a*
> *Small beer*
> *Table. He*
> *Held the one-piece*
> *To his ear and said:*
> *'Hello, Madness.'*
> *Love.*

Of course, this is really quite a simple exercise. The true
master of modern poetry prefers to draw his inspirational
paragraphs from far more arcane sources, like SBS movie
reviews, Australian Tax Office brochures, or best of all,
those really whacked-out instructions that come with every
cheap Chinese-made electrical appliance.

Now all you have to do is grow a scraggy beard, buy a
Tibetan yaks-wool vest, and stop wearing shoes. Poets don't
make much money – but a reputation for sensitivity, deep-
mindedness and mystic obscurity can turn you into a real
magnet for women of the yoghurt-brained herbal tea crystal-
gargling feng shui and Wiccan astronomy for spirit-chan-
nelling pussycats sort ... if you can stand it.

§

CHAPTER SIX

Making Yourself
Unfeasibly Wealthy

§

MONEY CAN'T BUY YOU LOVE, sure, but it'll let you park your yacht right next to it. – *David Gilmour* (lead guitar, Pink Floyd).

§

LET'S BE HONEST. NOBODY WANTS to be poor. The hours suck, the food is no good, the accommodation is miserable, and it's hell trying to interest women. Being Unfeasibly Wealthy has its problems too – but on the balance, we'd be prepared to exchange our current set of difficulties for those of, say, the Sultan of Brunei. What would you prefer: waking up and having to decide whether you can wear your last pair of intact underpants for the eighth day straight, or waking up and deciding which of your four hundred strong harem of Überbabes to tumble before settling down to another day of having your bum kissed by expert sycophants.

4 PATHS TO UNFEASIBLE WEALTH

1) **GENETICS.** The easiest way is the road taken by the very sensible young James Packer. Before he was born, he saw his future old cheese and thought, 'Hmmm that ugly fat man is rolling in it. I think I'll hang out with him', and after that, it was all downhill. Sadly, most of us appear to have been too damned stupid to take that option, and thus we have to look somewhere else for the bucks.

2) **WORK HARD.** The next easiest path is, I'm very sorry to say, a life of hard graft. Thrift, savings, investment, enthusiastic application to a reasonably well-paid job, eventually a business of your own, and finally, a comfortable retirement with investments which you continue to manage carefully. The big problem with this is easily identified: It sucks. By the time you've actually got any money to enjoy, you are well past the age where you could have really enjoyed it.

3) **CRIME.** Another possibility – even more difficult than hard work and thrift – is crime. On the face of it, crime looks quite attractive. Relatively short hours, fast cars, and lotsa horny, morally flexible babes. Sadly, it turns out that the path to riches in crime is depressingly familiar: thrift, savings, investment, and enthusiastic application to your job, eventually turning it into your own business. Added problems arise because a lot of busybodies and spoil sports disapprove of your chosen lifestyle, and they've appointed a whole bunch of other heavily armed, anti-fun types to block your progress up the happy staircase to success.

4) **ENTER POLITICS.** A reasonable compromise between hard work, crime, and Unfeasible Wealth lies in the realm of politics. It's a hard graft actually getting yourself into the game, but once you're in, it's all gravy

and blowjobs. Great pay, your own hours and regular 'fact-finding tours' overseas. You can cheat like a bastard on your taxes and your expenses, throw business to your mates and family, write laws to make you even richer, and get kickbacks for protecting the Unfeasible Wealth of others, and almost nobody ever takes any notice. The only real problem – if the contempt of your fellow human beings means nothing to you – is that while you'll become quite comfortable, Really Unfeasible Wealth is probably beyond your grasp. Still, if you're willing to sacrifice every shred of self-respect; if you're as willing to bend over and spread your cheeks for the guy above you as you are prepared to stick it to the guy below; if you have the morals of a drug-addled weasel and the ethics of a rabid Bhagwan; well, you may just have what it takes for a career in Parliament.

So, do we really want Unfeasible Wealth? Well, yes, of course we do. What a stupid question. Once again, though, let's be brutally honest. Poverty sucks, but the amount of time, energy and involvement required to become as Unfeasibly Wealthy as a Kerry Packer or a Rupert Murdoch, if you start from scratch, leaves you pretty much without a life to speak of. That being the case, I'm going to lay down a few simple ground rules that you can follow as far as you like. Push them long and hard enough, and with just a little luck, in this nominally free-market Capitalist state of ours, you too can become grotesquely rich. However, if like most of us you just want to own your own home, do a little travelling, and not have to hide from the credit-card Nazis, you can probably manage with rather less monomaniacal obsession and still get what you want.

6 PATHS TO FEASIBLE WEALTH

1) **YER GONNA HAVE TO WORK FOR A LIVING.** This deserves a chapter of its own and it's got one. See Chapter 2.
2) **ANY TIME IS EARNING TIME.** No point in working hard if you're never going to seize the day and make something out of it. Consider the concept of 'spare time'. What do you do with it? Take a walk? Play squash? Hit the beach? Watch television? Lost time is lost money. An hour a day in front of 'Home and Away' and 'Neighbours' is an hour a day that a smarter, more motivated person could be putting into study, a cottage business, or a potentially profitable hobby.

Use your spare time, don't abuse it. If you want to play squash, see if you can't arrange a regular social game wih some of the people from work. Form contacts. Establish a network. Want to take a walk? Make it a long, energetic walk, and see if you can't improve your fitness. Feel like just sitting down and reading? Read something useful – books by people who have succeeded in your chosen field, courses of study, references or whatever.

Small stuff adds up. Naturally, you'll always need a bit of time for relaxing and socialising, but you'd be surprised at how much time you simply waste, if you really look. If you get into the habit of using your 'down time' for productive ends, you'll find that seemingly without effort, you accumulate valuable skills, abilities and contacts which will make your road to Unfeasible Wealth a lot easier to travel.

3) **KNOW WHERE YOUR MONEY GOES.** Many, many people who earn quite respectable salaries are virtually always broke. At $60k per annum, they find that they have very little more to show for it than they did when they first started out as a junior clerk at $16k per annum. Earning elephant bucks is meaningless if you don't hold onto the elephant, bub.

Set yourself a budget. Recognise that word? It's a simple list of expenditures balanced against your income. The most important rule of any functional budget is simple and ironclad: you cannot spend more than you earn. Deficit spending works only for governments, and as near as anyone can tell, it only works for them because nobody questions what's holding the whole scheme up in the air in the first place.

When you set down your budget, the first things you account for are the essentials – things you absolutely, utterly cannot do without. Food, clothing, accommodation, transport and education are the only genuine essentials. What's left is non-essential. Trust us. Even recreational drugs.

Once you've eliminated the essentials, you're left with a sum of money and a host of non-essentials. (If you aren't left with a sum of money after budgeting for the necessities, you've got a problem. Get a new job. Find a way to pay less rent. Eat less. Buy your clothes from St Vincent de Paul.) From this sum of money, you must immediately earmark a regular amount to be saved. Doesn't have to be much. 20% of your post-tax income is nice, but for most people, 10% is more feasible. Anyway, the trick is to settle on a figure, and put it away without fail.

Saving is essential. It provides you with capital that you'll be using later, and it acts as a bulwark against genuine emergencies like sudden medical crises, deaths in the family and invasion by any ruthless, pan-galactic space monkey civilisations. Put the money away, however much it hurts, and keep on doing it.

AAIIIEEE!!!

Jeremy's accountant tells him how much his expenditure on socks was in the last financial year.

After you've done all this, any money remaining in the budget is yours. If you've done your budgeting correctly, you're going to hate the result – most likely, it will appear to be a pitiful stipend, insufficient to lead the life of an honest Monk, let alone the kind of raucous, rakehell existence to which you aspire. However, this is where the sacrifice bit comes in, see? Once you've put your budget together, *stick to it like fat sticks to a sumo wrestler!* The savings will eventually add up. And when they do, that's when you can try putting into practise some of the ideas that follow.

4) **DON'T GET EXCITABLE.** So, you got a promotion. An extra $2,000 per year. Brilliant! You can get a new set of Doc Martens, buy some decent wine for a change, catch a couple of movies, get a pair of Ray-Bans, replace your old surfboard, upgrade your modem to 56k …

Or you can put it away, just like you're doing with a chunk of what you were earning before. Parkinson's Law says: Expenditure rises to meet income. If you let it do that, you're no better off after that promotion than you were before. You may well have a new set of Docs and a taste for something better than Chateau Ratpiss, but you're not actually earning any more money.

The famous Bottom Line is precisely that: the bottom line of the sum created by income less expenses. It equals the net profit of the business, or lifestyle, or whatever. If you keep the bottom line in mind, you'll see that when your income increases, if you can keep your expenditures down, you get a whole lot of extra money to put into useful wealth creation.

Granted, when your income increases you may well feel a reward is in order. And why not? Most of us aren't here to become Unfeasibly Wealthy, after all – we're looking for a life, as well. When the extra bucks turn up, the trick is not to spend them all on making yourself feel better. Hang onto that old budget of yours, and before you look at increasing anything else on it, see how much you can bear to shunt into the savings and investment section. It all adds up after a while.

5) STAY OUT OF DEBT. This is really part of the budgeting concept, but with credit available to almost everybody, and with things like cars considered an essential life component, these days it's regarded as perfectly reasonable to spend the greater part of your life in one form of debt or another. This is deeply stupid.

Possibly the worst form of debt is credit card debt. It's an insidious sort of trap; the bank provides you with a groovy little piece of plastic which, when waved under the nose of various purveyors of goods and chattels, entitles you to all kinds of neat stuff. Unfortunately, it also entitles you in the short term to spend a little more than you earn, and as you recall, that only works for governments. With a credit card in your life, it's altogether too easy to wind up $100 to $1,000 in the hole at the end of every fortnight – and that sum costs you interest payments which are well in excess of the kind of interest the bank pays you on any savings. If this description applies to you – consistently a couple of hundred in the red – my advice is simple. Set your credit card on fire and watch it burn. Pay off what you owe. And don't get another credit card.

The other really useless form of debt is borrowing for items which depreciate. Borrow to buy a new car, and within five minutes of driving it off the lot, your $24,000 investment is worth $20,000. Not only that, but the debt of $10,000 you established at the bank to cover the gap between your savings and your purchase is still there – and bleeding you for 12% interest, or thereabouts. You have, in effect, instantly lost $4,000, plus the ongoing loss for interest repayments, not to mention the 'opportunity costs' of having your otherwise hardworking capital tied up in this rapidly-depreciating chunk of steel and plastic.

There are times to consider going into debt, investments wherein you can minimise your ongoing repayments and all – but you can't even consider getting into something like that if you've already got a red-ink albatross hanging around your financial neck. Straighten out your debt situation through hard work and thrift, and then you can consider the next rule.

6) MONEY'S NO GOOD UNDER THE MATTRESS. So, you've been putting the money aside for a while. Now what? Well, you can leave it in the bank, and hope to accumulate interest, or you can take it out and try to find an investment of some sort.

In the bank, assuming you've done some shopping around and looked for the account with the best return, your money will accumulate *compound interest*. Essentially, this means that if you lock up $10,000 in a 10% term deposit for three years, you'll get not $13,000 at the end, but $13,310. This is because the interest is paid not only on the principle, but on the accumulated interest as well.

Excitingly, compound interest produces an exponential curve of returns. Every year, the interest repaid is proportionately larger than the year before. If you know your Malthus, it will be obvious that

§

WHAT GOES UP, MUST COME DOWN.

You can't usually tell a liar by their demeanour. Liars are practised at it, they make a living by it. Looking back to Alan Bond, some of the deals he claimed to have pulled off and made huge profits on seemed too good to be true. Deals of the sort that make hundreds of millions of dollars profit overnight just aren't very common and certainly the sorts that he had just seemed utterly unlikely. You knew he was lying just from experience of the world over the years.

What helped me was having been through the seventies in Britain, which was very similar to the eighties here. There was a huge property boom and a stock market boom and then it all went bust and everyone went down with it. And the same sorts of things were said about the entrepreneurs in the early seventies, about how fucking brilliant they were. It just gave me a sense of déjà vu seeing the same things written about Bond and Skase here. They really were portrayed as the same sort of geniuses.

Many young journalists in the eighties had never known a bust. They were all in their twenties and had never experienced a recession. You just have to go through these things so you know when you see the same patterns.

Never trust anyone. High rewards involve high risks whatever people tell you. What goes up must come down. The wheel will turn. – *Paul Barry*

§

eventually, the accumulating interest will be positively gargantuan, and you will be Unfeasibly Wealthy. In the short term, at least, it's worth remembering the Rule of 72: take the number 72, divide it by your interest rate, and that yields the number of years it will take for your money to double. At 10%, the figure is 7.2 years. At 5%, it's 14.4 years. And if you can get it going at 20%, your money will double in only 3.6 years. Cool, eh?

Naturally, it's not that simple. Firstly, there's tax to consider. Interest is income, so far as the government is concerned. Every year, they're going to take a bite out of it. Then there's inflation, that mysterious tendency of prices to rise for no adequately explained reason. If the inflation rate is 5%, and you're earning at 10% you'll still come out ahead – but it won't be nearly so inspiring to watch. And if inflation climbs up a little, between that and the government's bite, you stand quite a good chance of going nowhere at all. As a rule, leaving money in the bank and relying on compound interest is not a useful way to become Unfeasibly Wealthy.

At the time of writing, most Australian workers had their compulsory superannuation levy paid into a fund selected by their employer. This is supposed to change over the next few years to give you more freedom in how your money is invested. So the following tips on investment could be relevant even if you haven't saved anything voluntarily.

You can borrow money to buy a non-depreciating (or even one which appreciates, hopefully) asset such as land. When you do this, if you make rapid and regular payments to defeat the fact that compound interest is now working against you, your money can really begin to do you some good. Better still, if your asset is income-producing, such as a rental property, you can even offset the interest on the loan against your income for tax purposes. This is known as *negative gearing*, and represents one of the Holy Grails of investment. Do this a few times, using acquired assets as security against your borrowings, and over the course of a reasonable working life, you should be able to put away a very reasonable nest egg.

How To Do Tricks With Money: Investments

INVESTMENTS ARE GAUGED ACCORDING TO factors of risk versus possible returns on your money. This means pretty much what it sounds like: high-risk investments are those in which you stand a substantial chance of doing your dough cold. High-return investments are those which increase your capital at a relatively high rate. In general the rule is: low-risk, low-return. And of course, high returns are related to high risks.

There are two basic types of investment: debt investment, and equity investment. In the first, you are essentially loaning out your money; buying a debt from someone else. This is largely the case with any bank investment. You put your money in a bank account. The bank loans money to someone with a home loan. They repay the loan with interest, and a smaller portion of the interest is returned to you. In the meantime, the house and property in question represent security to the bank and its investors (you) should the borrower default on the loan.

Debt investment is relatively low-risk, because it is supposed to be secured against some form of hard asset. It follows, therefore, that it's also relatively low-return. Also, because the terms of a bank loan or an investment with the bank such as a term deposit are worked out in advance in the form of a contract, debt investment isn't strongly affected by short-term market movements. Most financial consultants suggest that thirty to forty percent of your investment capital should be kept in debt investment – term deposits, bank bonds, high-yield bank accounts – as a hedge against possible market fluctuations.

Equity investment represents a purchase of sorts. Shares are a good example. When you buy shares, you are literally buying a piece of the company, assets, liabilities, income and all. However, when you buy into ownership of something, you expose yourself to the possibility that the value of your purchase will actually decline if market conditions become unfavourable. Equity investments are on the whole less safe and stable than debt investments, and as a result, generally return a higher yield. Shares and stocks are the classic moneymaking equity investments, along with real estate, unit trusts, precious metals, and foreign currencies.

Making big bucks on equity investment is a hit or miss proposition. Some equities offer a return simply on the investment – shares, for exam-

§

Be wary of great investment opportunities

You should always check out the person's record in business. You want to hear good things about that person. But that person is selling themselves to sell their product. If people would only do their homework on these con schemes they'd generally find the most horrific track records. You've really got to do your detective work. Don't rely on the authorities to do it for you. They're pretty tight with information.

If they're an accountant or builder go to their professional associations and ask about them. You may not get anything substantial but you may get a sniff of trouble. Always set out with a very healthy scepticism. Don't set off thinking, 'Oh this person's great I'm going to find out what else they've done'. Don't start with a positive attitude. I'm afraid you've got to start pulling that person down. Trust nobody. Get to basics.

Then you've got to strip back the deal itself. You've really got to focus in on what the deal is. Separate the promises from the reality. If there are people already involved you've got to ring them up and ask how they feel, what the problems are. Really bear down on them but do it subtly so they open up to you. – *Helen Wellings*

§

ple, repay dividends to their owners when the company declares a profit. Usually the dividends are quite small; no more than one or two percent of the face value of the shares. Similarly, investing in a unit trust which handles a large block of rental properties will generally offer an ongoing return. Seven percent per annum is not uncommon at the moment. The serious money in equities is made by buying and selling in accordance with the movements of the market. That's where the *real* black magic enters the picture.

Obviously, you don't want too much of your investment capital sunk into dangerously unstable shares and stocks. A good compromise, once you've put your thirty percent into safe, stable, debt investment, is to put another thirty percent or so into relatively safe equities – bank shares, for example. You'll pick up a steady return, which should be at least a little higher than the premium rates on debt investment, and if the value of your shares should increase as well, you score a windfall.

The final thirty to forty percent of your investment capital can be used for genuine speculation. You can be just as serious as you like about this idea, but apart from carefully avoiding obvious disasters such as ostrich  farming, the degree to which you can really affect your own fortune is kind of moot. There have been any number of whimsical studies involving chimpanzees, dartboards, and computer programmes which demonstrate that you're more likely to come out ahead in the share market by sheer luck than you are by trusting investment advisers. Try yourself out: buy a block of land in an area you think is going to increase in value, for example. Or play the stock market – try to guess which shares are likely to rise, and buy them early, while simultaneously selling the shares you think are likely to go down in value.

In the end, it's probably worth your while to remember one thing: the more money you have invested around the place, the more time you have to spend keeping an eye on it. 'Your money or your life' is more than just an expression …

So, that's the Bottom Line: choose something you are prepared to enjoy doing, and do it hard and well, and as often as possibe. Set yourself a savings goal, and stick firmly to your budget. When your earnings increase, try not to increase your expenditure accordingly. Keep a firm hand on your debt level, and use your savings to acquire assets which will work for you. Follow those five rules with everything you've got, and at the very least, you should be able to retire comfortably at a reasonable age.

BUT BACK TO THAT UNFEASIBLE WEALTH …

We did promise you a shot at the brass ring. Well, the really important thing to know in trying for the big time is that you'll never, ever get there working for someone else. So long as another person is writing your paycheque, there are simply never going to be enough zeroes on it – even if you push your way up to CEO of BHP.

Why? Well, consider a small business in accounting. As a top accountant yourself, you've been pulling down $50 an hour. Which means that the best you can do, if you work ten hours a day, six days a week, is $3,000 a week. On the other hand, what if you get a bunch of less brilliant accountants working for you at $25 an hour, plus a few cheaper trainees and office workers, but you contract the whole scheme out at $40 an hour against each of these workers? You're supervising and managing, putting your imprimatur on each job, of course, to keep the customers happy – but you're supervising half-a-dozen jobs and teams at once, so that the profits are coming in from six directions simultaneously, not just from your own, sole efforts. *Now* the big bikkies start to roll in.

Sure, business is a minefield of new expenses and laws you'd never anticipated. Sure, hiring employees is a complete bastard of a task, and firing them is deeply traumatising for all concerned. On the other hand, whoever heard of a nice multi-billionaire? The trick here is to get started early. Running a business isn't the same as doing whatever it was that you did so well for someone else. Running a business requires skills in marketing, arranging materials, pricing, fulfilling contracts, dealing with clientele, accounting, budgeting, and a bunch of other stuff. Naturally, you can study up on all this crap at TAFE or university – but nothing works so well as starting a small business for yourself at the first opportunity. Get in there and learn as you go.

MONEY MISCELLANY

• **TRY NOT TO BUY A CAR UNTIL IT BECOMES UNAVOIDABLE.** The most widely accepted estimate is that a car is going to cost you $100 a week to own and operate. You need a decent income to handle that.

• **CHEQUE ACCOUNTS ARE AN EXCELLENT WAY OF KEEPING TRACK OF YOUR FUNDS.** They pay little or no interest, but if you shop around,

> §
>
> **A bank is a place that will lend you money if you can prove that you don't need it.** – *Bob Hope.*
>
> §

you'll find one that doesn't suck too much money out of you, and you can handle bills quickly and conveniently with your chequebook. Which leaves a very nice paper trail to help you manage your money.

• **DEBIT CARDS AREN'T NEARLY SUCH A BAD THING AS CREDIT CARDS.** They're quick and convenient, can't be used by others, and since they have no credit facility, can't get you into trouble.

• **REAL ESTATE AND SHARE INVESTMENTS MAKE AN EXCELLENT BASIS FOR LONG TERM INVESTMENT.** Ignore the short-term market movements, and over five or ten years, chances are good you'll come out ahead.

• **CANCELLING OUTSTANDING DEBT** in things like personal loans or credit cards is a better short-term investment than practically anything else.

• *NEVER LOAN MONEY TO ANYONE NAMED 'DAVE'.*

• **OWNING A RACEHORSE IS NOT AN INVESTMENT.** It is a guaranteed way to lose money.

• **SAFE, HIGH-INTEREST SAVINGS ACCOUNTS** such as cash management accounts are a good place to put the money you're saving for a car or a house deposit. In the short term, it's better to be protected from brokerage fees and market fluctuations than it is to invest in long-range profits.

• **RENT AND SAVE.** Rent money is dead money, true. But if you rent cheap, and put money away, and buy carefully, you can be better off spending $100 a week in rent for a few years than you would be if you had to pay the extra $150 or so per week you would have accumulated in interest on your bank home loan.

• **DON'T MESS AROUND WITH EXTRA SUPERANNUATION.** Your employer will have you in some sort of scheme, by law. Put extra money there now, and you can't touch it until you're 60. That's a lot of potential opportunities you'll be missing.

• **PICK YOUR BUSINESS PARTNERS CAREFULLY.** Pooling your money with a few trusted friends might seem like a great way to buy a house and save on rent, but how many of those friends do you really trust to stay with the deal for the length of time necessary to bring it off? As a general rule, any sort of business partnership is a big risk. Stay solo if you can.

• **BANKS ARE NOT YOUR FRIENDS.** They don't loan you money out of the decency of their hearts, no matter what their advertising may suggest. When you decide to go for that big loan, take a good, long, hard look around. Don't forget the building societies, credit unions, and other trustworthy sources of credit. These days, many of them are much more competitive than the banks have ever been. Most importantly Never Sign Anything until your lawyer has okayed the deal. For instance, did you that most home mortgages come with a clause saying that *you* will be one hundred percent liable for the bank's legal costs if they decide to fuck you over in court. Remember, just because they're giving you money they are not your friend. The Mafia will give you money too and it's a toss up as to which of them is more ruthless about getting it back.

Finally, the best piece of advice of all:

> IF A THING LOOKS TOO GOOD TO BE TRUE,
> YOU CAN BE SURE THAT IT IS.

See you on Wall Street.

CHAPTER SEVEN

The Manly Art of Biff

IT'S NOT A NICE WORLD. As a bloke, unfortunately, you're likely to come into personal physical conflict with somebody else more than once in your life. And sadly, it's not always possible to play it cool, give the other guy what he wants, and walk away unharmed. There's just no way to be sure what an attacker really wants. If it was just a matter of money, or a bit of 'face' – a few rough words at the pub – then sure, it might be better to give in gracefully and gently. But there's no way to know.

You can get *killed* in something as commonplace as a fight down the pub – get pushed backwards over a chair, for example, and you smack your head on a sharp-cornered table. Curtain falls. Harp music fades in. And what about the bloke who gets out of his car with a spanner in his hand after that little prang in the car-park; how certain are you that you can talk him round? Why leave the outcome of the matter entirely in your attacker's hands?

There are things you can do to minimise the possibility of getting into real, physical trouble. First and best is to enrol in an accredited self-defence training course, or a decent martial art. Failing that, though, at the very least you can read through this section and try to put into practice some of the advice. It's not as good as really knowing how to handle yourself in the rough stuff, but it's a start. Just a start.

How To Not Get Beaten Up

MOST OF SELF-DEFENCE LIES in avoiding trouble in the first place. Thought and observation are your keys to achieving that much desired end. The majority of all confrontations need not occur if simple precautions are taken before you enter an environment where you believe you may be at hazard.

- **THINK ABOUT YOUR APPEARANCE.** Are you presenting an obvious target, ie, carrying bags or luggage when you could leave them in a locker? Wearing expensive clothes, but preparing to travel on foot through a 'rough' area? Travelling alone at night? Wearing a big sign that says 'Take My Stuff'?
- **THINK ABOUT YOUR DESTINATION.** Do you know where it is, or are you going to have to stop and ask someone? What kind of place is it? Could you find a telephone quickly? Is it a 'rough' area? Is it well-lit? Well-travelled? Poorly inhabited? Should you be going there? Should

Think about your appearance. Are you presenting an obvious target?

you be taking your girlfriend there? When do the buses or trains run? Can you park a car safely near to your destination? How long are you planning to stay in the area? Should you tell someone where you're going to be?

This is not paranoid behaviour. These are simple questions to ask yourself, easily answered, which can save you a great deal of trouble. It is worth your while to cultivate the habit of asking yourself such questions before you go anywhere; it takes next to no time, and once you get into the habit, it will quickly become second nature.

- **OBSERVING YOUR ENVIRONMENT.** As you walk, or ride, or simply stay in one place, you should be noticing what is around you. What kind of a place is it? Where are the exits? Is anyone around behaving oddly – watching you, for instance? Is there anyone you should take note of – drunks, or persons behaving aggressively, or even people who are simply out of place in terms of dress or behaviour? Are there any 'blind spots', such as shadowed or densely vegetated areas?

- **OBSERVING THE POTENTIAL ARENA.** When you've settled into a position for a while, think about what it might hold if violence were to erupt. Are there any potential weapons about – things that might be of use to you, or which might be seized by an attacker? What's the furniture like – light, heavy, mobile, fixed? Have you got a clear view of anyone who might want to approach you, or have you sat with your back to a door, or a dance floor, or such? What's the footing like? Are there any hazards to free movement, such as power cords, or spilt drinks?

- **OBSERVING YOUR ATTACKER.** Assuming that things have reached a critical stage, and you are confronted by an attacker, or a potential attacker, there are things to be learned even before hostilities commence. Is he right or left handed? Is he on his own, or does he have a friend or two nearby? Is he armed? Drunk? Agitated? Does he 'set up' like a boxer? Does he show signs of being a frequent fighter – scars, broken nose, prison tattoos?

TEST YOUR OBSERVATION

Observation means using your senses to pick up useful information, and though it sounds simple, very few people really practise it at all. As a test of your own skills, try asking yourself a few questions about a place that is well-known to you, such as a workplace. Could you find the fire extinguishers without looking around? Do you know where the emergency exits are? How about the fuse-box? Do you know where the alarms are? Where is the nearest fire hose?

These questions are about fire, because fire is a hazard accepted by everyone. Despite this, very few people take the time to prepare themselves for the possibility. If you had difficulties with those questions about fire precautions, think how much you may be missing in the case of possible violence. Observation can mean the difference between life and death.

DEFENCE SYSTEMS ACTIVATED:
9 WAYS TO DEFEND YOURSELF

1) **BE PREPARED TO RUN!** Here's a very important tip: there's nothing to be lost by running away. It's healthy, good for you, and comes recommended by more martial artists than any other form of self-defence. For a lot of men, there seems to be some shame or stigma in the idea of running away. In terms of self-defence, though, the rule is: 'He who fights and runs away, lives to run away again another day.' Fighting is absolutely a last resort. Do it wrong, and you get hurt. Do it right and you'll probably have to explain yourself to a jury of your peers. Why not just run like a bastard at the first opportunity?

Naturally, there are times when running away like a big squealing girlie isn't an option. You may be responsible for the safety of another person, for example, or there may be a number of attackers ranged about. Or you may simply be a truly terrible runner. Nonetheless, most of the time your first priority should be just to get out and get away.

When you do decide to run, be careful that decision doesn't compromise your safety. Don't turn your back on an opponent who's anywhere near striking distance. Don't try to slip past an aware, alert

§

SELF-DEFENCE TECHNIQUE #1: STAY CALM.

Frank is this semi-famous rock star I know. You'd probably recognise him on the street. This guy isn't effeminate, but he is one those guys who likes to think he's in touch with his feminine side. Even though he doesn't look the slightest bit gay, he'd like to think that he does.

In truth he's probably one of the most insensitive people you could ever meet. Anyway we were walking through town one day and this guy was wearing a very stupid-looking pork pie hat. These two huge Maoris came looming over the horizon. I noticed them, but this was over near Bondi, which is full of Maoris, so I didn't pay much attention. As we drew closer however, my friend nudged me and whispered, 'Don't worry about these guys. It'll be cool.'

But he was a long way from cool. He was cruising the ragged edge of a major freak-out. I could hear a bad spaghetti western sound track in my head and I started thinking, 'He's giving off fear. He's giving off fear.' And he was too. He was giving it off in waves. Gushing out thick ropey strands of pure terror like streams of hot plasma from a collapsing star. And it was affecting him in a really odd way. The closer these uglies came to us and the greater his fear, the camper he seemed to become, swishing his hips and

opponent – or even past someone whose part in the matter you're not sure of. Bystanders aren't always innocent; you may find your attacker has friends you weren't expecting.

Don't allow yourself to be 'herded'; if it looks as though your attacker wants you to take the fight to some other location, you're probably better off where you are. Don't run between attackers, as a rule. And don't run over broken or uncertain ground, especially in bad light; it's extremely difficult to effectively defend yourself – let alone run away – with a broken ankle.

Remember: running away doesn't just mean sprinting like crazy. It also means getting up and leaving the pub before the fur starts to fly, or going home early from a party which has begun an obvious spiral into flapping his hands until he'd transformed himself into this weird sort of fear-crazed vaudeville drag queen in a dumb hat.

Well these huge guys came within reach and BANG! one of them belted him without missing a step. This huge fist, about a foot across, just smashed into his face and sent him flying back through the air. It was one of the few times I've seen a man literally knocked off his feet. I've still got a vivid image of the white soles of his Nikes flying through the air. He landed, spread-eagled on the bonnet of a parked car. Most impressive of all though was his hat. That stupid little pork pie hat had gone flying into the air at the moment of impact allowing this enormous Maori to pull off a magic trick where he seemed to pluck it out of the air in mid-flight, make it roll up his own arm and plop down on top of his massive head. Where it sat, diminutive and ridiculous. He didn't miss a beat, just carried on past us, turned around and smiled. When they were a safe distance away I helped Frank off the car bonnet. He tried to wipe the blood from his face and said shakily, 'Thanks for that.' I thought he was accusing me of not doing anything but no, he was genuine. He went on, 'Thanks for not doing anything, that was really good of you. That could have been a very ugly situation.'

§

ugliness. Any time you walk away from a potential fight without anyone getting hurt at all, you've as good as won the fight on points so far as most of us are concerned. After all: 'Violence is the last refuge of the incompetent.'

2) **STOP THE FIGHT BEFORE IT STARTS.** Practise non-confrontational behaviour. Frequently, violence can occur even where no-one involved really wants it. This is especially true in the matter of arguments, insults and confrontations – people lose their tempers, or feel as though they've been shamed in front of their friends, and they are 'forced' to respond with violence. It is therefore very important that nothing in your manner of speech or in your body language should indicate aggression, or provoke a response.

§

SELF-DEFENCE TECHNIQUE #2: TAMING THE BEAST.

When I was at art college we had this awful day trip to this hokey theme park. Everyone had to find something down there to 'interpret' via their own medium. It was a really bloody cold and windy Wednesday in the middle of winter and the place was devoid of life. It was death on a stick. So most of us just went to the pub and 'interpreted' a few rum and Cokes. My friend Rachel was really into the theme park experience though and insisted on seeing every attraction. Her big moment came when this little electric golf cart pulled up and Bobby the Bunyip offered her a lift. Bobby was the mascot for this place. He was just some guy wrapped up in a stinky old brown shag pile carpet with a papier-mâché bunyip's head on him but Rachel was stoked. She hopped right in and asked Bobby to drive her to the roller coaster. Bobby said, 'Sure babe', which wasn't what she'd expected. Nor did she expect the strong smell of whisky, the erratic driving, or the heavy bunyip's paw which fell on her leg and started stroking back and forth. She's going, 'Stop it Bobby, stop it!' but this bunyip just rubbed faster and tried to nuzzle her breast. Rachel screamed and thumped him in the head. Left a big dent. Almost as big as the one in the golf buggy after it crashed into a gum tree, giving Rachel a chance to escape while Bobby the Bunyip rolled about on the grass laughing hysterically. Until he threw up inside his own suit. – *Lorrie*

§

When attempting to defuse or scale down a situation, your gestures and posture should remain open and relaxed. Even if you do feel it necessary to raise a protective 'guard' in front of you, try to do it without closing your fists. Open hands are conciliatory and non-threatening, and they work just as well as fists in a fight; better, in some ways. Threatening or provocative gestures, such as pointing fingers or pushing should be avoided at all costs.

Your voice should remain similarly restrained. Shouting, threatening, even raising your voice; these things are of no use, and can very easily provoke a violent response. Returning insults is similarly valueless; if you can't find anything useful to say, (as your mother would have said) you're better off saying nothing at all.

On the other hand, if you keep your voice low and measured, a man who wants to hear what you are saying will need to moderate his own voice to pick up your words. And when he's not shouting at you any more, you may both be surprised to discover that you're not nearly as angry as you thought. In any case, if you keep your voice down before any fighting happens, it will enhance the effect of your voice as a weapon should you come to need it.

3) BODY SAFETY – positioning yourself for survival. Okay, so none of the above has worked. You're in a fight. What do you do? The most effective stance for self-defence is your usual standing posture – knees slightly bent, feet a little more than shoulder width apart, with feet slightly splayed. What is very important, though, is your body position in relation to your attacker. Body safety is a consideration which should never be far from your mind. No technique of self-defence – no matter how effective or devastating – can be considered valid if it exposes our own selves to an attack in the process. An important part of self-defence training lies in learning reflexively to move yourself to a safe position as soon as anything happens. You should consider two things: orientation and distance.

Orientation refers to how your body is aligned in relation to that of your attacker. When you suspect that trouble is in the air, it is useful to turn your body side-on, reducing the overall target area presented to your attacker. This also shifts vulnerable areas such as solar plexus, groin and throat out of the direct line of attack. It is not helpful to assume an obvious fighting stance; this is exactly the kind of behaviour which may provoke an unwanted response from your opponent.

The other half of safe body positioning – distance – is a little more complex. Essentially, for each person, and each attacker, there is a 'safe distance'. If you stand too close to your attacker – within that 'safe distance' – by the time you see the punch coming, it will already be too late. Ideally, you should be just outside the useful range of your attackers longest-range assault, be it a punch, a kick, or a swing of an axe.

At that distance, your attacker cannot harm you without first moving into range, even if it's only a single step. That gives you time to see the attack coming, and to prepare a response. Remember, if you feel you are in danger from another person, even the act of closing the gap between you on their behalf constitutes a threat. In other words, you are justified in taking action to defend yourself if you believe that their move towards you is a prelude to hostile action.

If 'just out of range' is good, isn't 'well beyond reach' even better? Strange as it may seem, this is not true. By standing just outside of their effective striking range, you present a plausible target to your attacker. They 'know' they can reach you with a single, quick step, and so if they decide to commit an attack, it will probably be a quick and direct one.

While this may not sound like a good idea, it *does* mean that you know where their attack is going to be directed. If you were farther back, the attack may be more carefully thought out, or may come from an unexpected direction. You want it to be easy for them to commit an attack, if that's what they're determined to do – but not so easy that the attack will succeed.

4) **SURPRISE: THE GREAT EQUALIZER.** Nobody who attacks you does so thinking they are going to be beaten. If that was the case, they wouldn't attack. When you are attacked, your opponent has already 'seen' how the situation will unfold. They see you on the ground in a broken, bleeding pile and themselves at the pub spending your money. In defending yourself at all, you alter the scenario, and surprise the attacker. It's not much of an advantage, but it's one of the few you've got.

Surprise isn't good for much past the first couple of moments, so you have to follow up on it decisively. Either you finish the encounter during that moment of surprise, or you make a sufficient break that you can safely escape. Once the surprise of your resistance is over, if you're still fighting with your attacker, he is likely to come back at you more strongly than before.

Not expecting real resistance, your attacker is likely to give you an early opportunity. This is part of the element of surprise – that initial over-confidence on his part, which can lead to sloppiness. Therefore, when you seize that first opportunity, you must do so with complete intent, and follow through as thoroughly as the situation requires. Violence is an act of will. Politeness and the Marquis of Queensberry can get stuffed.

Some things you can do will enhance the value of surprise. A sharp shout – called 'Kiai' by martial artists – can momentarily 'freeze' an opponent. Similarly, a 'softening' attack, such as a kick to the shins, or a slap to the nose, can break your attacker's concentration long enough for you to utilize a decisive technique such as a knee to the groin. It is vital that you understand both how to achieve surprise, and how to follow up on the opportunities presented by a surprised opponent.

§

SELF-DEFENCE TECHNIQUE #3:
RESISTANCE: HOW MUCH IS ENOUGH?

My friends Scary Bill, Harry and Thompson were staggering through St Kilda early one morning when they came across two fat karate experts hassling some woman. Harry, being a drunken madman, decided to intervene. He's not much of a fighter, kind of weedy and prone to heart palpitations in fact, but he figured they had the numbers. So he rolled over and started giving these villains some lip, secure in the knowledge that his friends would be backing him up 'a hunnert percent'. Unfortunately his friends were backing him up about fifteen percent. Thompson was swaying menacingly behind him, threatening to fall flat on his face at any moment. Scary Bill had disappeared under a car. When Harry confronted the bad guys they stopped hassling the woman and started kicking six kinds of shit out him and Thompson instead. Their lady friend helped out with a few quick ones to the ribs with her stilettos. There was a fair bit of screaming and grunting before Scary Bill crawled out and sort of half-yelled, half-pleaded with them to stop killing his friends. They did, because Bill was waving a handfull of bright pink five dollar notes at them. He said he'd pay them five dollars each to stop bashing his friends. The fat karate experts were so taken aback by this that they both shook their heads like dogs emerging from a pool. Finally, the bigger one shrugged and said, 'Okay.' They took the money, gave Harry one last little nudge and wandered off into the cruel night.

'A little something I learned in primary school,' said Bill as he helped his friends to their unsteady feet. 'You can sometimes get away by squealing for mercy and giving a bully all of your stuff.'

§

5) RESISTANCE HOW MUCH IS ENOUGH? Self-defence is a tricky idea. It is not something you can afford to take in half-measures. Once you set out to defend yourself, you are taking a step which cannot be withdrawn. There's no stopping to take a breather, no picking up your attacker and apologising for hurting him, and no starting over if you get it wrong. Real violence is not a video game.

If you manage to injure, hurt or annoy – but not stop – an attacker, the results can be far worse than if you had never shown any resistance at all. Therefore, when you set out to convince your attacker that you are not a profitable or enjoyable target, you must continue to work towards that end, whatever the cost – until you are sure of your safety.

For many people, this is a difficult thing to consider. It is certainly not a matter of 'fighting fair'. In fact, your only real chance of escape may require the 'dirtiest' tactics you have ever contemplated. It might mean breaking someone's arm, or smashing their face into a wall. It might mean literally gouging out the eye of another person with your thumb-nail. If you are not genuinely committed 100% to saving your life, whatever the cost, then you might as well not try at all.

The worst thing is, until you are put into a situation where this kind of thing is demanded of you, there is no way to know how you will react. Seasoned martial artists have been known to freeze solid in a 'real' situation. Shy, retiring women can become spitting, screaming, scratching whirlwinds of fury. There's just no way to tell.

All the training in the world is completely useless if you don't put it into action. There's no 'invincible fighting art' outside of the Bruce Lee movies. The only thing that self-defence training can give to you is a simple and effective arsenal of techniques to help you, if you decide to help yourself. The ultimate decision, and the all-important commitment to that decision must come from within.

6) KIAI: THE ART OF NOISE. One of the most valuable and effective weapons available in self-defence is your voice. In martial arts, the penetrating shout which often accompanies an attack is called 'Kiai', and it serves a number of purposes. In terms of self-defence, shouting can do for you exactly what it does for a martial artist, plus one more valuable thing: it may serve to attract attention, or at least, cause the attacker to fear attention being drawn to the scene.

To make your Kiai as effective as possible, you should keep your voice even and level when negotiating in a potential attack situation. That way, you gain maximum surprise value when you do use your voice, accompanying your defensive techniques with a loud, penetrating shout. Surprise value is what you're after: one of the most important functions of Kiai in self-defence is that of startling your opponent. The sudden, loud, shrill tones of the shout serve to jolt your opponent's nervous system, momentarily 'freezing' him, and giving you an opening in which to attack.

Using your voice in this manner also has valuable effects on you. By tightening the abdominal muscles for the shout, you provide a strong base in your body to support and power your attack. The muscular tension and the exhalation also serve to protect your abdomen and torso from impact, to a degree. And finally, the very act of shouting can bolster your own commitment, helping you to overcome hesitation and uncertainty in the attack.

7) **STICKS AND STONES: IMPROVISING A WEAPON.** Having a weapon can be a great advantage when trying to defend yourself. Of course, using a weapon can be a great advantage to an attacker as well, which is why the law has forbidden the carrying of most weapons. Nonetheless, that doesn't mean that you can't carry some kind of object which can be usefully put to the task as a weapon – and as a matter of fact, almost all of us routinely carry about things which can be very effectively used in this manner.

A weapon is any object which increases your own fighting effectiveness, in terms of reach, or precision, or sheer damage-creating potential. If you think briefly, you'll be able to easily list a number of objects which you might have ready to hand which can be used as weapons. The list below is far from exhaustive:

- **UMBRELLA.** Sharp end for jabbing, also useful for blocking, tripping, strangling, joint-locking and pressure points.
- **NEWSPAPER OR MAGAZINE.** Tightly rolled for jabbing and blocking.
- **KEYS.** Gripped tightly between the fingers as a formidable gouging attack to augment a punch.
- **PENS, PENCILS, SMALL BOTTLES.** Gripped in the fist with ends protruding for gouging, jabbing, and work against pressure points.
- **ATTACHÉ CASE.** Reinforced edges and corners make a very effective club.
- **BELT.** Especially studded, works wonders wrapped tightly around the fist. If there's a heavy buckle, can be used as a flail. Favourite of bikers and punks.

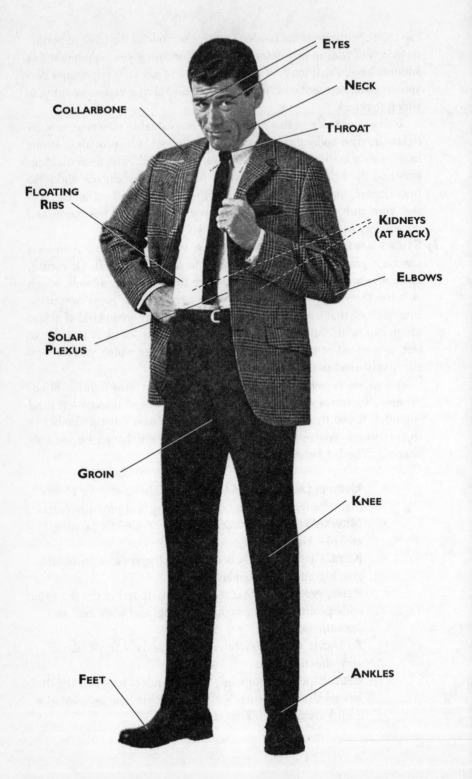

EYES

NECK

COLLARBONE

THROAT

FLOATING
RIBS

KIDNEYS
(AT BACK)

ELBOWS

SOLAR
PLEXUS

GROIN

KNEE

FEET

ANKLES

8) HOT SPOTS: HURTING YOUR OPPONENT WHILE SAVING YOUR OWN SKIN. If you want to stop a car running, the easiest way is not to take a hammer and beat the bodywork into a shapeless lump. It's much simpler to open the bonnet and rip the rotor arm out of the distributor, right?

So too, with the human body. A practised boxer can withstand extensive pummelling to the body and head, where a single kick to the groin will stop him cold. A wrestler, with that strong, muscular neck, might be able to spend all day in a headlock and come up smiling – but if you gouge his eyes, his sense of humour will disappear instantly. It is therefore very useful to know something about the body's weaknesses – not only to help neutralise an attacker, but to help you protect those same bits on your own body.

- **EYES.** Vital sensory apparatus, extremely sensitive to pressure. Gouging and jabbing are most effective.
- **THROAT.** Holds the windpipe, the carotid arteries and jugular veins. Extremely vulnerable to strikes and strangles. Great care should be taken in attacking the throat, as it is surprisingly easy to cause death with a mis-managed technique.
- **NECK.** The vertebrae protect the spinal cord, which carries information between the brain and the rest of the body. Vulnerable to strikes, but once again, great care must be taken not to accidentally kill or cripple with a mis-managed technique.
- **COLLARBONE.** Relatively weak and exposed bone, supporting the action of the shoulders. Easily broken with correct technique.
- **ELBOWS.** Easily broken if the arm is straight.
- **SOLAR PLEXUS.** Open to a penetrating strike, which will affect the attacker's ability to breathe for a few minutes.
- **FLOATING RIBS.** Easily broken, very sensitive to a sharp blow.
- **KIDNEYS.** Very sensitive to strikes; a strong blow to the kidney area will result in intense, disabling pain.
- **GROIN.** Extremely sensitive, in both men and women.
- **KNEE.** Vulnerable, exposed joint, relatively weak. Easily destroyed with an accurate kick.
- **ANKLES AND FEET.** Vulnerable, exposed joints and bone. A good stomping will finish things quickly.

§
Genius is 1% inspiration and 99% plastique

I went to an all-boys high school. Three hundred teenage boys, a real discipline problem as you can imagine. We were always testing the authority of the Powers That Be. It was mostly pathetic stuff, smoking behind the dunnies, putting potatoes in the teachers' exhaust pipes, stuff like that. But we did have one guy who was a real professional. He was a mad bomber. Blew up lockers and school bags and garbage bins in the playground. He must have been some geeky chemistry/physics honours student because he'd always time these things to go off when everyone was in class, so nobody got hurt. It'd be about two thirty in the afternoon usually. That really sleepy part of the day. You'd be thinking of catching a few zzz's when the teacher's back was turned and all of a sudden ... BOOM! Another locker would bite the dust and cheers would go up all over the school. It drove the teachers nuts.

They had searches and interrogations, all sorts of Gestapo-like tactics. Finally we're sitting in class one day when the PA crackles up and the headmaster comes on, says they've caught the mad bomber and there'll be a special punishment parade in the last period that day. About an hour away. Man, we couldn't wait to find out who this character was. The hour rolled round and we all assembled. The headmaster stood in front of us on this raised dais they had. There was a big, ugly uniformed cop standing next to him, looking really heavy and stern, but they didn't have the mad bomber with them. I figured they might have already locked

9) **BIFF AND THE LAW: WHERE SELF-DEFENCE STOPS AND EXCESSIVE FORCE BEGINS.** Let's assume you are involved in a confrontation. Your attacker is a large man with a club, and in defending yourself, you smash his knee and dislocate his shoulder, hospitalising him, and leaving him with permanent injuries. Where do you stand when the matter comes to court? What if he had no weapon? What if there were two or three of you in the group he attacked? What if you had used a knife to defend yourself?

him up or something. But no, that wasn't it. Those fucking hosers tried the oldest trick in the book. The headmaster fired up his microphone and said they knew who the guy was, they could see him in the assembly, and they were going to give him one chance, and only one chance, to come forward and give himself up like a man. They said he had one minute. Well, this silence fell over us. Unnatural it was. And nobody was moving an inch in case they got tagged as the bomber. I'm standing there thinking this could go on all day when all of a sudden ... BOOM! Three desks exploded in the teachers' common room.

They never caught him. That mad bomber is alive and free and walking amongst us today. – *PJ*

Elmer smiled with grim satisfaction. By the end of big lunch the teachers' common room would be a smoking crater. Those fools would rue the day they passed him over for the chemistry prize, superglued a stupid traindriver's cap to his head, and painted 'Property of Fudd' in big bright purple letters on his butt.

§

Self-defence is a legal minefield. The key to negotiating that minefield lies in the phrase 'appropriate or necessary force'. In essence, that means that where you have reason to fear for your own safety – or the safety of a person for whom you may be responsible, you have the right to respond to the perceived threat with force which is necessary, sufficient and appropriate to end that threat.

A hard-and-fast interpretation of that rule which can be applied to all cases is simply not possible. A drunken man with a broken bottle may be more of a threat to himself than to anyone around him. If that were the case, it would certainly not be appropriate or necessary to smash up your own bottle to 'take him apart'.

On the other hand, a fit, determined, but completely unarmed man may conceivably require deadly force to counter him, especially if you are smaller and less able than he is. There is simply no really sure way to stay in the right. There are practices you can follow, though:

• **TRY NOT TO INITIATE VIOLENCE.** While it is true that a perceived threat can exist in something as simple as someone approaching you with their hands raised, if there are witnesses around, it is best to be seen to be trying to minimise the situation. Use non-threatening body language, keep your voice low and reasonable, and don't make or return threats.

• **DON'T ESCALATE MATTERS.** If he's barehanded, while you might use a stick defensively, you shouldn't be trying to club him senseless with it. If he's pushing you around, the best response is probably *not* to knock him down and stomp on his head. Your response should not be more dangerous than his initial attack.

• **ENOUGH IS ENOUGH.** There is no way to justify, in a court of law, behaviour such as stomping an unconscious or neutralised attacker, or slashing a downed man with a knife.

• **REPORT THE MATTER AS QUICKLY AS POSSIBLE.** If you're the one to take it to the authorities, it's your story they'll hear first, and it will minimise your attacker's chance to concoct a counter-story.

BIFF FOR BEGINNERS

ASSUMING YOU'VE NEVER DONE anything like this before, here's a few pointers on how to get started. If you follow them, at least you'll look good as you get the living snot beaten out of you ...

• **SETTING YOUR GUARD.** Take a stance facing your body forty-five degrees away from your opponent, and turn your head so that you can see him over the top of one shoulder. Keep your knees slightly bent, feet about shoulder-width apart. Drop your head slightly, and keep your jaw firmly closed. It will save on dental work if you get hit.

Don't raise your fists; keep your hands open instead. It's better body language for a start – but more importantly, you can do more with an open hand than with a closed one. Fists can only pummel. They can't grab, slap, poke, or fend. One hand should come up to just about eye level, the elbow down to protect your ribs. The other hand stays a little lower, fore-arm across your body defensively. Lead hand is for softening and jabbing. Lower hand is for the big follow-up punch, if you get the opportunity.

• **THROWING A PUNCH.** First, make a fist by rolling your fingertips tightly into the palm of your hand, and folding your thumb across the front. Make it tight as you can, and remember that the thumb stays outside the fingers. Putting it inside is a good way to get it broken.

Your striking surface with the fist is a small oval surrounding your first and second knuckles. Third and fourth knuckles should just stay out of the way. When delivering a punch, don't haul your fist back near your ear first. It doesn't make the blow any more powerful. It slows you down, and it advertises what you're about to do. John Wayne only did it that way for the cameras.

With your feet well planted, pick your target area, and drive your fist forward with a snap. At the point of impact, try to roll your fist over so that the back of your hand is aimed at the sky. To get the best penetration, you should be trying to hit a spot about five centimetres *under* your opponent's skin.

Never hit anyone in the mouth. You'll cut your hand badly enough to require stitches, and if you're unlucky, rip up enough nerves and tendons to impair function in the hand for the remainder of your life. Target the eyes, nose, side of the jaw, groin and solar plexus.

> §
>
> ### THROWING A PUNCH CAN BE
> ### AS HARD AS TAKING ONE
>
> **Boxing is not like other tests in sport between one athlete and another; it arouses two of the deepest anxieties we contain. There is not only the fear of getting hurt, which is profound in more men than will admit to it, but there is the opposite panic, equally unadmitted, of hurting others. — *Norman Mailer***
>
> §

- **THROWING A KICK.** If it's a serious self-defence matter, the rules go out the window. Kick the bastard. Don't swing your leg from the hip, as though you were Mal Meninga trying to convert from the touch-line. This is slow, obvious to the watcher, and surprisingly lacking in power. Instead, aim by lifting your knee, then snapping your foot forward so that the toe of your shoe drives into your target.

  Never use a high kick. Even if you're well trained, it jeopardises your balance. Also, it advertises the fact that you have martial training, which takes away the element of surprise. Even the groin is too high a target – and besides, as you know, men are terribly, terribly good at protecting their groin. No, the thing you want to kick is either his kneecap, his shin, or his ankle. Knees are best.

- **FALLING DOWN.** It may very well happen. And if you don't know how to deal with it, you could be badly hurt, or at least stunned long enough for your opponent to step in and kick you white.

  If you get knocked over, immediately tuck your chin into your chest and keep it there. This will stop your head bouncing off the ground when you hit. Try to turn your body onto your side as you go over, so that you can take the impact on the muscular, padded hip and shoulder areas, rather than on your face or your back. Keep your arms tucked up in a guard position, and bring your knees up slightly as you hit. These actions will help you protect your face, belly and groin from the inevitable kicking which will follow.

THE TAO OF BIFF: MARTIAL ARTS.

WHAT, YOU DON'T WANT TO practise a martial art? What kind of a man are you, anyway?

Once upon a time, it was fair and reasonable for certain kinds of men to dodge their martial obligations. Back before 1940, say, when the only art available was boxing. Sure, not everyone is cut out to hang around sweaty gyms, being periodically punched around the head. These days, though, with the proliferation of exciting martial forms from all over the world, there's an art that's right for every man – and every 21st century man needs a martial art.

Why? A truckload of reasons, really. First, you need something to talk about with all the other martial arts freaks. That's really vital. Then, of course, there's all the physical benefits – fitness, co-ordination, relaxation and good stuff like that. Also, there's always the outside chance that you may need to beat the snot out of somebody at some stage. Nothing better than a bit of handy training before you get into the biff-o; it can save you a world of hurt.

Then, finally, there's the real kicker: a lot of women practise martial arts these days. And if you practise alongside them, you'll be grappling, wrestling, and struggling with them at extra close range. This can be a Very Good Thing ...

Of course, it's important to choose the right martial art for your needs. In the Shaolin temples in China, a new acolyte is observed very closely and given a variety of challenging physical tasks and chores before he is assigned to his branch of the art. Note that we say assigned. The acolyte doesn't choose at all. In fact, a bunch of bald, hairy-eyebrowed octogenarian monsters watch him like a hawk, and decide what kind of art suits his body type and musculature. Then the acolyte learns that art. And no other.

You get the idea. Anyway, in order to help you choose, here's a summary of the major martial arts:

AIKIDO

Developed by the master Morihei Ueshiba from a couple of different strands of Ju-jitsu, Aikido was codified as a martial art in the early 1950s, making it one of the most recent genuine arts. Aikido translates roughly as 'way of body and spirit harmony', which pretty well describes what old Ueshiba was trying to achieve. Aikido is especially effective in the areas of joint-locking and restraining techniques.

GOOD STUFF. Reasonably easy to find. Also reasonably non-violent, and pleasant to practise. The range of armlocks and holds is fantastic, allowing you a very subtle but powerful alternative to beating the snot out of your opponent. Very good for balance, and learning to fall safely. Think Steven Seagal – though not the damned ponytail.

NOT-SO-GOOD-STUFF. Ueshiba was a genuine master. He doesn't seem to have understood (or perhaps his followers have missed the point) that some of the techniques he used personally look a lot like black magic to the rest of us. As a result, many Aikido schools tend to be a little – well, fuzzy. Striking and kicking are practically disregarded. Extremely subtle techniques are occasionally taught far too early, and often by people who don't themselves fully understand what they're doing. (An exception to most of these is Yoshinkan Aikido, a rather harder and more rigorous style developed by one of Ueshiba's early student/partners.)

BOXING

This is the classic western martial art, subject of a hundred movies and a thousand bad novels. Oriented most especially towards punching things, the rules of boxing were formalised by a nice man called the Marquis of Queensberry way back in England, at the end of the 19th century. Boxing has long been an Olympic sport, and is also one of the most widely recognised professional sports.

GOOD STUFF. Widely available, with boxing instructors hanging around almost every decent gym in the country. Excellent sporting opportunities available – professional boxers are among those athletes who occasionally become unforgettable household names. Very, very good indeed for cardio-vascular fitness, endurance, and upper-body strength. Quick, deft footwork, best hand-striking and blocking techniques available outside k'ung fu. And if it weren't for the bloody gloves and rules, it would probably be better.

NOT-SO-GOOD-STUFF. Where to begin? Unless you're a major name professional, boxing is a completely crap way to meet women. Not many women box, and of those that do, you don't really want to know most of them.

Also, since boxing concentrates on introducing fist to head, there is a fair-to-middling chance that if you stick with it for any length of time, you're going to get punched. As in broken nose, split eyebrow ... scars. This may – if you're lucky – make you look 'interesting' to some women, but on the whole, will probably just make you lumpy.

JUDO

Famous martial art developed by Prof Jigoro Kano in the late 19th century. Derived from the contemporary Ju-jitsu, which had been declared illegal by the emperor, Judo emphasises grappling, wrestling and throwing. For many years, Judo was the official martial art of the Japanese navy, and was one of the very first Japanese martial arts to move to the west. It has been an official Olympic sport since 1964.

GOOD STUFF. Readily available. High degree of fitness involved. Excellent for ground-fighting, and positively uncanny with regard to over-balancing and throwing the opponent. Fantastic sporting opportunities available. Very, very good for overall balance and co-ordination – learn Judo and you will never again trip over your own feet. Also, most of your practice is done with a partner, which gives you a real feel for how the stuff works.

NOT-SO-GOOD-STUFF. Not too hot for self-defence. You have to be quite close to your opponent to apply judo techniques, and your opponent has to be prepared to grapple with you – or you have to be very good at convincing him to grapple. Very little in the way of striking or kicking is taught, and the blocking is pretty minimal as well. These days, the sporting orientation of judo has largely overwhelmed the older, more martial aspects.

JU-JITSU

The grandaddy of the Japanese martial arts, elements of Ju-jitsu can be found in illustrations and writings of nine hundred years ago. It is the least specialised of any of the arts, utilising techniques of striking, blocking, kicking, strangling, locking, grappling, throwing and anything else they can think of to formulate a very effective art of self-defence.

GOOD STUFF. These are the lads you want to talk to if your interest is in self-protection. It's often not pretty, but the bottom line is that it works. If it didn't, they wouldn't do it. Ju-jitsu is very well-rounded, with considerable practical training in most aspects of self-defence.

NOT-SO-GOOD-STUFF. Can be hard to find. Also, with its emphasis on self-defence, it's not so focused on fitness. If you want to get really fit, you do it on your own time. It helps – but if you have to be fit to win a fight, then all fights would be won on the basis of fitness, right?

There's a reasonably limited sporting side to Ju-jitsu as well. Many of the techniques are simply too nasty and dangerous to introduce to a sport, so practising sport Ju-jitsu is kind of like … errr – taking a shower in a raincoat.

The other real problem with ju-jitsu is the sheer volume of material you have to learn. Unlike most of the arts, which specialise in a single aspect of fighting technique and barely touch on the others, Ju-jitsu tries to get a handle on them all. Grading in a serious Ju-jitsu school is a lengthy, slow, difficult and frequently painful procedure, to be undertaken only by those who are prepared to think long and hard about what they're doing.

KARATE

A widespread art, specialising in striking and kicking techniques. Originated in Okinawa, in Southern Japan, where it developed from Chinese forms that came across from the mainland. Roughly translated, 'Karate-do' means 'way of the empty hand', and the original hard-style Okinawan karate schools are still some of the toughest and most exacting groups around.

GOOD STUFF. Readily available. Karate is excellent for fitness, and quite reasonable for flexibility. It will also develop strength, co-ordination and accuracy. Not yet an Olympic sport, but plenty of sporting opportunities available.

NOT-SO-GOOD-STUFF. Very little throwing or grappling involved. Not much good once you get knocked to the ground. Not much use if the situation doesn't call for punching or kicking a big fat hole in the middle of your opponent. Also, as most of the practise is done in a ritualised solo fashion referred to as 'kata', it can be difficult to bring your skills into play when faced with a real live opponent.

KICK-BOXING

A very powerful and physical art most commonly associated with Thailand. Kick-boxing has shot into the public eye in the last few years, cropping up in bad films, terrible books, and an increasingly active international sporting scene. It's another specialist striking art, paying special attention to the use of the extremely powerful elbows and knees as devastating close-quarter weapons.

GOOD STUFF. Lots of fitness and endurance here, as well as wide availability and a high sporting profile. There's still not a whole lot of money in kick-boxing, but things are getting better. The striking techniques developed in kick-boxing – especially those of elbow, knee and shin – are among the most powerful in any martial art, well and truly capable of getting the job done in a few quick shots.

NOT-SO-GOOD-STUFF. Lots of aggro in kick-boxing. It seems to attract blokes with attitude problems, and it does very little to alleviate or control those problems. Low babe quotient, although a reputation in kick-boxing will help you pick up a nice line in rough trade, if your tastes run that way.

The 'toughening' techniques in Thai kick-boxing are pretty stupid. There's a lot of slamming shins into things that ordinarily don't get that kind of treatment, like trees, pillars and walls. Hands and feet and elbows get that sort of thing too – less so in the West, thankfully. Anyway, long-term kickboxers are the martial artists most likely to develop arthritis and other exciting problems.

As is usual with the striking-oriented arts, kick-boxers pretty much leave out the grappling, throwing, and wrestling techniques, and wouldn't know an armlock or restraint grip if it bit them.

K'UNG FU

You're thinking Bruce Lee, right? Actually, 'k'ung fu' means something like 'healthful exercise', and has been adapted by the West as a blanket term to cover several hundred distinct fighting arts originating in China. This makes classification and summary of the 'art' a real cow. However, most of the k'ung fu styles emphasise striking and blocking techniques over grappling or throwing.

More often, work with the hands and fists is developed more fully than kicking and sweeping techniques. As there are so very many styles of k'ung fu – including Wing Chun, T'ong Long, Choy Li Fut, and all the variations of the Shaolin school – it isn't possible to say a great deal about any of them. However, Bruce Lee got his start in Wing Chun, and later developed his own version, which he named Jeet Kune Do.

All k'ung fu styles call for a very high degree of fitness and co-ordination from their students. Few, if any, do any real work on the ground, however – and some k'ung fu styles actively eschew groundwork, because they believe you should never be caught on the ground ... idiots.

NINJITSU

Another very old Japanese art, with a real history about it. Back in the bad old days of medieval Japan, a number of clans started supporting themselves by acting as assassins and spies for hire. Now, as Japan has always placed a very high value on 'honour', the Ninja were widely reviled for their activities. They were also in extremely high demand.

Since the Ninja clans existed in a kind of shadowy underworld, dependent upon their illegal skills for survival, it was thought that the arts of ninjitsu died out sometime in the 19th century, as things modernised in Japan. At least one man, however, Dr Masaaki Hatsumi, lays claim to being a direct linear grandmaster of one of the major Ninja clans, and his Togakure Ryu Ninjitsu has gained a worldwide following.

GOOD STUFF. Fitness, balance, adaptability, and a certain bizarre kamikaze mindset aimed at out-weirding your opponent if you can't beat him any other way. Modern ninja work long and hard with an exciting array of weaponry, including chains, nunchaku, swords, daggers, claws, bows ...

NOT-SO-GOOD-STUFF. Can be hard to find. Also, there remain doubts about the genuine-ness of the modern ninja's background. Actually, there's quite a number of out-and-out fakes, who sprang up after Dr Hatsumi's school excited the popular imagination.

Then there's the expense. All those weapons, plus the black pyjamas, plus the exciting boots, and all the ninja gadgets ... the costs add up at a phenomenal rate.

Also, there's that crack-brained mindset. Ninja traditionally are a sneaky, much-despised bunch who live by their skills in lurking in shadows and clobbering people. Now in the twentieth century, there's really not a whole lot of call for that kind of thing outside the armed forces and various shady intelligence groups. However, the Ninjitsu schools still work very hard at establishing that ultra-paranoid black-jammies sneakyduck mindset in their students. Which can really, really put the zap on your social life.

Finally, there's another point. Push comes to shove, and the ninja tend to get a bit complicated. They like to leap, dive and roll where taking a simple forward step would be less painful. They like to lob smoke grenades where most of us would just ask the waiter for the bill. And they're just as likely to pull out some weird Ninja weapon when the situation is screaming for nothing more complicated than a biff in the snout.

Ninja are strange.

SUMO
You're kidding, right?

TAE-KWON DO
Korean national martial art, formalised many years ago. It's a beautiful, high-flying art to watch, full of spectacular leaps and kicks, with a strong line in brick and board smashing. Tae-kwon Do has been an Olympic demonstration sport once already, and as a sport, has a very strong international following.

GOOD STUFF. Fitness, and most especially, flexibility. These puppies just love to do the splits. Also, Tae-kwon Do is widely available, and provides good sporting opportunities. And they can teach you more about kicking than anybody else, including the French and their Savate-kicks. We're telling you, what the Tae-kwon Do people can do with their feet defies the laws of physics and gravity.

NOT-SO-GOOD-STUFF. A lot of it doesn't work. Unless you're working out with another Tae-kwon Do practitioner, that is. Jumping spinning kicks look sensational on television and in the cinema, but in reality, they're just

§

USES FOR MARTIAL ARTS #2:
WHAT TO DO WHEN CONFRONTED BY
AN ANGRY LEOPARD.

- **Maintain eye contact.**
- **Do not make any sudden movements.**
- **Hope the leopard is not hungry.** – *John Davis*,
Keeper of the big cats, Western Plains Zoo.

§

a good way to lose your balance and get beaten up. And as Tae-kwon Do places especial emphasis on kicking, it follows that they're a little weak in other areas – grappling, throwing, wrestling, locking ... even their punching isn't too good at close range. Boy, they sure can kick, though.

Finally, this proviso: take all of the above with a grain of salt. In the long run, the most important part of any study of the martial arts is the teacher-student relationship. Frankly, if you have a certain amount of talent and you 'click' with your teacher in, say, ballet or basketball or rock-climbing, you'll probably become just as able in terms of self-defence as most martial arts students. It comes down to nothing more complex than that: a good teacher, a little talent, and a great deal of effort.

CHAPTER EIGHT

Cooking: Food as Foreplay.

THERE ARE A NUMBER OF excellent reasons for the Man of the New Millennium to learn the art of cooking. It's cheaper than eating out, for starters. And considerably healthier than trying to live on burgers and Mars Bars. Generations of Men have learned to cook, however, for one main reason: it's a top way to impress the babes.

Think about it. In the first place, women don't expect us to be able to cook. At best, they expect to see scorched meat, boiled potatoes and soggy vegetables, in the best British tradition. A Man who can rustle up a quick and elegant Thai salad, or perhaps a Cantonese crab-and-sweet-corn soup, or even a platter of rich, piquant spaghetti bolognaise – this is a surprising Man, a competent Man, a sensitive Man who has a fast-track to the bedrooms of his choice.

Food is suggestive stuff, you see. Remember all those films where food and sex are brought into combination? All the sequences you've seen with whipped cream and cherries, noodles and canoodling? It's an established idea within our culture – the sexuality of food. Men who know how to stimulate the senses with food – smell, taste, sight and touch. Men who are prepared to indulge in the sensuality of a fine meal are (in the mind of women). Men who may well be able to demonstrate sensitivity, creativity and sensuality in other, more intimate situations. 'Men who can cook', said Jane, when we asked her. 'Well, you know – they're just ...' And then she produced a slow smile that could have ignited the Pope's boxers.

A really good meal is practically a metaphor for sex in its own right. From the foreplay of soups and entrées, which build the appetite and arouse the senses, to the climactic satisfaction of the main course, down through the lazy, sensual afterplay of dessert. A well constructed dinner is a complete seduction, engaging the senses to their fullest and delivering a rich palette of pleasures to the participants. It *will* get you laid.

And what about the simple tactical advantages of knowing how to run up an impressive meal? Suppose you meet The Killer Babe at work, or get to know her on the bus, or through a bunch of friends – in fact, anywhere but in the classic pickup spots of pub and nightclub, where the rules of approach are already clearly defined. You get to know her, moving slowly and carefully, and when you figure enough time has passed, you move in. What will you do? Is it going to be a film? A show? A night at the restaurant?

Passé, gentlemen. All of the above have one disadvantage: they are clearly *dates*, and a Man who asks a woman out on a *date* has (let's be honest with one another, shall we?) only one goal. She knows it. He knows she knows it. She probably even knows he knows ... and so on. Anyway, suddenly the situation has gone from 'friends in a social context' to 'sniffing

§

Cooking for sex: The don'ts.

We were driving around the country and we fetched up in
Kings Cross. We had this huge old mobile home which was
coming apart at the seams. It was tied together with ropes
and bungee cords and it had blown two motors in two weeks.
I got rid of it in Victoria Street. Swapped it for a new
Gemini, a grand in cash and a five hundred dollar camera
from some German backpackers. Told them that because it
was classified as a house it didn't actually need a road-wor-
thy in Queensland. You couldn't even lock the door on this
thing. It'd fall off every time you started the engine.

   We cashed up and went for a giant breakfast at this café.
You wouldn't believe these breakfasts. They must have
killed three or four different sorts of animal to make a pile
that high. And they hardly cost anything. When I told my
girlfriend about it over the phone she suggested the waiter
might be a fag, trying to get onto me. She was just joking.
But the next day we were woken up by the camper being
rocked back and forth and it was this waiter warning us that
the parking guys were coming to ping us. A bit later he
dropped in and said he had a couple of T-bones. Did we feel
like a feed? Well we'd been in this camper for days. No
showers. No deodorant. We reeked. He said we could use
his bathroom if we wanted. So I'm thinking, what's the worst
that can happen? I'll have a feed with a fag. It's a new world,
right? You have to be ready to embrace diversity.

each others butts'. End result? Going on a *date* is one of the most arduous
and traumatic social experiences a Man can undertake outside of polar
expeditions and a stint in the Foreign Legion.

   The Man who can cook, though – he's got more options. He can, for
example, suggest something far more innocuous – a trip to the cricket or
rugby, or a day at the races together, if she happens to like that kind of
thing. Or a day jaunt to the beach, or maybe a drive to the hinterlands with
a couple of friends to check out the local craft markets. Now *that's* not really a date, no sir. Craft markets are about as sexually non-threatening as it

So Tod and I agreed to go to this guy's house. We get there and discover he's laid on this huge feast with tons of food and wine. A real Henry VIII spread. And the meal was sensational. But I can see from this guy's expression that this is not a free lunch. He's been cool so I don't want to have to tell him to fuck off or anything, but there is no way on Earth I'm going to bite his lilac pillows. So when we're out on the balcony after the meal I start acting the yob, talking about girls girls girls and beer beer beer. And he was like, 'Oh you're not really like that James. You really love people. You have such kind, beautiful eyes.'

We were blind drunk by now and he was saying why didn't we make ourselves comfortable, take off our shoes. I said no, I'd burned my feet earlier in the day kicking a footy round the street. But before I could stop him he'd disappeared. Then he reappeared and grabbed my feet. Ripped the shoes right off and started rubbing all this oil into the soles. I was panicking. Toddy was laughing his head off, whispering to me to calm down, to relax and just enjoy it. I jumped up and said I was ready for my shower. The gay guy thought that was a great idea but I dashed in and closed the door before he could follow me. While I was getting cleaned up I noticed all of these sex mags lying around. Like they'd been left there for me to see. When I came out Toddy was gone and this guy was powdering my shoes. I got dressed and flew out of that place like a bat out of Hell. *– Jimmy*

§

gets. And if our Man happened to bring a picnic basket, carefully loaded with the right goodies plus one or two niftily prepared dishes ... well, picnics are *romantic*, you see. Not like a date at all. Not with those other friends along. Make those specially prepared dishes really impressive, let the wine flow, and soon the non-date picnic will take on an altogether more intimate atmosphere.

The non-date dinner is an even better scam. Work the conversation around to food and cooking, let slip the fact that you can put together a really authentic Beef Rendang, and pretty soon, the pair of you will be making casual arrangements for her to come around for dinner some time. No pressure; no expectations – of *course* she can bring a friend if she wants. Hell, your flatmate will probably be there, right? It's just a social thing, to show off your talent in the kitchen and indulge your mutual liking for Malaysian food.

Mind you, there will be wine, naturally. Lots of it. And your flatmate can run interference with her friend (if she's actually brought one). Thus, as the non-date dinner progresses, you immediately have several very important advantages over the regular 'date' system. She's relaxed. You're relaxed. There's no question about who's paying for what. There's no fear of Restaurant Disaster intervening. Your entire bar stock (carefully supplemented for the evening – have you read the section on cocktails yet?) is close at hand. Atmosphere is easy to achieve with a few candles and some thoughtfully-chosen music. Most importantly, there will be *absolutely no embarrassment* about trying to get her back to your place for the night. *She's already there!*

Look, in a book this size, we're not even going to try to teach you to be a cordon bleu chef. Never gonna happen. What you will get, though, is a quick grounding in the essentials you need to make a good first impression. Because let's face it: an impression is all most of you will really want to give. You don't actually have to be a good cook to score the points – you just have to look like one, and to produce a limited number of reasonable results. Left to ourselves, most Men are happy and healthy with a very basic diet. Beer, rice, vegetables, chilli, and the odd chunk of meat – that's a Man's diet. It isn't going to pull the babes, though, so pay close attention to what follows.

THE RIGHT STUFF

Here's a list of the Absolute Minimum you *must have* in your kitchen. We have a lot more flash gear in our respective loveshacks because we are complete fucking wizards who know that thousands of bucks spent in the kitchen pay off admirably in the boudoir. But you are a hopeless joke who needs to be led through a kindergarten level cookery course. So costs and basic purposes of each object are included. Note that stove, oven, and refrigerator with freezer compartment go without saying. A kitchen without those three is just a spare bedroom.

- **WOK: CARBON STEEL, FLAT BASED.** Costs about $30 from K-Mart. Get one with a nice big wooden handle, and a well-fitted lid. Season it before use by washing it, then slowly heating it with a thin layer of peanut oil. After that, you should never soap it again – wash it with an abrasive pad and hot water, and wipe another fine layer of peanut oil on it after each use. Your wok is your best buddy in the kitchen: you can stir-fry, deep-fry, and steam with it. At a pinch, you can even use it in Western-style cooking.

- **MEDIUM SAUCEPAN** (about 2-3 litre capacity): Stainless steel, or at worst, (and it really is worst) enamelled metal. It will cost you about $20-$30 from K-Mart. Make sure the lid fits well and has a steam vent, and that the handle is sound and well attached. Medium saucepans are where your pasta and sauces get done. Small saucepans are cute, but they're a pain in the arse, and anything you can do in one of them, you can do in a medium saucepan.

- **LARGE SAUCEPAN/STOCK-POT** (5-10 litre capacity): Stainless steel. No substitutes. Costs about $30-$50 at K-Mart. This is where you'll make your soups and stocks, bulk pasta, and extra-large portions of chilli con carne or bolognaise sauce.

- **FRYING PAN.** Costs maybe $10 at disposal stores and army surplus places. About 25cm across on the inside cooking surface. Cast iron – no substitutes at all. And make absolutely certain it has a wooden han-dle, well attached. Cast iron gets hot, and if you haven't got something to grip it with, you'll do yourself a serious injury one day. With sand-paper, remove any surface rust. Then season your frying pan exactly as you did your wok, and treat it in the same manner. Well-treated cast iron eventually becomes nearly as smooth and slick as teflon-coated aluminium – which you must *never* waste your time with! Your frying pan is where you'll manage your bacon and eggs, and pancakes, and where'll you'll turn out the occasional, beautifully rare steak.

- **MIXING BOWLS.** At least three, of 4-5 litres capacity each. Spun stainless steel is best. They'll cost you around $5 each at any super-market. You need these for holding ingredients, mixing batters, and whipping cream.

- **SALAD BOWLS.** Two, large wood-laminate bowls. Cost about $5 each, again from K-Mart or any of the larger supermarkets. These are for serving salads of all kinds, and nothing else. Find another container for your stash.

- **CUTTING BOARD.** The super-duper toughened glass variety is best, because it washes easily, and doesn't harbour Evil Germs. Expensive, though – about $25. Dense plastic is next, but has a much shorter lifes-pan. Wood is not a good idea for anything but vegetables and breads. Don't make us tell you what a chopping board is for.

- **ROLLING PIN.** Cheap wooden ones cost about $3 from any supermarket, but a $30 marble or granite job from a kitchen shop will make your life a lot easier. An absolute necessity for pastries and pizza crusts.
- **WHISK.** Solid handle, preferably stainless steel. Don't get the kind with the wrapped-wire spring handles. They rust out from the inside. A good whisk is about $10. You need it for working with sauces, whipping cream, and most importantly, for beating eggs.
- **WOODEN SPOONS.** At least three, with fairly long handles. These are for stirring rich sauces and heavy batters as you cook, and for tossing stir-fry. Cost is negligible.
- **MEASURING JUG.** Just the one will do, but it should be graded both metric and imperial, and should show cup measurements as well. Costs about $5-$10. Pyrex glass or dense, transparent, heat-resistant plastic.
- **SPATULA.** stainless steel, with a dense plastic handle. Cost is negligible. Used for dealing with hot stuff on your frying pan, like pancakes and omelettes.
- **SHORT, SHARP KNIFE.** About the size of a paring knife, perhaps a little longer. Costs maybe $5 if you buy one of those laser-cut never-sharpen jobs at the supermarket. You need this for fiddly cutting jobs.
- **DECENT CLEAVER.** Chinese-style tong-axes in mild steel can be bought from the larger Chinese groceries for about $15. This is your all-purpose knife. After the wok, your cleaver is your next-best mate in the kitchen – all your chopping, dicing, slicing, cutting, and

§

FOOD ETIQUETTE #1: DON'T PLAY WITH YOUR FOOD.

I was working Casualty one night when they brought this guy in from a disco. He'd fallen over and broken his leg on the dance floor. He was green with the pain but he thrashed around something terrible when we told him we had to cut his pants off. He was screaming that they were a five hundred dollar pair of leather pants and he couldn't afford to lose them. He was really freaking out. We figured it was just shock. But when we shot him full of painkiller and cut them off we understood his reluctance.

He'd taped a whole salami to the inside of his leg. – *Barnes*

§

bone-cracking will be done with the cleaver. It's perfect for home defence too. Keep it sharp, keep it oiled, and keep it handy. If you can afford a really authoritative cleaver with a heavy spine, a wooden handle, and a curved cutting edge (about $50-$60, minimum) you'll have a friend for life. It also slices hot pizza like a dream.

- **LONG, SERRATED BREAD KNIFE.** Just a cheap one will do, at under $20. You need this for slicing bread, and carving the occasional roast.
- **ROASTING PANS.** Two of them, about 10cm deep, and maybe 40cm x 25cm in size. Go for stainless steel. These are for roasting and baking.
- **BAMBOO STEAMERS.** Two, plus one lid. (They stack on top of each other.) Buy them to fit in your wok. It will cost you maybe $10 for the pair. Very useful for quickly preparing tasty vegetables, and occasionally running up Chinese-style dumplings.
- **MISCELLANEOUS KITCHEN DRAWER STUFF.** Two pairs of stainless steel salad tongs, a good can-opener, and a corkscrew.
- **SEALABLE TUPPERWARE BOWLS.** At least three, of 3-5 litres capacity each. Vital for storing leftovers in the refrigerator. You should also start hanging on to those plastic containers that you get take-away Chinese in. They're excellent for storing things in the freezer.
- **GOOD, STRONG, SHARP KITCHEN SCISSORS.** Cost about $10-20 at a hardware store, if you appropriate something like Tullen Snips. After the cleaver, these are your next-best friend in the kitchen. They are just the absolute best things for preparing meat for stir-fries, clipping bits off things, trimming fat, and a dozen other operations.
- **COLANDER.** Solid plastic job. Costs under $10. Drains pasta, tosses salads, makes a great helmet in war games.
- **LADLE.** It's really hard to serve soups and sauces without this.
- **PYREX CASSEROLE DISH WITH LID.** Get the right size for making pies as well as small casseroles and two-person lasagne. It'll cost you about $20, and be absolutely certain it's pyrex.
- **RICE COOKER.** Even a moron could use one.

This list is an absolute minimum for absolute beginners. Don't cut anything out of it. Don't start inviting potential victims over for dinner until you've got it all, learned to use it, and put everything on it away in a place where you can always find it again. If you've done all that, though, and you find yourself liking this habit of cooking, you should consider getting a few more items which, while not absolutely essential, will make your life in the kitchen a lot easier and more fun.

- **MORTAR AND PESTLE.** Granite. For grinding spice pastes.
- **FOOD PROCESSOR.** At least $150. They're brilliant, but the cheap ones fall apart within three months.

- **KITCHEN SCALES.**
- **OVEN MITTS.**
- **FONDUE SET.** (Enormous fun.)
- **PIPING BAG.** (Hard to fill profiteroles without it – and oh, how women adore a good profiterole in the bed, heh-heh-heh.)
- **PORTABLE GAS RING AND BOTTLE.** cooking on electricity sucks. A mobile gas ring is fantastic, especially for picnics, but also for cooking at the table.
- **FLAT BAKING SHEETS.** For biscuits!
- **CAKE AND BREAD TINS.**
- **ELECTRIC MIXER.** Whips cream and beats eggs really quickly.
- **BASTING/PASTRY BRUSH.**
- **HIBACHI OR KETTLE BARBECUE.** Really tasty charcoal-cooked dishes
- **WEIRD METAL-MESH LADLE.** for getting things into and out of really hot fat.
- **MICROWAVE OVEN.** For defrosting and reheating only. The one exception is for melting Mars Bars and we never do this unless we know the young lady very well. Do we, gentlemen?

Don't forget that you have to serve the food as well. You can get away with Salvation Army stuff when you're a poor and shaggy student, but if you've got an actual job and an income, it looks much more convincing if your plates match, if your glasses are all from the same set, and your cutlery is all of the same pattern. Don't overdo it, though. We are, after all, Men. It's the practicality of the situation we're supposed to master. If you actually own your own full Wedgwood dinner set and matched crystal glasses, don't get it out for a casual dinner. You're only going to frighten your guest or make her think you are a bit of a closet case. Simple matched ceramic plates and half-way decent glasses or goblets will do very nicely. You might think about a couple of champagne glasses too. Champagne is what women drink instead of beer.

COOKING FOR SEX: TECHNIQUES

THE MOST IMPORTANT THING ABOUT cooking for sex is that it should never look like a gigantic struggle. Ideally, when you're ready to serve the food, your kitchen should look pretty much as it did when you started – neat, tidy and clean, except for the various containers actually holding the food. To achieve this, you need to chop and prepare everything well beforehand, and clean up your preparation surfaces and tools as you go. Then, as

§

HOW TO MAKE TEA

There are eleven rules for this process. On perhaps two of them there would be pretty general agreement, but at least four others are acutely controversial. The pot should be warmed beforehand. This is better done by placing it on the hob than by the usual method of swilling it out with hot water. The tea should be strong. I maintain that one strong cup of tea is better than 20 weak ones. All true tea-lovers not only like their tea strong, but like it a little stronger with each year that passes. One should take the teapot to the kettle and not the other way about. The water should be actually boiling at the moment of impact, which means that one should keep it on the flame while one pours. One should pour tea into the cup first. This is one of the most controversial points of all. The milk-first school can bring forward some fairly strong arguments, but I maintain that my own argument is unanswerable. This is that, by putting the tea in first and then stirring as one pours, one can exactly regulate the amount of milk whereas one is liable to put in too much milk if one does it the other way round. – *George Orwell*

§

you use the prepared ingredients, the containers that were holding them should be put neatly on the sink for washing. Saucepans should be rinsed with water immediately after dispatching their contents, and should be left to soak so that they can be easily washed at the first convenient moment.

Nothing about your cooking will impress a woman more than your ability to leave behind a neat and tidy kitchen. Aside from that, though, the whole matter of hygiene is reasonably important. Keeping your kitchen clean will cut down on incidents of food poisoning and will usually stop maggots from popping up to cha-cha in the corners. (Maggots are very off-putting to even the most determinedly romantic.) Except where otherwise noted, all your dishes and pans should be washed in detergent and very hot water. They should then be rinsed in really hot water, and left to drain on a dish-rack. Wipe all your counters and surfaces with disinfectant after each use. Dismantle the stove-top and clean it completely at least once every six months. Empty the fridge, clean it thoroughly, and wipe the interior with vanilla essence (mostly alcohol – strong disinfectant that smells really groovy) at least once every three months. And for God's sake, get rid of that weird greenish-black stuff in the bottom of the crisper.

Meat and poultry should never be cut on the same board as foodstuffs that are not going to be cooked, such as salad vegetables and breads. Also, leftover cooked meats should be returned to the refrigerator reasonably promptly, in a sealed container. For later use, leftovers should be very thoroughly reheated to prevent the growth of exciting things like salmonella. And you should never, ever, under any circumstances use anything from a tin which appears to be holed, rusted, or bloated.

Cooking itself is actually a whole lot simpler than it looks to most people. The trick is to see it not as a single, mysterious process which converts mere ingredients into food, but as a set of short, simple operations which are performed in an appropriate order to achieve best effect. A short list and description of some basic cooking techniques follows. Of course, there's about a zillion different techniques and variations in each of the world's great cuisines, and as there's at least twenty really different and interesting cuisine styles, you could make a career out of learning this stuff – but not out of this book.

10 COOL THINGS YOU CAN DO IN YOUR KITCHEN

1) DICING. Use your cleaver. Hold the stuff on the cutting board with your off-hand, fingers tucked up claw-style rather than stretched out, and slide the material under the cleaver as you cut. In your dominant hand, you hold the cleaver with your index finger on the uppermost corner at the top, your palm wrapped around the spine, the handle pointing towards you. As

your off-hand slides the stuff under the cleaver, you rapidly raise and lower the cleaver with a simple wrist action, pivoting it around the lower corner at the top end – like a paper guillotine, if you can imagine that. Get the hang of this technique, and you'll be awed at how quickly you can vanquish a bag of carrots. Same basic technique works when you're using one of those lovely, triangular bladed chef's knives.

2) STIR-FRYING. Calls for maybe two tablespoons of peanut oil in the bottom of the wok. Crank up the heat until the oil smokes. Never stir-fry more than a decent handful of meat at any one time, and add the vegetables and sauces only after the meat is lightly fried; you really only want the veggies warmed through, so they keep their crispness. Keep the whole lot in constant motion, either with your wooden spoons, or more flashily, by 'flipping' the wok as you would a frying pan with a pancake.

3) DEEP-FRYING. Not something you should be doing a lot of, as can make for fattening, unhealthy foods. When you do it, use clean oil, and use just enough to mostly cover whatever it is you're frying. Very high heat is necessary, and the food should not be added until the oil is at the right temperature. (Test by very, very carefully allowing a single drop of water into the oil. If it hisses, spits, and explodes, things are ready to go. Use your tongs, or preferably, your Weird Metal-Mesh Ladle for getting things into and out of the oil.)

4) FRYING. Calls for a little butter in the fry-pan (screw the cholesterol; margarine tastes like shit) and medium heat. Use your spatula to prevent the food sticking to the pan, although the butter, the use of medium heat, and a well-prepared pan will go a long way to help.

5) STEAMING. Put the food into one of those bamboo steamers. Put about a centimetre of water in the bottom of the wok, and turn up the heat. When the water is boiling happily, put the steamer in, with its lid on, and cover up the wok as well. A two-person serving of vegetables will steam very nicely within sixty seconds. Dumplings will need about three minutes.

6) POACHING. Lightly simmering in a liquid – usually water. Produces very nasty eggs, but you can get some interesting effects with other foods if you use wine as your liquid. Use your medium saucepan, and just enough liquid to half-cover whatever you're poaching. Don't go for a full, savage boil – try to keep the liquid gently simmering. Poaching usually doesn't take more than three minutes.

§

FOOD ETIQUETTE #2: KEEP IT SIMPLE, STUPID

I saw this guy recently at this Egyptian restaurant. It was a pretty cool place, had really great food, but it also had a belly dancer. And I hate that belly dancer stuff. Just hate it, you know. There isn't a white man alive feels comfortable in the presence of a belly dancer. Anyway, there's about half a dozen of us there, all late twenties, all established couples. So there is zero sexual tension, it's a dead issue. All we want is a feed and to be left alone by the belly dancer.

Sitting at the table next to us is this young white male. And he's got a date with this incredibly horny-looking Arab girl. A real seven veils character, but only sixteen years old. One of those girls who can actually give you chest pains because your heart constricts when you first see her and you realise that you will never even say hello. And this poor bastard had a date with her. He wasn't good-looking. Had no charisma. Had nothing going for him really. Except a pair of balls. He'd done the one thing that no other man had done on this particular night, he'd asked her for a date. Got past her awful, intimidating beauty and put the question. At first I thought, 'Good on you pal', because I wasn't even jealous. It was not an issue.

But after a while I realised it just wasn't going to happen. She wasn't very impressed with this middle eastern restaurant. That was his first mistake, operating on her territory.

7) BAKING. Application of all-round heat in the oven. Usually for cakes and breads, to drive off the moisture in the dough or batter, and to coagulate the protein in the flour to hold the whole thing in shape. Oddly, though, if you prepare whole fish in this manner, with a little aluminium foil to keep the moisture in, it's referred to as 'baked fish'. If you do the same thing with any other meat or fowl, however, the process is called 'roasting'. Go figure.

8) ROASTING (see Baking.) Takes quite a long time, and requires careful observation if you're going to produce a roast which is crisply glazed outside, and moistly tender inside. Easiest way of achieving this is to slow-

He should have taken her out to a dance or a pub, hooked into a bit of surf and turf. But he's tried to make her comfortable, tried to do the multiculturally correct thing, and now all these fried donkey dicks and roasted grasshoppers are turning up and he's just losing it. After ten minutes they run out of small talk. And then the belly dancer sees him. And these belly dancers are cruel women, you know. They can smell fear. And she flies over and starts giving it to him, the belly dance thing, and he's hopelessly embarrassed. He's sitting there burning up. His girl goes off to the bathroom. He can feel every eye on the place watching him. Everyone in the joint knows. I'm sitting there feeling for this kid. It was like a bond, you know. A brother was hurting. And I'm thinking if only there was some way I could do the Vulcan mind meld. Like reach over and grab his carotid or something, effect a direct transfer of knowledge and power, pour out all my hard won years of bitter frustration and fucking it up until I got it right.

I wanted to give it all to him. But I couldn't of course. We finished eating and we left. I kept looking back as we walked up the street. I was praying that she would lead him from the place, take him in hand, take him home and do incredible middle eastern sex things to him. But I know that just didn't happen. I know he probably dives into shops to avoid meeting her gaze on the street now.

§

roast the beast in a roasting pan, while covered with foil, at a relatively low temperature. Then, when the juices that run out after you poke the thing with a skewer are clear and colourless, remove the foil, and crank the heat up to blastissimo for about five-ten minutes. This should crisp up the outside quite nicely.

9) BOILING. For pasta and rice especially. (Although you really should think about getting a rice cooker.) Crank up the stove, get a half-pot of water so hot that it's jumping around in the saucepan, bubbling and roiling. Then throw in your food and watch it cook. Anyone who boils sausages or meat is weird.

10) WHISKING, BEATING AND BLENDING. Variations on a theme. Generally, the idea is either to aerate or thoroughly mix whatever it is you're working on. Should always be done with a light, rapid action from the wrist. Electric implements can be an enormous help here. Always whisk, beat or blend in a bowl at least a size larger than you would think necessary at first glance – it minimises fallout.

COOKING FOR SEX: THE GAME PLAN.

OKAY, LADS – THIS IS A very basic set of dishes to work with. You need an awful lot more, but these will get you started, break the ice, and establish the beginnings of a reputation as a true Kitchen Samurai. After you read them, go and buy yourself two cookbooks; Stephanie Alexander's *The Cook's Companion* and Marcella Hazan's *The Classic Italian Cookbook*. They'll teach you more about getting laid than a mountain of instructional sex videos. Just displaying them prominently in your batchpad will probably score you a few quickies.

• **KNOW YOUR TARGET.** No point serving mushrooms if she hates the things, right? Worse still, if she's seriously allergic to something you're cooking, you'll discover there's nothing like a trip to the Emergency Room to ruin the mood. Ask her first!

• **BETTER TO HAVE A LITTLE LEFT OVER** than not enough. Remember, she may bring a friend unexpectedly. She may turn out to be a monster trencherwoman, capable of eating like the entire Wallabies front row. Keep the servings small, but make enough so there's some left over, just in case.

• **LEFTOVERS MAKE GREAT LUNCHES.** If you've got your eye on a babe at work, try turning up to lunch with a selection of really nifty home-cooked Thai, Malay, and Italian dishes in your lunchbox. By about day three, the smell that wafts from the tea-room microwave as you reheat your Char Kway Teow will be driving her crazy with curiosity. A dinner invitation is a sure thing from there.

• **DO WE HAVE TO TELL YOU TO MIND THE SPICES?** You may be an iron-gulleted chilli monster, but she's probably not. Also, the effects of overly spicy food on your digestive tract, especially if combined with

Natasha was a sucker for the gang's 'Satan's Own Chocolate Mousse' evenings.

vigorous exercise, can make the bed a pretty nasty place to be a couple of hours later. (Mr Flinthart recommends that all parties eat a teaspoon of fennel seed after dinner, if you're concerned. Does absolute miracles for digestion. Mr Birmingham suggests a good port and damn the consequences!)

• **LEARN TO SHOP.** Find your local deli. Check out the range of fresh fruit and veg at the nearer supermarkets, and compare them with the greengrocers. Find a source of organic fruit and veggies. Will the neighbourhood fruit-and-veg place get special stuff in if you request it? What days do the Tasmanian trout turn up at the fish place? Very, very few foods benefit from extended refrigeration. Try to get what you need fresh for the day you intend to use it. Build your menu around what you can get locally that's of good quality – the same way the best chefs work their restaurants.

• **ABOVE ALL, HAVE FUN.** If it all looks too serious, she's going to suspect that it was hard work, which will shatter that impression of careless competence you were trying to establish. At least look like you enjoy what you're doing.

RECIPES

A dinner isn't just one recipe. Usually it's as many as half-a-dozen, ranging from the simple 'boil rice, then rinse and drain', to the drastically complex. To plan a meal properly, you need to think about all the different flavours and textures you're presenting, and most especially about balance. The Chinese in particular are very, very choosy about the balance of their meals. The whole yin-yang thing comes into play, with some foods being classed as 'heating' (of the blood) and some as 'cooling', and God help the cook who doesn't neatly play off the one against the other.

Put in less esoteric terms, a dinner which consists entirely of rich, meaty dishes may taste great, but nobody is going to be able to finish it and you can forget about the bedroom gymnastics afterwards. Remember your nice, healthy food-group balance, go for a good proportion of grains to vegetables to meats, and when you're trying to impress, don't be afraid to step just a little onto the naughty-but-tasty side of the ledger.

Remember that when cooking for the purpose of getting laid, the ideal meal is one which looks and tastes as impressive as all hell, but doesn't really require all that much effort. You don't want to be exhausted after you've done all that groundwork. Likewise, you don't want everyone lying around, clutching their distended bellies and burping gently, so keep the servings reasonably small. You can always whip up a quick snack later if the situation calls for it.

BREAKFASTS

The importance of breakfast cannot be overstressed. If you've made the grade the night before, and that stunning babe is currently reposing in fetching disarray upon your sheets, there is nothing at all in the world more likely to score you a replay than fronting up with a platter of something tasty while she's still rubbing the sleep out of her eyes. Friends, if ever you meet a woman anywhere in the world who doesn't have a deep-seated weakness for a really fine breakfast brought to her in bed, take care: she is almost certainly an alien body snatcher.

THE OMELETTE

An omelette consists of two things – a crisp-skinned, but light and fluffy egg 'shell', and an optional savoury filling. (Those who espouse the concept of sweet omelettes are very, very sad and inept Men indeed.)

To make the 'shell', or omelette proper, you will need:

- **2 eggs**
- **pinch of salt**
- **half-teaspoon fresh minced garlic**
- **heaped tablespoon finely grated parmesan cheese**
- **tablespoon finely diced eschallot**
- **dessertspoon coarse-ground black pepper**
- **tablespoon milk**

Crack the eggs into a mixing bowl, and with your whisk, rapidly and thoroughly blend all of the ingredients into a thick, fluffy goo. Put your frying pan on medium-high, and melt a pat of butter in it. Don't let the butter burn. Pour the egg-mix into the pan, and move the pan gently around the heat. When bubbles start to appear and the mixture is thickened, gently and carefully use your spatula to fold the omelette in half, sort of like a taco shell. Leave it like this, cooking on one side for another twenty or thirty seconds. Then tilt the pan and use the spatula to guide the omelette as you turn it over and fry the other side for twenty seconds or so. This should ensure the outside is crisp and golden brown, while the inside is moist, fluffy, and absolutely delicious.

Filled omelettes aren't much harder. Your savoury filling should be pre-cooked, and there should be no more than a handful of it. A little smoked, diced ham, perhaps, or leftover chicken, or even some diced bacon lightly fried with some mushrooms. Add just a tablespoon of fresh, grated, sharp cheddar cheese to the filling, and place it carefully in the centre of the omelette about ten seconds after you've first put it in the pan. Then fold the omelette and toast both sides as before. Serves two very easily – but don't cut it in half. Presentation is important; share a plate. Serve it up with a parsley garnish, and a glass of cold orange juice and champagne. If you're considering marriage, now is the time to ask the question.

FILLED CROISSANTS

These aren't quite as impressive as a masterful omelette, but can be prepared the day before – which makes them a lot easier to produce, if reaching the bedroom took more wine than you were expecting. Croissants (they're a pastry, stupid. Get them from the local bakery.) are very rich and buttery, and the fillings will make them even more so. No more than two per person are recommended.

Grab your croissants, and slice them crosswise like a hamburger bun, leaving a 'hinge' of pastry at the back. Load in your fillings. Put the beasts into the oven on a biscuit tray, and crank it up to 'high' for about five to ten minutes at most. Serve piping hot.

Suggested fillings:

- one slice of smoked ham, one wedge of brie, one slice of ripe avocado and a dash of pepper.
- slivers of smoked salmon, capers and brie.
- sliced tomato, grated sharp cheddar, and one rasher of pre-fried bacon.
- spoonful of strawberries, lightly sauced in brandy, butter and brown sugar, with fresh cream on the side.
- shredded leftover chicken with diced eschallots and coriander leaves.

Mr Flinthart's Infamous Monster Pancakes

Real hangover food. These beasties are easy to make, cheap, delicious, and very filling – just the thing if you decide to feed twenty or thirty people the morning after a really big one.
For each person, you will need:

- one cup self-raising flour (more or less)
- one egg
- tablespoon of icing sugar (definitely not icing mixture)
- about half a cup of milk

Whisk the whole lot together into a thick batter, adding a dash of vanilla essence. Get out your frying pan, and set it over medium heat. Melt a pat of butter, and ladle in the batter. About one and a half ladles will turn out a very serious pancake.

Let the batter cook until the edges look doughy, and you can see bubble-craters in the middle. Initially, you'll need to carefully turn the pancakes with your spatula so they can toast on the other side for about twenty seconds – but when you get better at it, a simple, arrogant flick of the wrist will turn the things over in the pan and make you look like a complete Kitchen Samurai.

Serve hot, with butter and real maple syrup. And tequila!

Salads

Salads are really great things to know. You can serve salads at practically any time of the day, and better still, since they're prepared well before the meal is served, you can have them standing by, to be produced with a flourish. They impress the hell out of the broads, who suspect that the closet most Men get to a salad is cocktail onions and hot chips.

There's all kinds of salads – crisp vegetable salads, pasta salads, fruit salads, salads with meat, salads with chicken or fish. They're a wonderfully versatile and tasty range of dishes in and of themselves. Be creative. Try out new and interesting vegetables. Throw in the odd cooked ingredient. Display your own ingenuity, and bask in the female admiration which comes your way.

Caesar Salad

This is an excellent accompaniment to almost any Italian meal. Alternatively, served with a little shredded grilled chicken, it makes a marvellous lunch in its own right. Recipe serves four to six.

- **lettuce**
- **red onion**
- **sliced black olives**
- **stick of celery**
- **coarse-grated cheese – mozzarella is nice**
- **capsicum**
- **hardboiled eggs – quail eggs, if you can get them.
  One per person (two if using quail eggs).**
- **sliced avocado**
- **croutons**
- **anchovies**

Line a large salad bowl with a double layer of crisp, washed lettuce leaves. Thinly slice the red onion. Cut the capsicum into strips. Chop the celery thinly. Toss these three together, and fill the bowl. Slice your avocado thinly, and spread it evenly over the top. Cut the hardboiled eggs in half lengthwise, and distribute them evenly. Take the anchovy fillets, and lay them between the eggs. Sprinkle a handful of grated cheese over the lot, and a handful of sliced olives over that. Arrange the croutons on top. Serve with an optional mustard dressing.

Note: really nice croutons can be made from a single French loaf, cut into 2cm slices. Spread both sides of each slice with olive oil, and arrange them in a roasting pan. Put the oven on medium, and when the slices turn golden brown, they're ready to go. If you want something extra-tasty, cheat by sprinkling a little commercial chicken stock powder over your croutons before they go in to the oven. Don't give away the secret, though: nobody is much impressed by chicken stock powder.

FLINTHART'S BODACIOUS POTATO SALAD

Fantastic at picnics. Guaranteed to attract admiring attention
– and you won't have to carry any of it home afterwards,
believe me. Recipe serves four to six.

- one dozen small, washed potatoes.
- punnet of cherry tomatoes.
- one red capsicum.
- six rashers of bacon.
- two eschallots.
- four large pickled gherkins – not sweet gherkins.
- teaspoon of finely minced fresh garlic.
- tablespoon coarse-ground black pepper.
- teaspoon cumin powder.
- about a cup of good mayonnaise.
- generous tablespoon of seeded Dijon mustard.
- quarter-kilo sharp cheddar cheese, cut into 1cm cubes.
- four eggs, hardboiled.

Boil the potatoes until they are cooked through, but still firm, and
plunge them immediately into cold water. Dice the bacon, fry it until it's
crisp and crunchy. Dice the pickled gherkins. Slice the cherry tomatoes in
half. Cut the capsicum into thin strips. Finely slice the eschallots.

Now cut the potatoes into quarters. Combine all these ingredients, with
the cheese, in a large salad bowl.

Thoroughly mix the garlic, mayonnaise, black pepper, cumin and mustard, and spoon it through the salad. Work it round until it's all nicely
mixed. Quarter the hardboiled eggs, and lay them decoratively atop the
salad. Garnish with fresh parsley.

SEAFOOD PASTA SALAD

This one is utterly delicious, and combines elements of Mediterranean
and Thai cooking. Serve chilled, as a light meal in its own right, or as an
accompaniment to a good curry. Recipe serves two.

- two cups interesting pasta – shells or spirals are nice. Macaroni
  will do. Spaghetti and fettuccine will not.
- one cup commercial pre-cooked seafood marinara mix –
  little octopods, mussels, prawns, and bits of squid.
- juice of two limes.
- tablespoon coarse black pepper.
- one medium-hot red chilli.

- **half-cup fresh coriander leaves.**
- **coarse sea salt.**

Cook the pasta as usual, strain, and cool. Toss the marinara mix through. Finely slice the chilli and the coriander leaves, and work them through the salad. Add the black pepper, and the lime juice, and toss again. Just before serving, sprinkle perhaps a dessertspoon of coarse sea salt over the salad and stir briefly.

MAIN COURSES

Centrepiece of your dinner, usually. You can either make them a real production number, like a major Thai stir-fry or Indian curry, or you can make them deceptively simple, and surround them with nifty salads and side-dishes. Remember, this is your showpiece meal, and you're cooking it with a purpose in mind, so take extra care and don't forget the value of presentation. A little patter about authenticity of recipes, cooking techniques, freshness of ingredients, personal touches, and good nutritional qualities is also helpful. Do some research before-hand. Also, check the section in this book on 'Wine' and try to pick something that will complement your meal, rather than clash with it.

BASIC RARE STEAK

This is a much under-rated dish. It is also not easy to do well. Good steak should always be served rare – dark, perhaps even charred outside, and pink and juicy inside. Pick a good cut – rump as a minimum, fillet better, rib eye better still – and make sure it's at least 3cm thick at the absolute minimum. Don't mess around with the supermarket when you're trying to impress someone; go and have a talk with your local butcher.

With the general downturn in consumption of red meat, a really good steak is getting harder to find in restaurants around the country. And to be fair, you don't need to eat them all that often. However, they are an excellent source of iron and protein, and for obvious reasons, many, many women occasionally find themselves craving a good piece of meat. Learn to do this one right.

Put two cloves of crushed garlic in a small jar with some light vegetable oil, at least 24 hours before you want to cook your steak. (Not olive oil. Good olive oil is a dressing oil. It's cold-pressed, and starts to burn at too low a temperature.) Prior to cooking the steak, you should also rub it down with a clove of crushed garlic.

Crank up your cast-iron frying-pan to Supernova, with just a couple of teaspoons of oil across the bottom to stop things sticking. Grab your steak, and slap it down in the middle of the pan. (Lots of hissing, smoke and steam.) At this time, add about a level dessertspoon of coarse-ground, fresh black pepper.

If your pan is correctly heated, and your steak is between 3cm and 4cm thick, you should need to leave it for at most two minutes. Then quickly turn it over, and sear the other side in the same manner, cooking it just a little longer as the pan will have lost some of its heat. Don't turn it again. Whip the pan off the heat, and put the steak on the plate. Using the pan juices, add just a little butter and garlic, and quickly fry up a handful of fresh, sliced mushrooms to accompany the steak. Serve with a baked potato and a large, fresh green salad. A nice, big cabernet sauvignon makes an excellent accompaniment.

If everything has gone well, the steak will be absolutely fantastic – meltingly tender inside, savoury, slightly crisp and smoky outside. You probably won't manage this the first two or three times you try it, so practice this recipe for yourself before trying it on anyone else. And never, ever, grill a really good quality steak – it dries out and behaves like leather.

MACKEREL STEAK POACHED IN WHITE WINE
(THANKS GERARD!)

Mackerel is a big, deep-water, muscular fish which produces lovely steaks about 3cm thick and 15cm across. This is one of those dishes that impresses everybody, but is laughably simple to do. First, put about 2cm of white wine – cheap chablis is best – in the bottom of your medium saucepan. Add half a clove of finely minced garlic. Bring the liquid to a light simmer, and place your mackerel steaks in it. Cooking takes about a minute each side.

Serve with fresh black pepper and a garnish of coriander leaves. A side dish of small pumpkins, individually stuffed and roasted, looks great. Don't forget to serve a nice, chilled, dry white wine with the meal. Try a three-year-old, well-oaked chardonnay.

MALAYSIAN RENDANG ASLI

This is an Indo-Malaysian dish best described as a slow, succulent
beef curry in coconut and lemon grass. It is absolutely delicious,
but takes about four or five hours of slow cooking time, so it's a major
showpiece. This recipe serves four fairly easily. Take note that it's
also quite a hot and spicy dish. Be sure your intended victim is
up to the challenge, or tone down the chilli.

- **one kg beef. Doesn't have to be the best cut – it's going to get
  extensive cooking!**
- **one large onion.**
- **eight large cloves garlic.**
- **chunk of fresh ginger the size of your thumb.**
- **two full tablespoons powdered coriander (minced fresh coriander root is better).**
- **two large tablespoons ground hot chilli.**
- **one dessertspoon ground fennel seed.**
- **one heaped teaspoon fine white pepper.**
- **ten cardamom seeds.**
- **a dozen cloves.**
- **one stick of cinnamon.**
- **one dessertspoon turmeric.**
- **two stalks fresh lemon grass, lightly crushed.**
- **two cups grated coconut.**
- **three tins of coconut cream.**
- **juice of three limes.**
- **three cups of water.**
- **salt to taste.**

Chop the meat into cubes about 3cm on the side. Mince the ginger and
the garlic, dice the onion. Put the meat, garlic, ginger and onions into a
big, heavy pot, and pour over the coconut cream, the lime juice, and all the
spices. ALL of them. Allow to marinate for a couple of hours.

Add the water and the grated coconut, and put the pot on low heat,
bringing it to a simmer. Simmer it for about four to six hours – stir regularly. When the meat is falling apart, and the sauce has become thick,
sticky, and somewhat dry in appearance, it is ready to serve. Pull out the
cinnamon stick and the lemon grass stalks. Best over long-grain rice.

Personally, we recommend this be served alongside a platter of sliced
vegetables such as cucumber and carrot, with perhaps a mild peanut sauce
for dipping the veggies. Accompany it with ice-cold Singha beer and fan-
tastically exaggerated anecdotes of your travels through the spice routes.

Mr Birmingham's Favourite Pasta for Two

A reasonable command of Italian cooking is absolutely crucial if you intend to make out like a bandit because of your culinary skills. This dish, a variation of Marcella Hazan's spaghetti alle vongole, is easy to whip up, seems a lot more exotic than it actually is, and won't weigh you down in the sack afterwards. If you make this one for the babe in your sights and she doesn't come across immediately you should think about dating someone other than a lesbian. You'll need:

- half a dozen of the smallest clams you can find.
- a clove of garlic, peeled and chopped.
- one and a half tablespoons of olive oil.
- half a teaspoon of anchovy paste.
- 200g of Italian peeled tomatoes in their own juices.
- three twists of pepper from the grinder.
- a pinch of salt.
- half a pound of fresh spaghetti (none of that packet stuff).

Clean your clams by standing them in a large bowl of cold water for five minutes. Drain. Pour in some new water and scrub the clams with a stiff brush. Just rub them together if you don't have one. Drain and repeat until the water stays clear.

Heat the clams in a covered pan until the shells open. Get the meat out, chop it finely and put it aside where the dog won't get it. Strain the clam juice through a sieve and set aside.

Sauté your garlic in olive oil over a medium heat. It'll go a little brown. Add the anchovy paste and stir. Add the chopped tomatoes and stir. Add the clam juice and stir. Get a bit of a stiffy at how much your date is going to dig this. Simmer uncovered for about twenty-five minutes until the oil and tomatoes separate. (A few minutes from the end of this process you boil up your fresh spaghetti. Note: it cooks a lot quicker than dry spaghetti. Ask the guy at the pasta shop for the timing.) Take sauce off the heat and add the clams. Make sure your babe is in the kitchen to pour you a glass of wine and reel at your Manly cooking skills as you drain the pasta. Transfer to big warm bowls and mix in the sauce. Don't stuff it up by adding cheese. Support the arm of your date who is now reeling with desire.

DESSERTS

Never, ever underestimate the power of a good dessert. Rich, sweet, heady, creamy confections laced and graced with sugar and chocolate will do more to establish a mood of decadence and sensuality than anything else you put on the table. Of course, the rule of balance applies: if your main course was rich and complex (like a rendang) your dessert should be simple and fresh – perhaps just a light fruit salad. If you want to show off your desserts with a major chocolate mousse, though, you should make the main course simple and light – fish and salad, for example. Whatever you do, though, don't skip the course altogether when you're entertaining. Just having a specialised dessert course turns a meal from simple food into a treat.

POACHED PEARS

Buy yourself a couple of nice, ripe, unblemished pears. Go for the soft kind, rather than the crunchy-hard ones. Peel the pears, halve them from top to bottom, remove the stems and the fibrous cores.

In your medium saucepan, place about a cup to a cup and a half of cheap red wine. A cask of hermitage will do. Add to the wine a stick of cinnamon, and a teaspoon of cloves. Bring the wine to a simmer and add the pear halves, flat side down. Simmer them gently for perhaps three minutes, then put them aside in a covered dish to stay warm.

Remove the cloves and the cinnamon from the wine. Add a tablespoon of white sugar, and bring to a boil until you have a light syrup. Place the pears in their serving bowls, spoon the syrup over the top, and serve with double cream – or better still, good quality vanilla ice cream.

It should be noted that Mr Birmingham violently disagrees with Mr Flinthart's use of cloves in this recipe. Mr Birmingham would use a vanilla bean instead of cinnamon and, controversially, half a teaspoon of saffron threads instead of cloves. Nor would he halve the pears. Wars have been fought over less.

SATAN'S OWN CHOCOLATE MOUSSE

Chances are, she'll hate you for this. But it will be a pleasant, obsessive sort of hatred not unmingled with lust, because this mousse is completely undeniable. Refusing to eat it is unthinkable, despite the fact that it contains more kilojoules and cholesterol than the collective arse-end of an entire Oprah audience.

- one egg per person.
- half-cup thickened cream per person, plus one extra half-cup for every two people.
- 150g dark chocolate per person.
- tablespoon brandy per person.
- sugar.

Prepare the brandy 24 hours in advance by soaking half a dozen good quality coffee beans in it.

Break the eggs, separating the whites from the yolks. Put the yolks away, add one dessertspoon of sugar for each egg to the eggwhites, and whisk them until they stand up in stiff, frothy peaks. Put the whipped eggwhites in the fridge.

Now whip a half-cup of thickened cream per each person, with just a teaspoon of vanilla essence and a dessertspoon of sugar for every cup of cream. Whip it until, like the eggwhites, it forms stiff peaks. Gently, carefully, thoroughly fold the cream into the bowl containing the eggwhites, and refrigerate the lot.

Break up all the chocolate. Put the remaining cream in a medium saucepan with the brandy (turf out the coffee beans first) over a low heat. Stir in the chocolate and the egg-yolks until you have a thick, smooth, dark sauce. Turn off the heat, and let the sauce come to just above room temperature. Now gently, carefully, thoroughly fold the sauce through the eggwhites and cream until the mixture is evenly coloured. Spoon into individual serving dishes and refrigerate. Serve with a dollop of whipped cream, some grated dark chocolate, and a couple of Italian sponge-finger biscuits.

SNACKS

Never neglect this one. Best if you've got a few put aside in advance, just in case. Snacks are for those moments late at night, when you need just a little extra on your side to convince her to stay for another bottle of wine, or a video, or whatever. They're also for those times when you need a little renewal of energy – say, about two hours after you finally hit the bed.

Just about any sort of finger food will do, of course – tasty cheeses, fresh bread, antipasto, and fruit – but it's always impressive if you can whip together a couple of personalised treats. Check out the following.

SERIOUS BAD-ASS GUACAMOLE

- two ripe avocadoes.
- teaspoon fresh minced garlic.
- two rashers of bacon, diced.
- one large tomato, diced.
- one medium onion, diced.
- one capsicum, diced finely.
- juice of two limes.

- **cup of sour light cream.**
- **tablespoon fresh black pepper.**

Fry the bacon until it's crisp, and put it in a salad bowl. Use the bacon grease to fry the onion and garlic briefly – just until the onion begins to turn clear – and toss them into the salad bowl too. Smush the avocadoes into a smooth pulp with the bacon and onion and garlic, and stir in the tomato and the capsicum. Stir in the sour cream, the black pepper and the lime juice. Add a dash of cumin powder too, if you like. Serve with super-fresh bread, or better still, plain corn chips.

DANGER! POPCORN ALLA FLINTHART!

- **one cup of popping corn per two people.**
- **tablespoon of garlic oil (made the same way as for the steak).**

In your stockpot, heat the garlic oil until a single kernel of popcorn in the bottom of the pan begins to spin around. At this point, add the rest of your popcorn, close the lid, and agitate the pan until the popping dies away. Pour the popcorn into a big salad bowl. Cheat like crazy: mix a dessertspoon of salt and a dessertspoon of chicken stock and sprinkle the lot over the popcorn. Meanwhile, melt about a tablespoon of butter in the pan, and pour it over the popcorn. Toss the lot lightly, sprinkle with finely grated parmesan cheese, and get out of the way of the stampede.

CHOCOLATE TRUFFLES

These things are the ultimate in high-calorie decadence.
Smooth, creamy, and rich with strong dark chocolate, they're practically a seduction all on their own. Have a couple of dozen on stand-by in the fridge for post-coital indulgences. You might also consider running up a batch and carefully wrapping them to make that thoughtful, personalised (cheap) gift.

- **200mls thickened cream.**
- **300g dark chocolate.**
- **box of bitter cocoa.**

Grate the chocolate. Then, in your medium saucepan, scald (bring to a boil and then remove from the heat) the cream. Whisk the grated chocolate into the hot cream until the mixture is smooth and thick. Allow to cool to room temperature. DO NOT REFRIGERATE.

When the mixture has set to a thick, smooth paste, pour the cocoa powder into a mixing bowl. Now dust your hands with cocoa powder. Roll gobs of the paste into balls about the size of a 20c piece, and liberally dust the balls with cocoa powder. These are your classic chocolate truffle, and can be presented and served just as they are. For now, you can store them in the refrigerator.

If you're feeling really adventurous, you can melt some more dark chocolate (take one of your steel mixing bowls and stand it in a large pot of water. Put the chocolate in the bowl. Bring the water to a boil. Don't let any water get into the bowl with the chocolate.) and using a tiny oyster fork, briefly dip each truffle in the melted chocolate. Stand the dipped truffles on greaseproof paper to set, and return them to the fridge.

The reaction you get when you feed these things to a normal human female is absolutely amazing ...

CHAPTER NINE

Cars – things that make you go brmm* – and Jumbos.

*By Mr Flinthart, as Mr Birmingham doesn't actually drive. He catches cabs.

CARS ARE GREAT, EH? THINK of all the things they represent: freedom, power, independence – and a hefty dose of purely Freudian symbolism, of course. Sure, they're expensive. Sure, they're destructive as all hell to the environment. And yes, they're a bastard to park, to maintain, and to keep fuelled. And they're a rotten investment, with most cars losing value the way English cricketers lose Tests. And they're noisy, and – hang on ... what was it we like about the things again?

Financially, it makes sense to avoid buying a car for as long as you possibly can. Think about it: depreciation, maintenance, insurance, registration, fuel, parking/garaging, occasional fines ... well after the purchase price is accounted for, the best estimates put the cost of owning even a cheapo wimp commuter car at $100 a week. Or more. $5,200 a year. Serious bucks, baby. You don't just go out and impulse-buy one of these puppies. If you've been sensible, and you've put off owning your first car until the need was positively painful, then for sure you're going to want to take just a little more time to make certain you get the best car you can.

BUYING YOUR CAR

- **NEVER BUY A BRAND-NEW CAR** That's only for mugs with money to burn. The moment you drive a new car off the lot, it depreciates by 10-15%. If you've bought a mid-range car, say, for $25,000, that means you've immediately dropped $2,500. Just like you'd ripped up twenty-five $100 bills on the spot. Does that sound stupid to you? It does to us. On top of that, you've got to go through all the strain of keeping it up to specs in order to keep your warranty valid: unfeasibly frequent servicing at expensive specialist outlets, all-genuine replacement parts ... if you so much as get a cheap aerial to replace the one the neighbour's stupid kid snapped off, you may find you've invalidated the warranty on your shiny new money-pit. Bummer.

  Ideally, you should be looking for a car from two to three years of age, one previous owner, books kept up to date. If you can do that, you'll have a vehicle that drives and performs like a new one, only better, since it's been properly broken in. Of course, this is a pretty expensive option too, so if you're in the same financial league as most of us, you're probably going to settle for something a bit less flash. (The average age of the Australian car on the road is ten years.)

It was the opening of the aerial moped routes that finally convinced Adam to trade in his Holden.

- **DECIDE WHAT YOU NEED**, and establish what you can afford. Going into debt over a depreciating asset like a car is a really dumb idea, but if you must arrange finance, at least remember to check the credit unions and building societies as well as the banks. Try to arrange a loan with flexible repayments, so that you can make extra payments when you have any spare cash; it makes the whole thing go an awful lot quicker.

  Assessing your needs can be quite difficult. You need to sit down with a piece of paper and a pen, and decide as objectively as possible what features your car absolutely has to have. Think about how often you'll be using it, and how far you intend to go. Do you need room for tools and materials? Is it purely a passenger car? Do you *really* need those extra four cylinders? Do you have to have AC? (That last may sound odd, but if you consider the needs of a commercial traveller in a Queensland summer, you'll see that air-conditioning can be an unavoidable necessity for at least some people. For the rest of us – it's a *luxury*.)

- **LOOK AROUND.** Once you know what you can spend and what you absolutely must have, the next thing you have to do is check out the market. Know current prices and values. Be aware of which cars represent value for money, and which are notorious money-suckers. Best way to do that is buy a couple of magazines. Here in Australia, the *Used Car Buyer's Guide* is mandatory – it gives you prices, comparisons, tips, descriptions, flaws, and a dozen other things. Another very useful publication is *Which Car?* If you pick up the most recent issue of those two and go through them with a pen, marking off the things in your price range, it won't take you long to narrow your search down to a fairly limited number of makes, models, and years.

Now you can start actually getting out there and looking at cars! Try these places:

FIVE WAYS TO FIND YOUR PERFECT MATE

1) CAR YARDS

ADVANTAGES. Vehicles frequently come with a warranty. Very small chance of getting a stolen car, or a car which is actually owned by some finance company somewhere. Lots of vehicles in a small area, making the search easier.

DISADVANTAGES. The most expensive way of acquiring a second-hand vehicle. Also, used-car salesmen are awesomely greasy, cunning, and as crooked as they think they can get away with. Finally, these fellows are absolute pros when it comes to making a dodgy, nasty piece of junk look like the finest charabanc on the roads. Can be a real problem unless you do your homework very carefully, and don't let yourself be pushed around.

2) PRIVATE SALES – NEWSPAPER ADS, WORD-OF-MOUTH.

ADVANTAGES. Generally 10-20% cheaper than going through a car yard. Potential for real bargain purchases, if the seller isn't clued-up as to the value of their vehicle. No greasy-moustached salesmen to deal with.

DISADVANTAGES. *Caveat emptor!* Sure, the car has to be roadworthy before the registration can be transferred, but there are plenty of mechanics out there prepared to put together a very suspect certificate of roadworthiness. Also, you may be buying a stolen vehicle, or one upon which the owner has lapsed their payments to the bank – which means that in reality, the bank owns the car, and if you buy it, you can expect to have it confiscated in the not-too-distant future. Also, since you can only visit one private owner at a time, the search for the Right Car is often a deadly slow process.

3) GOVERNMENT AUCTION

ADVANTAGES. Reasonably cheap – you're buying up ex-government vehicles, and cars which have been confiscated or impounded for whatever reason. The books are usually up to date, and you can be certain you're not getting an encumbered (stolen, or money-still-owing) vehicle. Lots of vehicles go under the hammer at one time, potentially shortening your search.

DISADVANTAGES. Relatively infrequent. Tend to favour certain models of vehicle, so if you're after something else, it can be an awfully long wait. And the bidding process is unfamiliar to most people, and downright nerve-wracking if you wind up in competition for a car you really want.

4) CAR MARKETS
    ADVANTAGES. Cheap as they come.
    DISADVANTAGES. Dodgy as it gets!

Okay. A week or two has passed. You've done your research, and picked out maybe half-a-dozen different types of car which fit your needs. You've cruised the car-yards, checked out the markets, watched an auction or two, and sussed out four or five private sales. Finally, you've found a car which looks as though it might work for you. What next?

VEHICLE INSPECTION FOR AMATEURS

- **LIE OF THE LAND.** If it's a private sale, and you've been let into the garage, see if you can't take a surreptitious look around the place. Things like touch-up paint, radiator stop-leak fluid, body putty (bog) or muffler-repair putty (more bog) are a very bad sign. If you see any of them in the garage, you should scale up the intensity of your inspection considerably.

- **INSPECT THE MERCHANDISE.** Next, look the entire car over in a very general way. You're looking for overall condition: old crash damage, heavy rust, broken windows, damaged interiors and the like. Make sure you check the tricky areas below the bumpers and the doors, while you're at it.

- **RUST IS THE ENEMY.** You're most likely to find rust on mudguards, door sills, and the bottom areas of car doors. Also check carefully around the rear door of hatch models and station wagons. Look for obvious holes, and bubbling paint. Lift the carpets and check the floor of the car. Look underneath the bonnet, and in the boot. If you come across areas of bodywork which look as though they've had a bit of repair-work done, apply a magnet. It will cling to metal, but not to quick-and-dirty rust repairs made of fibreglass or plastic.

- **GIVE THE INTERIOR A GOOD GOING OVER.** You may think that a few stains, tears and scratches are of little importance, but as a guide to the overall maintenance and condition of the vehicle, they can be invaluable. Check the electricals carefully, especially windows. Repairing electric windows is expensive. While you're in there, make sure the safety belts and buckles are up to scratch. They should fasten and release smoothly, and the belt should lock up nice and tight when you give it a sudden jerk, or when the car is parked on a moderately steep slope. Check any electrically operated adjustable seats as well; they're another very expensive item to fix. Don't forget the simple roadworthy stuff: lights, horn, wipers, indicators and hazard lights.

Sound systems can be a real problem to repair. If there's a good one in the car, don't just take it at face value. If you can get the owner's manual and put the stereo through a complete test, you may be saving yourself a lot of money. Remember that the current owner is probably loading up their price in expectation of a bit of haggling; if you come across something that doesn't work, make absolutely certain that you aren't paying for it.

- **TEST YOUR ENGINES.** Having come this far, you can now put the key in the ignition and give it a partial turn. Don't turn the engine over yet – you're just looking for exciting warning lights. Most of them should go out within a couple of seconds. If they don't – especially the ones for oil, coolant or brakes – start asking pointed questions.

  Before you start the car and drive it, you want to know about the brakes, and the tyres. Also the suspension and steering, if you can manage it. Push the brake pedal hard. If it sinks slowly to the floor, you've probably got a serious hydraulic problem – undriveably dangerous, big bucks to track down and fix. Check that the handbrake grips, while you're there.

- **THE BODY BEAUTIFUL?** Climb out of the car, and stand at the rear, then the front. Sight along the body panels to spot any sign of a ripply finish – which usually indicates serious panel-beating work has been done. Check that the paint matches all over the car; colour and texture both. Again, a mismatch can indicate body repair work, covering up crash damage. Another sign of repair work is paint overspray – stray paint on things like windows, bumpers, chrome strips and tyres. If you do come across evidence of repairwork – start asking questions. A proper repair should have brought the car up to as-new quality. A big crash, or a shoddy repair job, though, and the car may have serious structural problems. Get a professional inspection. (You were going to do that anyway, though, weren't you?)

- **LIFT THE BONNET.** A filthy engine is a bad sign, as it points to long neglect. On the other hand, a sparkly clean engine suggests a recent steam-clean, which may have been done to hide all kinds of defects. Look around for frayed or burnt wiring, damaged or poorly attached hoses, or streaks of oil. If you're in the garage, look under the car and see if there are any recent oil stains on the floor. Oil leaks eventually mean expensive repairs – or much worse.

- **CHECK THE RADIATOR** for water stains, rust or leaks. Especially check for seepage at the juncture of the cylinder heads and the engine block, and at the join between the radiator hose and engine or radiator proper. Pop the radiator cap (make sure the engine is cool, first, right? Steam burns are remarkably painful.) and check the water. A bit of rust colour is all right, as is a greenish or reddish tint from added coolant or conditioner. Be suspicious if it's perfectly clear – it's probably just been added. If there's oil in the radiator water, you've got a serious, major problem. Don't even think about buying the car without a full professional assessment.

- **LOOK AROUND THE CARBURETTOR AND FUEL LINES FOR PETROL LEAKS.** These are Very Bad. (In a fuel-injected car, be certain that the engine idles smoothly. Rough idling can be the first sign of fuel trouble.) Check for oil leaks under the transmission, the engine, and the differential. Again, these are potentially very bad news. Pull out all the dipsticks you can find (The engine has one. Power steering and transmission may also have them) and check the oil levels. Give it a sniff; burnt oil is a sign that things are running above the desired temperature, which is not good.

- **LOOK UNDER THE CAR** and make sure the muffler and exhaust systems are sound. Bring back Mr Magnet, if you have any doubts. Soft, brittle metal or areas of putty are rather bad news.

- **CHECK THE TYRES.** Minimum legal tread is 1.5mm. Check with the edge of a Bankcard, if you've got one – and don't even test-drive the car if it doesn't pass. Be certain the tyres aren't shedding chunks of tread, or

'No no,' said the salesman, 'wheels are not essential.'

missing pieces of sidewall, or anything else like that. While you're here, run your hand back and forth across the tyre treads. If you get more resistance one way than another, you've got uneven wear. This may indicate simple alignment problems, or it may point to serious suspension difficulties. Check the spare for similar problems – you never know, the seller may have swapped the spare across to make the car look better.

- **PUSH DOWN** on the front of the car as hard as you can, and let it rise back up. Do this a few times in rhythm, until you've got a nice bouncing action going, and then stop. If the car settles to level at once, all is well. A car that keeps bouncing has shock-absorber problems. Try this one on every corner of the car, if you can.
- **COLUMNS AND CLUTCHES.** Back inside the car, ascertain that when the steering wheel is centred, the front tyres are pointed dead straight ahead. Check that the clutch pedal works, that the accelerator doesn't stick, and that the gearshift is functional. Also, check that all the external lights are functioning, including brakelights, headlights, and indicators. When you get onto the road, check that the speedo, the tacho, and the temperature gauge are all working. Now is a good time to check out fuel gauges, battery indicators and everything else on the dash as well.

AN EXTREMELY IMPORTANT THING: Before you go for a test drive, ask about the car's insurance. Crashing an uninsured car on a test drive is very depressing.

- **START YOUR ENGINES.** Now you can actually start the car. Do it cold, if you can – it makes problems more noticeable. You want to hear that the starter motor turns over cheerfully and effectively. You also want the motor to 'catch' without a lot of prolonged turning of the starter. Listen for backfires, or rattly exhaust noises. Keep an eye on the oil pressure light, to be certain it goes off a couple of seconds after the engine fires up.
- **LISTEN TO THE ENGINE** and everything else. You don't want any weird noises which could indicate problems. Also, rattles and squeaks from the body and doors may indicate that the car has had a bit of rough-road usage, which is not good. The engine should pull smoothly when you accelerate, with no sudden power-losses, or stalls. And when you take your foot off the accelerator, the engine should power down nicely.
- **THE GEARBOX SHOULD ALSO OPERATE SMOOTHLY.** Try a couple of fast downchanges; if you get ugly great crunching noises, the gearbox

may be in need of an overhaul, or replacement. Now drive the car at a steady speed, and without lifting your foot off the accelerator, quickly pump the clutch. As soon as it disengages again, the engine should 'bite' with a good, solid thump. A slow return to speed probably indicates the clutch is on its way out. An automatic transmission should be just as smooth and groovy as a manual. Thumps, bumps, and unexpected gear-changes are not good signs.

- **TAKE THE CAR DOWN A NICE LONG HILL,** with your foot off the accelerator. At the bottom, step on the petrol big-time. If the engine is old and worn, it may not pick up acceleration promptly, and you might see a great big puff of smoke in the rear view mirror. Repairing this kind of problem may well run to replacing the entire engine.
- **CHECK THAT THE BRAKES PULL SMOOTHLY** and evenly, without pulling the car to either side. If the car is fitted with anti-lock brakes, stomp on the pedal for all you're worth. If the car goes into a skid, the anti-lock features are stuffed.
- **AFTER THE TEST DRIVE.** Pull the car over, but leave the engine running. Pop the bonnet and have another look at the motor. Now is the time to look for smoke, oil leaks, water leaks, or problems with the cooling or electricals.

Very, very carefully, check the water in the radiator. (Remove the radiator cap with a thick rag and great caution.) You're looking for two things – movement in the water, which indicates the pump is doing its thing, and bubbles – which indicate that the cylinder head is *not* doing its thing. Bubbles in the radiator water are Mondo Bad. Check the oil again, while you're here. If it was changed just before you examined it earlier, you might now be able to detect signs of burning. Now wander around the car, and check for tyres and wheels which are noticeably hotter than the others. This may indicate brake problems, or worse still, bearing trouble.

If you do all these things as ostentatiously as possible, with a serious expression on your face, there's a good chance that a private seller will start to panic, and volunteer valuable information about the car's history. In any event, even if the car passes your personal inspection, you should now insist on a full, professional inspection before purchase. Contact your local motoring organisation for information as to where such an inspection can be carried out, and how much it will cost.

While the car is being checked by the pros, you should ring the Registry of Encumbered Vehicles in your state. These are the chaps in charge of keeping track of cars which have big bucks owing on them in finance, or even in outstanding fines – and of ascertaining that the vehicle isn't stolen. If you miss on this one, simple telephone call, you are an utter wombat, and you deserve whatever happens to you.

When the inspection is done, you and the car's owner will be given a report sheet. The car cannot be sold with the licence plates attached if it isn't in roadworthy condition, so there may be some repairs to be carried out. These are the problem of the seller, as he or she can't offload the car until they're done. If you do agree to cover the repair costs – perhaps the seller is strapped for cash – you'd be a fool not to knock the costs off the price of the car. Haggle like crazy. At best, you save a lot of money. At worst, somebody you barely know takes a dislike to you. Who cares? Don't be afraid to walk away from a deal at any stage if it looks necessary. Remember: it's your money, and you're the one who's going to be stuck with the car once the papers are signed.

GETTING FROM A–B: HOW TO DRIVE YOUR CAR.

THERE'S A MILLION TRICKS TO driving a car. There's cunning ways to drive faster, extract more fuel economy, save wear on the engine, and keep your brakes in working order. I don't give a damn about any of them. So far as I'm concerned – and so far as you should be concerned, your first and only priority is reaching the end of the trip in one piece. Think about it: you're in command of a tonne or so of complicated metal and machinery, travelling at (legal) speeds of up to 110 km/hour. All around you, dozens of other very ordinary people – the kind of people who can't manage shopping trolleys or automatic banking machines – are doing exactly the same thing. You want to play driving tricks in that kind of set-up?

I don't think so. In the meantime, here's a few recommendations:

- **KEEP THE CAR WELL-MAINTAINED.** Driving an unsafe car is a very, very bad idea. Check the oil, water, and tyres at least once a week in newer cars, and more often in older models. Have the thing serviced regularly – and if you're the kind of cunningly mechanical swine who does his own servicing, get a professional to look it over at least once every six months in any case. Look, the human body is a brilliantly designed and self-repairing machine, based on a blueprint with about two million years of on-road testing, right? And they recommend you have a full medical examination at least once every twelve months,

§

You are not Peter Brock

The fundamentals of driving are very basic. Everyone does what Peter Brock does in his race car. He pushes the accelerator to make the car go. He pushes the brakes to make it stop. He turns the wheel to go around the twisty bits. Driving is not a physically demanding activity, like tennis for example, where you're running around and exerting yourself. When driving you're really just sitting there wiggling your hands and feet. So you don't need to be overly fit but you do need to know what you're doing. Driving is the single most dangerous thing most of us will do at any time in our lives. And we'll do it almost every day of our lives. The chances of making a mistake are large.

The problems arise from awareness and attitude. Most people are really unaware of the risks, of what a car can and can't do, until it's too late. Finding out for instance that their car can't go round that tight corner at two hundred miles per hour. We are all experts after the event.

Unfortunately, getting a driver's licence is absurdly easy. You go round the block, do a three-point turn, a parallel park, a handbrake start on a hill. None of it real life-threatening stuff. And then you don't get retested till you're eighty-five years of age.

In twenty-three years I've heard every reason as to why motor cars crash. And it's never the driver. They always say, 'The car went out of control.' That's one of the all-time classics. Or the tyres let go. I've heard that thousands of times, 'Ian, I was going round a corner and the Goodyears let go.' Or the brakes locked, the steering failed, it skidded, it went off the road and so on and so forth. The idea that they might just be a bad driver never occurs to them.

This is particularly so with men. There are some who shouldn't be driving at all. They've got the wrong attitude.

The wrong approach. The wrong skill level. And poor knowledge. But you can't tell them that because men believe that driving ability is something they were born with, or acquired through osmosis.

But nobody is born with natural skill. Peter Brock did not emerge into the world holding a steering wheel at the ten-to-two position. It's a load of garbage to think that people are natural drivers because they spent a lot of time in billycarts or tractors or on bikes as a kid. Unfortunately a lot of guys see the Johnsons and the Brocks doing it on TV and they want to prove their masculinity. They think, 'Well I could do that, probably better than they could.'

They're connecting with the power of a car. It's almost a sexual object. Why put mag wheels on a car? They are completely pointless, except as a sort of plumage, like peacock feathers. The car is almost primeval. These guys have hair on the back of their hands, on their chests and necks, and they climb aboard this beast and go cruising, looking for women. They want to stand out, they want people to look at them, and if they can hang a bit of a burn around a corner there's a degree of macho skill, when in fact it's all stupidity because mostly they go burning away thinking, 'I've got it, I've got it' and then they'll stick it into the nearest bin or telegraph pole.

There is a lot of cultural and psychological baggage with cars. Little boys grow up playing with matchbox cars, crashing them into things, making jumps, living out this fantasy. Dad goes out and buys his son a little pedal car. Men are brought up with cars as part of their world. They are exciting and fun and a form of release. As they grow older they want the real thing, but believe me a childhood spent with matchbox cars will not prepare you to control the real thing.
– *Ian Luff*, Advanced Driving Australia

§

right? What does that tell you about the reliability of your five-year-old car, designed by college graduates along principles established less than a century ago?

- **BE DEFENSIVE.** Unless you've had experience as a professional driver of some sort, pay for a good defensive driving course. They'll teach you a few things about controlling skids, emergency stops, and brake failures – but most importantly, they'll teach you to be paranoid.

- **BE PARANOID.** At least ninety-five percent of all road accidents are avoidable. You may be a law-abiding driver who follows the rules of the road to the letter, but it still won't help you when you encounter the sheer stupidity of some of the brain-dead human salamis on the road today. Being able to say 'It wasn't my fault' after an accident which kills three people is *very* small fuckin' comfort. It's not enough to be a law-abiding driver. You have to be an absolutely shit-scared, 100% certifiably crazy-arse paranoid driver, or you're in line to be a statistic.

Let me clarify this one, speaking from personal experience. I spent four years as a cab driver in the inner city. At that time, I was also riding a motorcycle to get around. I *strongly* recommend the motorcycle experience to anyone and everyone who is thinking of getting onto the road. On a motorcycle, there is no protection. And the number of times you hear people say 'Oh, I just didn't see you!' is starkly terrifying. Spend two years on a motorcycle, and you will have developed a kind of sixth sense on the road that most people won't even detect, let alone understand. You'll be hitting the brakes three blocks before the trouble starts. You'll spot the drunks and the mobile phone freaks before they even pull into the traffic. Accidents? Ha! By the time they happen, you will long since have moved to high ground.

This isn't just me. Ask the car insurance companies: the single best risk group they have is people who've spent three or more years on a motorcycle. Anyone who survives that long on a motorbike acquires reflexes to shame a jet fighter pilot, and a stone-crazy paranoid attitude. All their friends think they're a bunch of wussies, prone to driving like the mythical little old lady – but these people do *not* get involved in car smashes. Even those which are someone else's fault.

Keeping Your Car On The Road:
Quick And Dirty Diagnostics.

First thing you need to do is read the lights and gauges on the control panel. There's a reason the manufacturers put them there, you know.

PROBLEMS WITH LIGHTS

- **Temperature gauge** should never climb into the red. If it does so – even if it seriously threatens to do so – pull over and wait for half an hour. Then check the coolant in the radiator ... very, very carefully. Same drill as before, using a nice, heavy rag and a great deal of caution. No coolant? Minor problem, for the moment. Add water – but check to see all the hoses are connected first. You'll feel like an idiot if you add your last two litres of water only to discover a broken radiator hose has dumped it all onto the roadside. If there's still water in the radiator, though, you may have a problem. Call someone who can help.
- **Alternator light.** The alternator charges your battery as you drive. If the alternator goes, not much later your battery runs out of juice. No juice, no spark. No spark, no putt-putt-putt in the pistons, and your engine stops. Check the belt which drives the alternator. If it's loose, or broken, replace it. Otherwise, you have a problem either with the alternator or the wiring. Call an auto electrician.
- **Oil light.** Oil pressure is too low. Not enough oil in the system. STOP DRIVING THE CAR. Check your dipstick, then add some oil. If the level doesn't rise, look under the car for a major-disaster type oil leak. Don't drive the car until there is oil in it. Doing otherwise is guaranteed to convert your engine into a solid lump of useless metal.
- **Brake light.** You've left the handbrake on, stupid. Release it. If it doesn't release, jiggle it. If that fails, try driving forwards and backwards very briefly, and jiggle it again.

PROBLEMS WITHOUT LIGHTS

- **Car begins to pull to one side** while driving: most likely a flat tyre. Pull over. Change the tyre. If all the tyres are still good, check your alignment. (Do the front tyres point straight ahead with the steer-

> §
>
> ROBERT BENCHLEY CAME OUT OF a night club one evening and, tapping a uniformed figure on the shoulder, said, 'Get me a cab.' The uniformed figure turned around furiously and informed him that he was not a doorman but a rear admiral. 'Okay,' said Benchley, 'Get me a battleship.'
>
> §

ing wheel centred?) Alignment calls for a mechanic – but you can drive it there. If the alignment is okay, check the temperature of the wheels. You'll probably find one is *real* hot. This is a problem with brakes or bearings, and you're going to need a tow-truck.

- **ENGINE COUGHS AND DIES IN MID-JOURNEY.** Checked the fuel gauge recently, stupid? If you've still got fuel, and if you've still got lights and electricals, you've probably got a fuel-feed problem. Call a tow-truck.
- **CAR SCREAMS WHEN YOU TRY TO START IT.** Starter motor is getting worn. Turn the ignition off. Put the car in neutral. Push it forward half a metre. Try to start it again. Repeat process a few times. If nothing improves, call a mechanic.
- **SMOKE FROM UNDER THE BONNET.** Pull over. Get out. Run away. Observe from a safe distance. When the smoke stops, come back and check the damage. If you're lucky, it was just a little spilled oil burning off the top of the engine. If you're not lucky, a fire just burnt out your wiring, or worse. Call a mechanic.
- **YOU TURN THE KEY. NOTHING HAPPENS.** Electrical problems. Did you leave the lights on? Pull the leads off the battery, and carefully give them a good scrape with a pen-knife. Reconnect the leads. Roll-start the car, or get somebody with a more reliable vehicle to jump-start it.
- **STEERING WHEEL BEGINS TO VIBRATE AT SPEED.** Front end of the car may visibly oscillate when slowing down: possibly alignment, but more likely, a tyre has developed a bulge, or begun to shed tread. Get it replaced immediately.
- **OTHER MAINTENANCE PROBLEMS.** Actually, the best advice is to pay the mechanic to make these his problems. Keep up the oil, the water, and the petrol by yourself. Regularly check wiper fluid and brake fluid.

If you're feeling dangerously competent, change your own oil filters and air filters every 5,000 kilometres or so. Beyond that, unless you are yourself a qualified mechanic, send your car regularly to the spanner-men to have it thoroughly checked out. Haven't you got better things you could be doing with your life?

HOW TO PUSH-START YOUR CAR

In the life of every driver, there comes a time when you forget to turn the headlights off, and the battery changes from a magical energy storage device into a lump of plastic, acid and lead. When that happens, you need to know how to push-start your car.

Hills are helpful. If you've parked on a hill, you can probably do this by yourself. Get the car facing downhill. Put the car in *second* gear. Turn the key to the 'on' position. Put the clutch in, and roll forwards until you're doing about 15-20kph. Let the clutch out. The car should jerk, cough, and start running. DON'T TURN IT OFF. From this point on, the alternator should be recharging the battery. In about twenty minutes, if you have a decent electrical system, you should be able to start your car in the accepted manner. Until then, just keep driving.

If you're not on a hill, you'll probably need somebody to help you push the car until it reaches the requisite speed. And please – never try to push-start an automatic. You'll only annoy the people trying to help you when they find out how stupid you are.

HOW TO JUMP-START A CAR

First, you need jumper cables. You also need a functioning car, with the engine running. Park the functioning car front-bumper to front-bumper with the dead car. Now, very carefully clip one end of the RED cable to the POSITIVE terminal of the battery in the functioning car. Repeat the process using the other end of the RED cable, and the POSITIVE terminal of the battery in the dead car. Now take the BLACK cable, and clip one end to the NEGATIVE terminal of the battery in the functioning car. Repeat the process with the other end of the BLACK cable and the NEGATIVE terminal of the dead car. Start the dead car in the normal manner. Very carefully, disconnect the cables.

DO NOT AT ANY TIME PERMIT THE ENDS OF THE DIFFERENT-COLOURED CABLES TO COME INTO CONTACT WITH ONE ANOTHER. That will produce a lot of sparks, and probably a big bang. Bad News.

By the way: battery terminals are nicely coded. Usually, the insulation on the positive terminal is red, and the insulation on the negative terminal is black. If the insulation is missing, or not colour coded, all batteries are marked with a '+' at the positive terminal, and a '-' at the negative. If the battery is so old or worn these marks cannot be seen, abandon the exercise and replace the battery altogether. Don't throw it away, though – it's probably an antique.

HOW TO MAKE A BOOTLEGGER TURN

No, this is not a riddle with an answer like 'stick a pin through his navel and push on his head.' A Bootlegger Turn is actually a driving manoeuvre. It's reasonably easy to pull off once you know the basic technique and have had a little practise, and it looks impressive as all hell. To be precise, a Bootlegger Turn is that 180 degree handbrake turn that everyone is always using in the movies, and on television. It is so named because – supposedly – the first drivers to use it regularly were the booze-runners back in the days of the American Prohibition.

Seen from outside, a Bootlegger looks great. The car comes hurtling towards a roadblock, and without warning, spins end for end in a cloud of dust and squeal of tyres. Then it roars off again, as fast as possible, in the direction it came. If you've never secretly wanted to do exactly that at some stage or another, I can't figure what you're doing with this book in the first place.

Doing a Bootlegger is actually pretty easy, so long as you follow the rules. And the first rule is this: 60 kilometres per hour. No more, and preferably not a lot less. If you go much over sixty, you will find yourself doing not a quick, semi-controlled 180 degree turn, but an even quicker and far less controllable flat spin that could bring you out almost anywhere.

Rule two is equally simple: low wheel-base. Tall vehicles – vehicles with a lot of ground-clearance room under their chassis – are not at all good to Bootlegger in. If you try to do a Bootlegger turn in a vehicle with a high centre of gravity, you stand a very good chance of rolling the thing over, which is no fun at all.

To do your Bootlegger turn, you need a straight, very much unoccupied stretch of road. Bitumen road works best, but gravel road will do at a pinch, although you should reduce your speed to cut down on your chances of spinning more than 180 degrees. Bring your speed up to the desired 60km/h, and making certain you have at least fifty metres of clearance in front of the car, you do two things simultaneously: bring the steering wheel hard over, and yank the handbrake full-on.

The tyres will lock up instantly, and the car immediately begin to turn end-for-end. Release the handbrake again – basically you just yank it up and release it as soon as the tyres lock – and when the nose of the car is facing the direction you want, drop down a gear or so, and step on the accelerator. If your tyres have survived the ordeal; if you haven't rolled, or spun too far, or smashed into something unexpected, you should now be careening away in the direction from which you came.

Obviously, this is not something I recommend you do very often. In fact, I can't say that I recommend you do it at all. And if you do try it, and crash horribly in the process, it's your damned problem and nothing to do with me, right?

AUTOMOTIVE ACCOUTREMENT

• **WOMEN ARE NO WORSE THAN MEN ON THE ROAD.** Neither are they discernibly any better.

• **ANYONE WHO DRIVES WHILE WEARING ANY KIND OF A HAT** should be treated with the greatest of suspicion. Bowls hats and big country Akubras are the most dangerous, but you should never ignore the IQ implications of the baseball cap, especially if it is worn backwards.

• **VOLVOS ARE NO LONGER A SERIOUS STATUS CAR.** Currently, Volvo drivers are no worse than anyone else.

• **MERCEDES BENZ, BMW, SAAB, AUDI AND TO A LESSER EXTENT, JAGUAR ARE ALL EXECUTIVE-STATUS CARS.** Their owners cannot drive. Really. They are without a doubt the single most dangerous subgroup of

Currently, Volvo drivers are no worse than any-one else.

drivers on the road. I can't stress this enough. Any time you spot one of these loose cannons on the streets, give them all possible leeway. It's only a matter of time before they try to kill you, otherwise. And a big kiss-kiss to the wanker whose BMW tail-lights I kicked to pieces in Brisbane traffic about seven years ago. No good pretending you didn't see me just 'cos I was on a motorcycle, dickhead – I hope those lights cost you a packet!

• **PERFORMANCE SPORTS CARS** – Porsches, Ferraris, Lamborghinis, Maseratis and the like – are either too expensive to be crashed, or are driven by people who like driving performance vehicles, and know what they're doing. These people will not try to kill you in traffic. Admire the cars as they go past.

• **BRAKING DISTANCE IS IMPORTANT.** It's going to take you about two seconds to spot trouble ahead of you and start bringing the car to a halt, so you need to leave two seconds travel time between you and the car in front. Watch for one of the white paint-marks to come out from under the car in front. Count in your head: 'One, one thousand. Two, one thousand.' That's the length of time it should take you to reach that paint-mark. If it's any shorter, *slow the fuck down*. If it's longer – well, good. And in wet weather, you should think about doubling that distance.

• **DRIVING UNDER THE INFLUENCE OF ALCOHOL ISN'T THE SAME AS DRIVING DRUNK.** You may think you're in perfect control after three beers in half an hour. The reality is, your reflexes and your ability to react are impaired. Perhaps not enough for you to notice, sure – but enough to count in a crisis. Drink, drive – and die, please! (Before you kill someone who matters.)

• **IN ANY TRAFFIC, IT'S NOT THE SPEED LIMIT THAT MATTERS, BUT THE TRAFFIC SPEED.** One of the best defensive driving techniques of all is known to every motorcyclist still alive: *don't* stay with the traffic. Your best bet is to drive at about 5km/h above whatever the prevailing traffic-speed is. That way, most of your problems will come at you from the front, where you're constantly watching, and have the best chance of taking evasive action. If you drive slowly, and force the traffic to pass you, there's a constant stream of potential disasters creeping up on you from behind – and you have to try to spot them in your mirrors before they manage to kill you!

• **ALL CARS SHOULD HAVE A MINIMUM TOOL-KIT.** You'll have a jack and a spare tyre, obviously, as well as tyre-spanner for the wheel-nuts. You should also have jumper cables. Screwdrivers of various sizes, including both philips head and straight, are helpful. Also a bunch of spanners. Similarly, never go anywhere without a litre bottle of engine oil, and a couple of litres of water. A tin of WD-40 and an electric torch rounds things off. Having a fire extinguisher in the car is a very comforting thing.

• **MEMBERSHIP IN AN AUTOMOBILE ASSOCIATION**, such as the RACQ, the NRMA, or the RACV is cheap, and extraordinarily valuable. Neglect this at your peril!

And once you've got driving right …

HOW TO LAND A JUMBO

HEY, WE'VE ALL SEEN *Flying High*, right? And what about all those *Airport* flicks from the bad old days of the seventies? Doesn't matter what Dustin Hoffman says about Qantas' safety record; never mind the statistics that show it's safer to fly than it is to cross the street; we know the truth, don't we?

Gentlemen, the frightening reality of the situation is that one day, you are almost certainly going to be in one of those situations: terrorists gun down the pilot, food poisoning overcomes the co-pilot, the cabin crew bails out in terror, and the *only thing left* between a Jumbo Jet full of screaming passengers and a truly unpleasant interaction with the ground is you. And this book. Well, we're not going to let you down. Here's what you have to do:

1) **CLEAR THE CABIN OF TERRORISTS.** In our next book (*Armed Response for Every Situation*, coming soon from D&S) we'll talk about the best way to handle this. For the moment, try just asking them nicely, and pointing out that if they don't get out of your way, there's going to be rather a lot more martyrdom going on than they might have counted on.
2) **GRAB THE RADIO.** Scream for help.
3) **ENGAGE AUTOPILOT.** Look for three buttons marked 'CMD'. Press only one of them so that it lights up. Point the nose of the aircraft in a straight and level heading.
4) **DIG OUT THE CHECKLISTS.** These handy little buggers cover the basic procedures which must be followed for landing. They're usually tucked into a side pocket next to the pilot's seat. And the co-pilot's seat too.

Have a good look at the checklists. They'll help you identify exactly which subtype of Jumbo you're flying, which can simplify matters considerably – especially as some are equipped with an Automatic Landing System.

5) WHAT, THE TERRORISTS ATE THE CHECKLISTS? USE OURS. They're not exactly generic, but what the heck.

PRE-DESCENT:
- i) Complete EO system check.
- ii) Set pressurisation.
- iii) A/C packs on. Set the airfield altitude. This allows the 'plane to depressurise on landing. Trust us, this makes it considerably easier to open the doors.
- iv) Check and set landing data.
- v) Switch the Horizontal Situation Indicators to radio navigation mode.
- vi) Set auto brakes. That will help you stop, should you actually manage a touchdown.

APPROACH:
- i) Normally, you'd alert the cabin crew, switch on seatbelt signs and exit lights. Screw it.
- ii) Ignition on – gets the engines ready for landing.
- iii) Set fuel system for landing.
- iv) Fuel heat on – prevents fuel from freezing.
- v) Set QNH. Remember how you set the airfield altitude earlier? Well, this is the doohickey that actually keeps track of your altimeter and switches stuff on at the right height.

LANDING:
- i) Check the gear. Handle should be down and in, and the green gear-down lights should be showing.
- ii) Arm the speedbrakes. Hopefully, these will keep you from bouncing back off the runway.
- iii) Check hydraulics.
- iv) Set landing flaps at twenty-five degrees.
- v) Normally, you'd get a report from the Senior Cabin Crew about now. Unfortunately, they bailed out, remember?

6) DIG OUT THE JEPPESON CHARTS. These babies are life-savers. They're big, notebook-like things, full of maps and landing approaches for practically every airport in the world. What you have to do is figure out which one you want. Then you can find the radio frequency you need to communicate with their tower ... which would be a good idea, about now.

7) LOCATE THE FLIGHT MANAGEMENT SYSTEM. There should be some buttons on the mode control panel marked 'LNAV' and 'VNAV'.

8) FIND YOUR AIRPORT ON THE JEPPESON MAP. Ideally, the pilot and crew entered the appropriate data before their various depressing exits. What you have to do in that case is to put your map on a 100km scale using the EFIS control panel. When it's time to start going down, you'll get a yellow message on the middle screen, courtesy of this device.

9) ONCE THAT YELLOW MESSAGE COMES UP, check out the control display unit between the pilots' seats. The bottom line says 'Reset MCP altitude.' What you do is find the knob on the Mode Control Panel which sets the altitude. Turn the knob until the set altitude on the display is about 30 metres higher than the airfield altitude, as specified by the Jeppeson charts.

10) SET UP FOR LANDING. Depress the LOC and G/S buttons on the Mode Control Panel to engage the autoland functions. With any luck, all three autopilot buttons on the CMD will now light up.

11) TURN ON THE AUTOBRAKES. If you've done everything else properly, the aircraft will have come down to read the radio-based landing beam. The autopilot will take care of the landing, and the autobrakes should bring your beast to a halt. You may now change your underpants.

CHAPTER TEN

Cleaning and Hardware: Manly things to do around the House.

WHEN YOU COME RIGHT DOWN to it, women are probably responsible for the existence of civilisation as we know it. The key here is housework. Your primitive man – who is, lets face it, anyone with a Y-chromosome – is quite happy to live a nomadic lifestyle. Here today, gone tomorrow. It's an excellent life, but you don't get a whole lot done, except a bunch of hunting, eating, and sleeping.

Women, though – well, you can see their viewpoint. All this hunting, gathering and wandering is great, but if you're trying to carry a small child with you, it doesn't work very well. You need somewhere to sit down for a while, put your feet up, maybe have a cup of tea and a cigarette. You need to *stay in one place*.

So the idea gets put to the committee. Primitive man takes one look at this concept of staying in one spot, laughs out loud, and says something like: 'Tried that. Didn't work. The garbage piled up so high we couldn't see to hunt any more.'

And that's when Primitive Woman (who hasn't really changed much either) does her nana. By this stage, her feet are hurting, the kids are screaming, there's half a mammoth left to be peeled and burnt, and by the look of the way the Primitive Men have been hanging around the pot of fermented banana mush, she figures they're planning yet another enormous piss-up and singalong that night. Right at that moment, something goes 'ping!' way, way down in her hindbrain where the dinosaurs lurk. Suddenly, Primitive Woman doesn't give a damn any more about the way Primitive Man selflessly risks his life to hunt mammoth, beat off sabretooth tigers, and make ever bigger and more exciting fires. 'You lazy good-for-nothing bastard,' she screams in a voice that has been known to chip flint. 'If you think you're spending one more evening round that fire with your shiftless, no-hoper Cro-Magnon buddies, drinking banana beer while I'm left to feed your brats and scrape mammoth hides, you're carrion! Don't just moon around the place like an evolutionary dead end ... *go and take the garbage out!*'

In that moment, civilisation is born.

So, what are we, ten thousand years later? Has anything really changed? Not really. Given the choice most men would prefer to gnaw old chicken bones and drink beer until the landscape was awash in empties – then get in the ute and drive down the road until the pile of bottles and bones became invisible. Similarly, we'd quite happily wear the same shirt until it fell off, and then get around in what was left of our underwear.

Women, though – they're different. They have strange ideas on garbage removal, dishwashing, hygiene, laundry and things like that. For them, washing socks and jocks isn't a matter of wearing them into the shower. For women, doing the dishes never involves a fire-hose in the back yard. And since what we're trying to do is turn you into a magnet for the opposite sex, it seems you're gonna have to learn to do enough housework to make the womenfolk think you're not such a disgusting pig after all.

Of course, a life of celibacy could be balanced by the joys of all the beer, chicken, and television football you want to indulge in. But we wouldn't know. The price always seemed too high to us ...

HOUSEWORK MADE EASY

FIRST QUESTION: ARE YOU SUFFICIENTLY flush that you can pay some grotesquely poor Third World migrant to come in for a couple of hours a week? Many of them will do so for about $10 an hour, you know. And if you can live with yourself, that $20 per week will save you a lot of time and effort. Also, think how much fun you can have sitting in the lounge with a cold beer, watching Shane Warne eviscerate the Poms while somebody else struggles with last night's pizza debris ...

Assuming you have that $20 earmarked for better things, what you're going to have to do is get yourself organised. Housework, left alone long enough, turns into the kind of gigantic task the Greeks invented Hercules for. You can't afford to turn your back on it for a minute – especially in a share household. They're the absolute worst. The thing to do is understand what actually has to be done, and more importantly, how often. Then you can minimise the number of times you have to do it. Here's a simple break-down of household chores with which you can familiarise yourself.

BEDROOM
- **DAILY.** Check under bed for leftover pizza or girlfriends. Remove any found. Place all dirty clothing in one spot, so it can't get away.
- **WEEKLY.** Wash and change bedsheets. (More often during periods of frequent usage.) Wash clothing, and return to the cupboard, closet, or designated piece of floor.
- **MONTHLY.** Pick up everything on the floor and put it into either a bin, or a closet. Sweep or vacuum.
- **HOT-SPOTS.** Dust collects under a bed the way embarrassment clings to Alexander Downer. Include that space in your vacuuming or sweeping regime.

§

Clean up after yourself

I went out with this girl for a while and we had a lot of sex in the early days. Like you do. It was pretty good sex too. Always left me feeling shagged out. I was usually so tired afterwards that I would just take off the condom, wrap it in a tissue and drop it by the bed. I'm into safe sex but not necessarily neat sex. Anyway I thought Donna was cleaning these little packages up because they were generally gone when I got up in the morning, and she always beat me out of bed by half an hour. At any rate, we never discussed it. We should have. The full horror of the situation dawned after a month. Donna asked me whether I thought Astroboy, her tabby cat, was getting fat. I had to admit that, yes, he did look a little porkier than when I'd first met him. I suggested she shouldn't let him eat so much chocolate. Then at dinner that night, Astroboy lost it. Started mewling and yowling and scraping his bum on the carpet. When I gathered him up to have a look, the mystery of the missing condoms was explained. At that very moment one was emerging, half chewed, from his butt. – *Marty*

§

SHOWER/BATHROOM

- **DAILY.** Recap toothpaste. Replace soap in the holder.
- **WEEKLY.** Mop floor and clean shower/bath cubicle. Gather up old razors, empty toothpaste boxes, pointless slivers of soap, dead bandaids, elderly cotton-buds and all other debris. Remove ugly wads of hair from drains.
- **HOT-SPOTS.** Don't scrub too hard at an old-style enamelled tub. The enamel comes off, which is embarrassing. Best way to clean the bathroom properly is to put a Do Not Disturb sign on the door, and get nude with a bucket of disinfectant, a mop, a cloth, and scrubbing brush. That way you can take advantage of the water supply from the shower or bath. By the way: cheap commercial bleach does an excellent job removing mould from tile grout and anywhere else. Just don't spend too long breathing it in.

§

DON'T LET THINGS SLIDE

As a teenager living with my parents in Paddington, I witnessed a man gradually slide into a cesspit of seediness that still appals me when I think about it. His name was Jean Louis and he was a big, ugly, lumbering, French Noumean chef, practising his art in some Double Bay bistro. Somehow he ended up renting a room in my parent's house. I'll never know why they accepted him. I think there was some connection with friends of theirs, some people we never mention nowadays.

As teenagers, my friends and I thought it might be worth scouting the room of this mystery boarder. We found one of those places you see on the news or tabloid TV every so often. The one where there's so much shit piled up against the door that you can hardly open it, and when you do you find six Kampuchean kids or about three hundred beagles all squashed in together. We just went numb, staring at the mess and sucking in the foul fumes. A year's worth of dirty clothes and dozens of dinner plates lacquered with rockhard yellow scum covered the floor. The grass matting carpet was alive.

After the initial shock we started looking around. The first thing we spotted were these enormous glass jars, filled to the brim with silver coins. Good pinball money, we agreed. Someone who lives like this will never miss a few less coins, we thought. Then, the big find. Over near the bed was a stack of *Ribald* porno mags. These weren't your half-lame stick books like *Penthouse* or *Playboy*. These things didn't even bother with articles, the only written content was the

TOILET

- **WEEKLY.** Replace toilet paper. Remove debris. Mop the floor, and swish out the toilet bowl with disinfectant and one of those long-handled brushes. Give the toilet exterior a going-over with a cloth and some disinfectant.

most personal personal ads you'd ever see. For a group of 14-year-olds this was the find of the century. We must have spent two hours poring over them.

We didn't lose our senses completely though. We remembered to bag some coins on the way out, and leave the room the way we found it, which wasn't hard.

Of course now that we knew what was behind that door we made regular forays into the forbidden zone, whenever we'd hear him lumber down the stairs and off to work. The *Ribalds* were frequently updated, so we never got bored. We even took a bunch to school and made a killing charging the other kids for a peek. We also noticed that Jean Louis had been hard at work with the highlighter in the personal ads, marking off every desperate chick advertising her wares. They all seemed to want to meet a 'generous businessman with a big cock and credit card', so he obviously wouldn't be scoring too well. Over the year the bright yellow highlighter started drifting ever more downmarket. By the end of the first year, he was no longer circling the female ads, only the male ones.

Then the *Ribalds* disappeared and were replaced with hard core gay porn. Then the Philippino tour brochures started appearing. The man was getting desperate. We opened the door one day and sitting on his bedside table was this massive, shiny white vibrator. Finally we found out just how low he could sink when the vibrator was replaced by an electric styling wand.

That was it. We were out of there, faster than you could say 'psycho'.

Jean Louis left soon after. – *Paul*

§

• **HOT-SPOTS.** Make sure you get right in and mop behind the base of the toilet pedestal. If you don't, *things* start to accumulate there. Really Nasty Things.

KITCHEN: (THIS ONE'S A BASTARD.)

- **DAILY.** Clear food debris. Bag it, and take it out to the garbage. Or the compost. Or whatever. Wash the dishes. Dry them. Put them away. (None of this is optional.) Sponge off all food preparation surfaces, including the top of the stove, and the griller, if it has been used. Sweep the floor. Put away any spices or ingredients you aren't using *right this moment*. Check the fridge for food which has begun to mutate, evolve etc. and remove.

- **WEEKLY.** Mop the floor with disinfectant. Pull the crisper drawers out of the fridge and clean out the horrible substances which have begun to pool threateningly underneath. Check the freezer compartment for signs of freezing over. Full bio-hazard scan of the fridge, checking inside jars of tomato paste for mould, inside cartons of milk for lumps, and anything else you can think of. Gather all the limp, stinky tea-towels, wash them and dry them. Replace your old dishcloth with a clean new one. Use the old dishcloth in place of your old counter-wiping cloth. Throw your old counter-cloth away.

- **MONTHLY.** Lift the elements out of the stove top and give it a complete cleaning. Clean out the interior of the oven, using one of those savagely toxic oven-cleaner sprays. Completely clean the griller, too. Use disinfectant on all counter-tops and food preparation surfaces. Empty the fridge entirely, storing any perishables in the sink, with ice from the freezer. Allow the fridge to defrost, if necessary. Wipe the interior of the fridge with disinfectant, and let it dry. Then give it a wipe with some vanilla essence, and put everything back.

- **HALF-YEARLY.** Move the refrigerator. Sweep, then mop where it stood. Run a vacuum cleaner or a soft brush over the heat-exchange coils at the back. Those damned things *manufacture* dust, we're telling you.

- **HOT-SPOTS.** Sue kindly pointed out that it is helpful to wash *both sides* of the dishes, not just the surface you eat on. Otherwise, Terrible Crud gets caked onto the other bits, and you can't see the pattern on the china any more. Also, once a week at least, you should get a broom or a rag or a thin and hungry house pet, or *something* anyway, and try to grout around in the gap between the stove and the counter. In Mr Flinthart's first flat, they referred to that space as the Abyss of Horror – because it was dark, warm, and wet, and it smelt of fungus, and frequently, people felt something in there was watching them. His advice is get on top of it immediately with regular doses of bleach and ultra-violet light, if you can. Otherwise, nail a board over the gap, and festoon it with crucifixes and garlic and holy water, to keep imprisoned whatever lives there.

GENERAL HOUSE & COMMUNAL AREAS

- **DAILY.** Scavenger hunt through all communal areas of the house to retrieve coffee mugs, empty stubbies, drug refuse, congealed plates, disemboddied rats tails, discarded junk food artefacts, stray underpants, newspapers, books, forgotten guests and any other unnecessary debris. Sweep heavily trafficked areas.
- **WEEKLY.** Dust, sweep and vacuum everything. Move the furniture, including somnolent flatmates, when you do so. Remove dying pot plants.
- **MONTHLY.** Do the windows with a commercial window-wash liquid, and a soft cloth. Get a long attachment for the vacuum-cleaner, and suck up all those spiders hanging around the ceiling and the light fixtures. Vacuum the light-fixtures too. They fill up with dust and suicidal bugs very quickly, especially in the tropics.

HOUSEWORK: THE TECHNICAL STUFF.

LIKE MOST THINGS, THERE'S A right way and a wrong way to tackle almost every household task. Unfortunately, because we've been too busy building things and conquering people, Man has never learned the right way to do anything domestic. (Except for Gay Man of course, a tip o' the feather is due to those boys.) As a result, we have to work it out by trial and error, and in the process, we reinforce women's stereotyped ideas about Man's incompetence when it comes to housework.

LAUNDRY

- **PRACTISE APARTHEID.** It's a good idea to separate the whites from the coloureds, and do two separate washes. Trust us on this: there are few things more embarrassing than a bright pink karate uniform.

- **COLD WATER WORKS PRETTY DAMNED WELL.** It's cheaper. It doesn't 'cook' stains onto your clothing. It is also less likely to shrink anything, and less likely to make colours run. Really, hot water is only good for very greasy clothing.

- **READ THE MANUFACTURERS' LABEL CAREFULLY.** Some textiles shrink. Some hate being tumble-dried. Some like to be hand-washed in yak's milk. Never launder anything that says it needs to be dry-cleaned.

• **SEARCH THE BASTARDS.** All kinds of stuff collects in your pockets. Sending it through the wash is an extraordinarily bad idea. Empty the pockets. Do up the zips. Tie any drawstrings or sashes.

• **ZAP THE STAINS.** Rub or spray particularly ugly areas with some sort of enzyme pre-wash product, or with a little liquid detergent.

• **KEEP THE BALANCE.** Don't overload the machine. Try to distribute clothing evenly by weight around the centrepost. Failure to do this will make the machine either shut down during the spin cycle, or maybe walk across the floor like a big white square electric zombie.

• **BEWARE THE SUN.** if you're using an outdoor clothesline, consider turning your clothing inside out when you hang it, to prevent the sun fading the colours.

• **FOLD IT.** if you fold your clothing carefully, and hang it properly, you can minimise the amount of ironing you actually have to do. Mr Birmingham, for instance, has not used an iron since 1985.

IRONING

• **CAN YOU GET SOMEONE ELSE TO DO IT?** There are plenty of people around who do loads of ironing at very reasonable rates. This is an excellent idea. You don't have to buy an iron and an ironing board, and you never have to learn to iron a shirt.

• **DON'T IRON WHAT YOU DON'T HAVE TO.** Only obsessive-compulsive types iron their shorts, underwear, socks, or T-shirts. In reality, the only things that Men wear which need ironing are button-down shirts and slacks or chinos. Also, some artificial fabrics will drip-dry nicely into shape. Don't iron them, either.

• **READ THE LABELS AGAIN, STUPID.** The kind of heat it takes to deal with a heavy cotton will annihilate a nice light silk. Irons have variable heat-settings for a reason.

• **SHIRTS ARE EVIL.** If you can iron a long-sleeved, high-collared button-down shirt, you can iron anything. First, get one of those plant-misters, and spray the shirt with a little water. Fold out the collar, lie it flat, and iron only the back. Make it flat. Now stretch out the yoke of the shirt – the bit that goes over your shoulders on the back – and make it flat as well. Move to the sleeves, next. Good shirts never have a crease down the sleeves, so stuff a towel into the sleeve before you iron out the wrinkles. Now stretch the back of the shirt over the board, leaving all the bits you've ironed to hang over the edge. Flatten the back of the shirt. Do the same with both panels of the front. Finish up by ironing the placket down the front, in between all the buttons, and finally, do the cuffs. *Voila!* One flat shirt.

• **ALTERNATIVE TO IRONING.** Get two large, flat, smooth boards – about 2m x 2m. Lay one of them out in the front yard. Spray your items of clothing lightly with water, and arrange them on the board. Take care to straighten out any wrinkles, and set the clothes so that their creases are reinforced by their position. Now gently, carefully, lay the other board over the top of the clothing. Back your car onto the board, and leave it there for half an hour. When you retrieve the garments, they will be nicely pressed.

VACUUMING

• **USE ALL THE ATTACHMENTS.** Most vacuum cleaners come with all sorts of widgets that you can slap on the end of the hose. Used properly, these will make your job much easier. There's a long widget with a round brush for cobwebs, and a narrow widget to get in beside cupboards and things, as well as the usual broad-head widget for floors.

• **DON'T GET CARRIED AWAY.** Yes, vacuum cleaners can shlork up all kinds of things, like small change, old condoms, paper clips, mice, and popcorn. However, they don't really like any of these objects. If your floor is littered with chunky stuff, sweep it first. Then run the vacuum to get the small stuff. (Although, it *is* kinda fun matching your vacuum cleaner's suction against the sticking power of a really determined mouse.)

§

TAKE OUT THE RUBBISH REGULARLY

I'd gone to bed early, and I heard Johnny's car pull into the driveway. I heard his door, then two other doors. There was something wrong. Sure enough these deep voices boomed, 'Can we see your licence' and 'Do you live here', and so on. It's the cops. So whooosh I'm out of bed and freaking, because we had about two pounds of mull in this big green garbage bag on the kitchen table. I figured those little piggies could probably smell it from where they were standing.

There was nowhere to hide it. I couldn't smoke it or swallow it. Man, I was panicking. So I tied up the bag, tipped a whole bunch of garbage in there first though to cover the smell, and then, cool as a cucumber I walked down those stairs, past these two coppers, with ten years of hard labour in this big green garbage bag. I nodded to them, ignored Johnny, rocked on over to the wheelie bin and plonked it in. They were all looking at me. I could feel them burning holes in the back of my head with their X-ray vision.

'Evening,' I said on my way back past them.

'Evening,' they said.

'Just taking out the trash.'

'Right.' – *Max*

§

• **CHECK THE SETTING.** Most household vacuum cleaners have an inbuilt brush on their cleaning head. You can retract the brush with a lever on top of the head. Use the brush on smooth floors. Retract the brush to do carpets.

• **CHANGE THE BAG, STUPID.** Vacuum cleaners don't really work by magic. All that crud doesn't just vanish into the Twilight Zone once the machine sucks it up. In fact, it gets deposited into a bag in the guts of the device, which bag requires emptying or changing once it's full. Failure to do this will give your vacuum cleaner the Clintons. It will not inhale.

DISHWASHING

• **CRANK UP THE HEAT.** Hot water cuts grease more efficiently than most soaps. Make your wash-water just as hot as you can stand it, and wear rubber gloves. Also, if you rinse your dishes in extra-hot water, they'll probably be bone dry already when you come to apply the tea-towel.

• **DO THE LIGHT STUFF FIRST.** If you start out with greasy pots and pans, the water in the sink is going to turn horrible very quickly. Then, when you come to do things like drinking glasses and plates, you'll wind up leaving a film of ugly grease on them. The answer is to do your dishes in the right order. Start with drinking glasses and crystal. Move on to plates and bowls. Next, tackle the cutlery, and finish up with the heavy cooking gear.

• **SCRAPE AND RINSE.** If you let food 'set' on pots and plates, it's a lot harder to get off later. When you're through with any cooking gear, scrape it out and immediately fill it with hot water and leave it to stand. That way, when you come to do the dishes after the meal, the remnants of food will come off easily. Plates and bowls should get the same treatment.

DUSTING

Get serious! There's not a Man alive who really gives a damn about dust. If it gets to be too much, pull out the vacuum cleaner and shlork up the worst of it. Then use a damp cloth on items which have become unconscionably dusty.

MOPPING

Get a nice big bucket of hot water. Now splash a little cleaning fluid on the floor. Wet your mop thoroughly, and scrub away. Rinse and wring the mop at regular intervals. Change your bucket of hot water if it gets too grubby or sudsy. Your goal is to rinse away all of the cleaning fluid with your hot water and your mop, removing any stains and glort from the floor in the process. Note: always mop from the far corners of the room towards the door. You'll look like a right dickhead if you do it the other way.

STAIN REMOVAL

• **BOOZE, JUICE, COFFEE, AND ALL OTHER DRINKS.** Sponge with cleaning solvent. Soak in a solution of a teaspoon of dishwashing liquid, a tablespoon of vinegar, and a litre of water. Rinse. For tough stains, sponge with methylated spirits. For non-washable fabrics, sponge with water. Now add a couple of drops of vinegar and a mix of 1 part glycerine, 1 part dish-washing liquid, and 8 parts water (this mix is called *wet spotter*). Blot with a cloth moistened in vinegar and wet spotter. Flush with water. As a last resort, blot with methylated spirits.

• **BLOOD, PUS, VOMIT, FLECKS OF BRAIN MATTER AND OTHER NASTY SUBSTANCES.** Soak in a solution of 1 litre warm water, 1 teaspoon dish-washing liquid, and 1 tablespoon spirits of ammonia. Rinse. For non-wash-able fabrics, sponge with water, then blot with wet spotter and ammonia. Flush with water. Apply a little vinegar. Flush again.

• **GREASE, LIPSTICK, SHOE-POLISH AND OTHER OILY STUFF.** Get to it as soon as possible. Sponge with cleaning solvent. If stain remains, apply a few drops of a mix of 1 part coconut oil to 8 parts commercial cleaning solvent (*dry spotter*). Rinse with cleaning solvent. You can do gravy and meaty stuff this way too.

• **GRASS & VEGETATION.** Sponge with cleaning solvent. When dry, sponge with ethyl acetate (nail-polish remover), rinse with cleaning sol-vent. When dry, sponge with water, then add a few drops of wet spotter and vinegar. Now sponge with wet spotter.

HOW TO SHARE A HOUSE: EIGHT RULES YOU MUST NEVER BREAK.

AT SOME TIME IN YOUR life, unless you decide to live with your parents forever, or perhaps come into an unfeasibly large sum of money very early in your career as a Man, you'll wind up sharing a residence with someone else. More likely a whole bunch of someones, through a string of seedy addresses over a period of a decade or more.

Generally, it's done for money. Especially during the student days, real bucks can be very hard to come by. Renting your own flat involves a truck-load of ugly expenses, and if an emergency arises, you can find yourself without the necessary financial resources to pull through. The most com-mon answer to this is to rent a much nicer place, and get a few like-mind-ed souls to share the rent and expenses.

Share housing can be a lot of fun. You meet a lot of interesting people and their friends, and sooner or later, their friends' friends as well. You

§

Impress your flatmates: How to swallow a sword.

You really want to know how to do this? Well, okay. After all, Houdini could swallow and hold in his throat objects up to the size of a billiard ball, and bring them back on demand, without apparent discomfort. This kind of thing takes practice.

To protect the delicate tissues of the throat from damage, you will first need to swallow a guidance tube, or 'shim'. The shim is a thin tube of metal, about forty centimetres long, and perhaps two centimetres in diameter. Once it has been slipped securely down the throat, the sword can be safely 'swallowed' by sliding it down the inside of the tube.

Of course, getting that tube down your throat in the first place is pretty tricky. Practice with something small to begin with, to help you quell your gag reflex. Teaspoons work well enough. Basically, you open your mouth wide and tilt your head back to make a single, straight passage of your mouth and throat. Be careful that you put your spoon into your throat, and not the trachea, which leads to the lungs. This is a Bad Thing.

Once you're comfortable with spoons, try something longer, like a chopstick. (One of the rounded Chinese kind, not a pointy Japanese one, okay?) When you can comfortably deal with that, it's time to move on to the guidance tube.

And remember: you gotta be able to bring these things back up again. If you're at all nervous about your ability to do that (it's not so hard, really – a lot like vomiting ...) consider attaching a monofilament line to the upper end of the tube. You can keep the line hidden in your cheek, and use it to haul the tube back when you're ready.

§

lose track of who owes what money to whom. Your clothing goes missing, but you make up the shortfall by stealing someone else's. You get drunk a lot more often than you should. You – ahh, hell ... go and read *He Died With A Felafel In His Hand*, and *The Tasmanian Babes Fiasco*, both of which vastly entertaining books were written by Mr Birmingham, and are available through this august publishing house.

When you do read those books, you'll realise something else. Aside from being economically sound and potentially great fun, share housing is also fraught with dangers and traumas. If you're very lucky, your first share house experience will see you renting a room alongside a troupe of experienced groovers, who know the ins and outs well enough to show you the ropes and keep you disaster-free. Unfortunately, you'll probably just grab a couple of your friends, pool your cash, and rent the first sleazy dive you come across. When that happens, you should prepare for the worst. And at the very least, obey the following rules ... to the letter.

1) **NO JUNKIES.** Nothing personal. It's just that anyone with a serious habit needs serious money. And that means their rent-paying capacity is very unreliable. Likewise, their ability to chip in for telephone, gas, power, and food bills. After a while, they also tend to get very fast and loose about who owns things like stereos, refrigerators, CDs, cars ... anything that's not nailed down.

This rule isn't aimed solely at people using heroin; anyone with a solid addiction to anything illegal qualifies as a 'junkie' for purposes of flatmate-finding. Speed, coke and pills are all part of the Big Picture.

Playing 'spot the hop-head' at the initial flatmate-interview can be more tricky than you might expect. The thing to do is make the household policy very, very clear from the outset. That way, if somebody with a jones does slip by your scrutiny, you can just toss them out on their arses when they finally do give themselves away. As they inevitably will, sooner or later.

2) **SEX BREAKS UP MORE HOUSES THAN MONEY.** Making a move on a flatmate involves all kinds of tricky variables. Suppose she doesn't want to know? That's going to make it tough to continue sharing a house, especially if you've poured your heart out to her and she's had a good long laugh. What if she acquires a boyfriend (or even a girlfriend) after that? Can you handle the snogging, the baby-talking, and everything else that goes with it, or are you going to lose the plot and set fire to the brown couch while they're lying on it, pretending to watch *Truly, Madly, Deeply*?

On the other hand, if the two of you do get together, whose bedroom is it going to be? And are you going to keep renting the two rooms? How are your other flatmates going to feel about the incessant snogging and first-flush sex-a-thons?

Share-house dynamics are complicated enough in the first place. The last thing you need to do is get involved with one of your fellow-renters. Admittedly, this may be tricky to avoid, but it is a vitally important issue. If you really want to get it on with one of your flatmates, your best bet is to splinter off and either join another household as a couple, or start afresh in the same manner. Better yet, just forget about it and aim your love lizard somewhere else.

3) RENT MONEY ISN'T PIZZA MONEY. There are few things more depressing and irritating than a flatmate who's always a week or so behind with the rent – or the phone money, or the electricity bill, or any of the shared expenses. Okay, late at night when the munchies are coming on hard, it might seem like a great idea to borrow twenty bucks from the rent kitty in order to summon the minions of Pizza the Hutt, but in the morning, you'll regret it.

The reason you're involved in a share-house situation is because none of you can afford decent accommodation on your own. A good flatmate, therefore, is one who ponies up the bucks reliably and on time. Sure, sooner or later everybody gets caught short – but if you've established yourself as a solid bloke who pays his share, your flatmates will be a lot more relaxed about covering you until payday. On the other hand, a regular defaulter is a man who will very soon be looking for alternate accommodation.

4) NEVER LIVE WITH A LABEL NAZI. Label Nazis are people who can't go through life without clearly identifying who owns that last third of a bottle of milk at the back of the fridge, or exactly whose turn it is to go to the corner shop for more fish fingers. You can always tell a house with a Label Nazi in it. Aside from the fact that everything in the refrigerator has Nikko pen all over it, there are complicated rosters and diagrams in every room of the house detailing exactly who is supposed to do what and when. Then there's the tense, oppressive atmosphere of the place … a house with a Label Nazi in it is not a happy house. It is a simmering pot of bitter gall, a seething mass of discontent and resentment, awaiting only the slightest of trigger incidents to burst into outright rebellion.

It's true that some form of work-distribution arrangement has to be reached in a share household. However, it's much more important that the house maintain a cool, relaxed atmosphere. It's not easy sharing a residence with a bunch of rugged individualists. Personal space gets invaded. Ugly music crops up on the stereo from time to time. People will want to watch soap operas at unconscionable hours – and get

§

ANNOY YOUR FLATMATES: HOW TO CHEAT AT CARDS.

• THE MECHANIC'S GRIP

When preparing to deal, grip the deck in your off-hand. Curl your first three fingers over the top end of the deck, with the down-side facing your palm, and your thumb curled over the bottom end. This is known in the trade as the 'Mechanic's Grip', and it is essential for dealing from the bottom.

• DEALING FROM THE BOTTOM

While this is a little easier to spot than dealing 'seconds' (keeping the top card in place and dealing the card below), dealing from the bottom is also a lot easier to do than dealing seconds. Holding the deck in the mechanic's grip, use the thumb of your dominant hand to slip the top card free so that it can be pinched against the index finger and tossed with a flick of the wrist. This is the normal dealing action. To deal a card from the bottom, keep the wrist action the same, but instead of sliding the top card free with the thumb, slip your index finger under the deck, slip the *bottom* card free, and pinch it against the thumb.

The overall action is almost identical in appearance to the normal deal. If you do it quickly, without breaking the rhythm of your deal, it becomes practically impossible to spot. When a highly skilled practitioner does it, even an observer who knows what is happening will see nothing more than the usual top-deck deal in action.

• WHY DEAL FROM THE BOTTOM?

Simple. Because when you shuffled, you slipped an ace to

cranky if nobody remembers to videotape them. If you add to such a volatile mix the anal-retentive tendencies of a genuine Label Nazi, things move from tenuous to unlivable so fast you won't even have time to bunker down and take cover.

Let the work roster sort itself out. Feel free to liberally remind peo-

---

the bottom of the deck, and you want to deal it into your own hand.

So how did that ace get down there? Well, it's easy. When you were gathering the cards from the last hand, you watched carefully and noted the position of one of the aces. Then, in the process of gathering, while making a little easy small talk, you simply swept the cards together in such a way as to put that ace on the bottom.

• HOW DO YOU KEEP A CHOSEN CARD ON THE BOTTOM DURING THE SHUFFLE?

Remember the mechanic's grip? Your standard shuffle is a rapid back-and-forth between the gripping hand and the plucking hand. Each time your hands come together, your 'plucking' hand grabs a random clump of cards from the top of the deck and palms them, until gradually, the entire deck is transferred to the 'plucking' hand. Then you return the deck to the gripping hand and repeat the process four or five times. To keep a chosen card on the bottom, on your first 'pluck' of cards, instead of simply raking half-a-dozen off the top with your thumb, you also lightly 'pinch' the whole deck, with your index finger underneath. This will bring the bottom-most card indetectably along with the clump from the top – but it will remain on the bottom, and as this is your first 'pluck' of the shuffle, it is automatically the bottom-most card of the new line-up.

• RIFFLING AND MARRYING

Usually, after the 'pluck-shuffle' process, the dealer will separate the deck into two halves. Both halves are then bowed, face downwards, upper edges close together, and the cards are allowed to spring downwards to page 270 >

CLEANING AND HARDWARE 269

ple of the need to occasionally wash the dishes. Grin and get soapy when somebody turns the same torch on you. Do a little more than you think is necessary. If you get a genuinely unbearable slob in the place, call a house meeting and turf them out. Establish a kitty for milk and bread and butter, and be sure to pitch in regularly. Try to share the shopping as much as possible, and respect other people's cold Mars

< *from page 265* so they land flat, and the two halves 'marry' together by overlapping, card upon card.

In order to keep your bottom card here, you have to remember which half of the deck it's in. Then, as you tension the two halves so that they spring together, you must release the desired bottom-card fractionally before you release the bottom card of the other half. This will make sure that your chosen card remains on the bottom so that you can deal it at your leisure.

• WHAT IF MY OPPONENT INSISTS ON CUTTING THE DECK?

Well, now you've got a problem. Your best bet here is to actually mark the cards you want. The way to do this is not with a pen, but with your thumbnail. A very small crease in the edge of the card will make that card very easy to spot when the deck is in its normal stacked state. (The deck will separate very slightly at the level of the card.) If you want to mark a number of cards, use a system in which the higher the rank of the card, the closer to the corner the crease. Don't mark more than half-a-dozen cards, though. You don't need much of an advantage to tilt the odds.

Now, when your opponent insists on cutting the cards, very simply and casually re-cut afterwards, lifting the cards apart at the slight separation that marks your chosen card. And once again, it's back on the bottom where you want it.

• HOW TO SPOT A CARD CHEAT

You won't spot a professional doing their thing. Spotting amateurs isn't so hard, though. Look for the mechanic's grip, look for marked cards, and keep an eye out for distracting gestures – the spilled drink, or the funny routine of tossing the cigarette to the mouth. It's a lot easier to cheat

Bars in the fridge the same way you'd hope they would respect your own. And the moment somebody pulls out a Nikko pen and starts labelling things, throw them out on their arse.

By the way: if you're a Label Nazi yourself – go out and get a life. Pencil-neck!

5) MIX THE GENDERS. 'Male and female created He them ...' (Genesis,

---

if you have a 'shill', or partner, so watch for signs of co-operation between people, and don't let anybody stand behind you.

Spotting a professional, as I mentioned before, is next to impossible. What you have to look for is the odds. Luck is one thing. Bucking the odds – now that's another. In a game of, say, straight five-card stud poker, there's likely to be only one big hand at the table – if any. When you start to see full houses bumping into flushes, straights, and four-of-a-kind, it's time to be very, very suspicious. And remember: a run of odds in your favour is just as suspicious as a run for someone else. If there's money involved, it's possible you're being set up for a big sting.

• STOPPING CHEATS

Not difficult. Always cut the deck when the dealer has shuffled. Never permit a re-cut afterwards. Always open a new deck at the start of proceedings, and should the deck start to show signs of wear, immediately open another one. Brand-new. Still with the cellophane wrapping.

Check your environment. Sitting with your back to a mirror is plain stupid. So is sitting with your back to a glass surface – such as a window, door, or china cabinet. Don't hold your cards in front of you at chest height. Lift the corner nearest you to examine them, and leave them face-down on the table.

If you suspect you are being cheated, it's always best simply to get up and leave quietly rather than make a scene. You don't have to play cards with the cheat again, after all.

§

somewhere or another. Who really cares?) Men and women are very different animals. They have different strengths, and different weaknesses, and oddly enough, they rather complement one another. As Mr Birmingham has observed, living in a houseful of men is absolutely, balls-out disgusting. It's stained jocks and socks drying limply over the shower curtain rail. It's a midden-heap of stubbies piling up on the back deck. It's thick matter clogging the bottom of the kitchen sink, down under the dishes where nobody's been for a month. It's *horrible.*

All-woman households are every bit as ugly, but in a weird and subtle fashion. Women, acting in a pack, are capable of the utmost viciousness. The social dynamics of an all-female household are savage in a way that essentially easygoing and forthright male politics simply can-

§

COMMUNICATION WITH YOUR FLATMATES: HOW TO READ MORSE CODE.

Morse code is a very simple binary system used originally in telegraphy, and still in use over shortwave radio around the world today. The advantage of Morse is that you can signal it with just about anything: lights, sounds, radio pulses – anything you can turn on and off. In the Morse system, each letter of the alphabet is replaced by a number of dots and dashes, as follows:

A ._	J ._ _ _	S ...
B _...	K _._	T _
C _._.	L ._..	U .._
D _..	M _ _	V ..._
E .	N _.	W ._ _
F .._.	O _ _ _	X _.._
G _ _ .	P ._ _.	Y _._ _
H	Q _ _ ._	Z _ _ ..
I ..	R ._.	

Remember to leave a gap between letters. A constant stream of dots and dashes is not information, it's a disco light.

§

not achieve. And then there's the stuff women don't do very well – like pulling out all that long hair from the shower drain. And changing light-bulbs. Or remembering to take their stiletto heels off before they walk on the polished pine floor. Spiders and rats can become all-out emer-gencies in an all-female household. (Men don't much like them either, but have no real qualms about crunching them under a size ten Blunny.)

A share house comprising occupants of one sex only is a disaster waiting to happen. Leave that kind of bullshit for boarding schools, prisons, and uptight Catholic colleges, where it belongs. The only time it can work is if there are only two householders, and they go back a long, long way. More than two, and you need that alternate chromo-some. You can stave off the catastrophe by mixing straights and queers, but it is at best a temporary measure. The only way to achieve a stable, long-lived share household is to mix the sexes, and for both sides of the equation to make a real effort to learn to live with the other.

6) EVERYONE'S GOT PARENTS. Parents are the bane of decent share-houses. Most of us move out of home to uncramp lifestyles which have become severely inhibited by the presence of the Dear Old Things. It's considered remarkably bad form, however, to ban them outright from visiting their beloved son, especially when you probably still owe them for the car, the bond on the house, and last week's laundry.

Ground rules must be established and observed. It is legitimate to require that visiting parents give notice of their intent – and in the case of a surprise visit, it is also legitimate for you to hide and get your flat-mates to insist that you're actually out. You are also required to return this favour whenever necessary.

Formal parent visits require a full house-cleaning, and a painstak-ing effort to conceal any aspects of your lifestyle which may distress them. (Hide the bucket-bong. Put the stroke mags in a box under the house. Get rid of the mountain of beer bottles.) Once again, you are obliged to assist in these efforts, no matter whose parents are visiting.

Finally, during the period of a parental visit, all householders are expected to be on their mettle. Disgusting bathroom stories are out. Sculling competitions are out. Prawn and Porn nights must be post-poned. Genuinely barbaric housemates must be shepherded elsewhere until the Oldies have gone away. Personal household dislikes, vendet-tas and duels should be held in unconditional ceasefire mode for the duration of the crisis.

7) NOT EVERYONE IS CELIBATE. In share houses, everyone knows about your love-life. This isn't something to worry about, or to avoid – in a good share house, having your flatmates onside is one of the best

§

SOLVING SHARE HOUSE ARGUMENTS: THE DUEL.

Sure, it's not done much any more — but think how much cooler you look getting into a duel instead of your everyday pub brawl. So what if somebody gets killed? It's the *image* that counts, remember?

You can get involved in a duel in one of two roles; either as the insulted person, who becomes the challenger, or the insulter, who receives the challenge. Assuming your manhood has been impugned for the final time by that unspeakable boor Jeppeson, from Accounting, you must immediately seek redress, or run the risk of being ostracised as a loathesome coward by your peers. The accepted method of requesting satisfaction from Jeppeson is to remove the glove of your off-hand, and slap him across the cheek with it, once, twice. Cast the soiled glove to the ground at his feet. Remove your other glove, and tuck it into your belt.

As the challenged party, Jeppeson should then lift your glove on the tip of his sword and offer it back to you. Don't put it on again; it's *touched* him, remember? Tuck it into your belt with its mate.

Jeppeson now has the right to nominate the time and place of the duel, and most importantly, the choice of weapons with which you will fight. Gentlemen usually rely on sword or pistol, but duels have been fought with weapons as unlikely and diverse as hurled billiard balls. As ever, restraint is considered mannerly. It is legitimate, of course, for the challenged party to insist on duelling with howitzers from twenty kilometres range, but most unsporting, and likely to disturb the slumber of better gentlemen than either of you, thus provoking still more duels.

At this point, both parties should name their seconds, and decide on a neutral referee. Seconds are good mates who come along to carry the corpses away, and make sure weapons are all in order. It's worth remembering that if for some reason, the principal cannot attend the duel, his second is required to take his place. Your second should be someone you trust. If there's no-one who fits that description, your opponent should be genteel enough to offer you one of his own acquaintances. If neither of you has anyone who will take on the job, maybe you should consider just wrestling in the gutter like the scum you are ...

At least 24 hours should pass between the issuing of the challenge and the duel itself. There are sundry reasons for this, the best being that you should be either putting your affairs in order, or running away to join the French Foreign Legion like the coward you are. In any case, the traditional time for a duel to be held is at dawn, the first full day after the original insult.

Before the duel proper, the referee should examine both weapons to see that they are equal. As the choice of weapon type went to the challenged party, it is the challenger who gets to choose which of the pair of swords or pistols (or billiard balls, or howitzers) he wishes to kill his opponent with. The referee also needs to ascertain that the seconds are willing to act for their principals, and is required to ask the duellers if they're absolutely certain the matter cannot be settled without bloodshed. This is, of course, purely a *pro forma* question. Anyone who wimps out at this stage of the matter may never hold his head up again in the civilised world.

With pistols, it is customary for the duellists to stand back to back, take a measure eleven paces as counted off by the referee, turn and fire on his command. With swords, you just find a clear spot and go for it. Any other weapons, and you work out the logistics for yourself as you go. Remember this: while it is technically acceptable to duel to the first blood only, this option is reserved for loathesome cowards. There is only one kind of duel, and that is, of course, to the death.

§

advantages you can have in the seduction stakes. They're your friends and your allies. Give them the word, and they'll help set the scene, get out of the way at crucial moments, and not stand outside your bedroom door cheering when they hear your shoes hit the floor. (Unless you live with Mr Birmingham of course).

It's important to reciprocate these favours. Give your flatmates space when they're bringing home a hot prospect. Say good things about them to the hot prospect when the flatmate disappears to the toilet. Be nice to girlfriends/boyfriends or whatever. Even if one of your flatmates decides to get it on with an absolute barker – a two-bag monster from the Planet of the Dogs – you are required to behave with as much decency and respect as possible. There may come a time when you are equally desperate.

8 **GET WHILE THE GETTING'S GOOD.** The final word on share housing is this: you may be doing it to save money, but that doesn't mean you have to suffer. When you stop enjoying the place you live in, unless you can fix the problem, it's time to go. Doesn't matter what the reason. If you're particularly happy with any of your flatmates, you can shamelessly attempt to poach them away to a new household somewhere else. Never stay in an unhappy household. If you don't split, sooner or later the atmosphere of doom and gloom will get rid of anyone else in the house with an ounce of brains, and you'll be left holding the bag.

DAMAGE CONTROL: MAINTENANCE, REPAIR, & RECONSTRUCTION.

IT'S A SAD FACT OF life that even though Men are becoming much more intimate with bizarre household cleaning rites than ever before, women are not learning to change lightbulbs, unstop drains, plaster holes in walls, change tap washers, or repair door hinges. Now of course all of us blokes know that we weren't born with a hammer in hand – but women don't seem to know that. Nor do we really want them to know that. So long as the world of home repair and DIY is a mystery to them, we will always have that last, great retreat open to us – the garage, or the toolshed.

That being the case, you are morally obliged as a Man to maintain the deception. If you're genuinely incompetent with all things mechanical, at least by the time you're done with this section, you'll be able to do the vital stuff and pretend like you know how to do the rest of it.

HARDWARE

Hardware is fun. It's probably genetic. There comes a time in every Man's life when he find himself in a hardware store with a warm, dopy smile smoothing out his craggy features. He is home. Home to a hugely complicated sort of area, capable of sucking up enormous sums of money from the overly enthusiastic. If you decide you want to be a serious DIY and home hardware freak, go and get yourself some specialty books on it. What we're concerned with here is making you sufficiently hardware-literate to fool the babes into thinking you're an appropriately Manly sort of man. To that end, we're going to talk you through the Minimalist Home Toolbox. If any of the tools listed here are unfamiliar to you, just head down to your local hardware store and ask to see an example. If you think the hardware guys are sniggering and pointing at the pantywaist who just walked in, you're right.

- **SAWS.** Required for cutting wood, plasterboard, plastics, and light metals. Powered saws are for Serious Hardware Users only – except for a powered jigsaw. If you find you need a jigsaw at all, get the electrical sort. The old kind is practically useless for all practical purposes.
  ABSOLUTE MINIMUM. One standard wood saw, and one hack-saw.

- **HAMMERS.** Required for driving nails, flattening things, breaking stuff, and hitting things you don't like. Also useful for home defence.
  ABSOLUTE MINIMUM. One nice, strong claw-hammer.

- **SPANNERS.** Required for tightening and loosening nuts and bolts.
  ABSOLUTE MINIMUM. Three shifting spanners, small, medium and large.
  BETTER. Two sets of spanners, one metric and one imperial. One end of each spanner open crescent-shaped, the other closed-circle shaped.

- **MEASURING IMPLEMENTS.** Needed for figuring lengths and angles.
  ABSOLUTE MINIMUM. 5m tape measure, 50cm steel ruler, carpenter's square.

- **SCREWDRIVERS.** Necessary for emplacing and removing screws.
  ABSOLUTE MINIMUM set of six flat-head screwdrivers; set of six phillips-head; set of allen keys.

- **DRILL.** Vital implement for putting holes in things. Can also be used as a powered screwdriver.

ABSOLUTE MINIMUM. Don't screw around with anything that hasn't got an electric motor in it. What you want is a 9-volt rechargeable cordless drill, with keyless chuck and range of wood-bits. Buy some of those attachments that let it drive screws, too.

- **CROWBAR.** For prying things apart.
  ABSOLUTE MINIMUM. High-tensile steel clawed s-bar, approx 1m total length.

- **CHISELS.** Needed for gouging chunks out of wood to make nifty joins, and disguise klutzy carpentry.
  ABSOLUTE MINIMUM. Three different-sized flat head chisels, with the steel cores so you can hit 'em with your hammer.

- **PLIERS.** For gripping, holding, and bending.
  ABSOLUTE MINIMUM. One pair long-nose, one good solid standard pair with wire-cutter, and one decent-sized multigrip pliers.

- **SANDING BLOCK.** Needed for support of sandpaper. Sandpaper smooths things up.
  ABSOLUTE MINIMUM. Your basic wooden block about the size of a blackboard duster, plus half a dozen different grades of sandpaper.

With this basic set of tools, you'll be able to answer pretty much every household requirement. You'll be able to build a set of shelves, for example, or hang pictures, replace hinges, and fix sticking doors or windows. You're certainly not going to be a master of DIY Ninja Carpentry, but at least you won't look like an utter wally.

By the way: you will also need a decent toolbox to keep all these goodies in, and a workspace, with a decent bench. Go and commandeer the garage right now!

THE 9 LABOURS OF HERCULES

1) Dripping tap

Probable cause: Worn washer on the jumper valve.
Solution: Change the washer.
Tools needed: Adjustable spanner – or none at all.

PROCEDURE. FIRST, FIND THE MASTER TAP AND TURN OFF THE WATER SUPPLY! The master tap is usually out in the front yard, next to the water meter. If you're a resident of a block of flats which shares one master tap, it's polite to tell your neighbours that you're about to mess with their water supply.

Next, unscrew the little decorative doohickey on the top of the tap-handle. This may require an adjustable spanner, or a pair of pliers. Once you've done this, you can take the handle off, and get at the mechanism below. You'll find that it's a generally cylindrical assembly, and at the very bottom of it all is a nylon washer. This is your culprit. Remove it, take it straight to your nearest hardware store, and buy a replacement of the same type. In fact, buy a whole bunch of them.

Come home again. Put the new washer in the place of the old, and replace the mechanism. Put the little decorative doohickey back in place, turn the tap carefully to the 'off' position, and turn on the water supply again.

2) Dribbly toilet

Probable cause: Worn washer in the cistern.
Solution: Change the washer.
Tools needed: None.

PROCEDURE. There's usually a flow-control tap outside the toilet cistern. Turn it off completely. Now unscrew the flush button, and lift off the cistern lid. You'll see a large float on a lever arm. The lever is supposed to drive a washer, at the bottom of a long, skinny, cylindrical assembly, flush into the intake, cutting off the water supply.

Pull out the skinny cylindrical affair, remove the washer from the bottom, and proceed exactly as above. NB: Fixing a dud toilet is almost as impressive to Woman as a mastery of Italian cooking.

3) SHITTY TV RECEPTION

Probable cause: No outdoor aerial.
Solution: Install aerial on roof.
Tools needed: Drill, screwdriver, ladder, silicone sealant.

PROCEDURE. Buy a nice combination VHF/UHF aerial from somewhere like K-Mart or Chandlers. Pick a place on the side of your residence, preferably near the TV set, and away from power lines, trees, and obstructions. You'll probably be able to get away with a 5m 16-gauge mast for your aerial, which will only require the two mounting brackets supplied by the manufacturer – but if your aerial itself is more than 5m from its upper mounting bracket, you'll need to add three steel-cable guy wires to the rig to hold it steady.

Follow the manufacturer's instructions for mounting the aerial. Now run a coaxial aerial wire through the nearest convenient window to the TV. Turn it on, connect it up, and get somebody to sit inside watching television while you stay on the roof and rotate the aerial until you get the clearest possible signal. Use silicone sealant around all screws which enter the exterior of the house. You may want to drill clever holes in the wall to conceal the aerial wire – but you certainly don't have to. If you do so, make sure that you leave about 15cm of aerial wire hanging down in a loop below the entry point to the wall, to prevent rainwater dripping into the wall by way of the wire.

If you're using your aerial to pick up more than one signal type (VHF, UHF and/or FM) you'll need to get a *signal splitter* from Tandy or Dick Smith. This is a little black box. The wire from the aerial goes in at one end, and out the other you run a separate aerial wire for each signal. These separate wires are connected to the appropriate aerial screws on your TV and/or radio.

To protect against lightning, it's a good idea to install a static discharger – also available from any electronics supplier. Connect a copper wire to the mast of the aerial, run it down with the aerial wire to the discharger, then earth the copper wire.

4) SINGLE LIGHT FAILS TO COME ON

Probable cause: Bulb trouble.
Solution: Replace the bulb.
Tools needed: Hands only.

PROCEDURE. Look, anyone can change a standard Tom Edison-type incandescent bulb. They're designed that way. Wrap it in a tea-towel, push it gently but firmly into the socket until you feel it move very slightly, then give it a quarter turn counter-clockwise, and it should pop right out. Screw-fitting bulbs are even easier. Older bulbs may be 'frozen' into position. Turn off the power, and give them a quick spray with something like WD-40. They should free up after a couple of minutes.

Fluoro bulbs are trickier. If the bulb fails to light, or flickers epileptically, give it a bit of a twist back and forth to make sure it's properly seated. If that doesn't do the trick, turn off the power, give the tube a quarter turn towards you, and gently pull it out. Bent tube pins can be carefully straightened with pliers. Try spraying the socket and the pins with electric contact cleaner. Tighten all the socket screws.

Now line up the pins with the socket slots, push the tube into place and give it a quarter turn away from you. Still no luck? Replace the tube, using the original as a model. If that doesn't help, pull out the little cylindrical starter, and replace it with one of the same wattage and type. If you're still without light, it's time to call an electrician.

One point, though: most fluoro lights won't work below 10 degrees Celsius.

5) HOLE IN A PLASTER-BOARD WALL

Probable cause: clumsy or stupid householder.
Solution: Install a plaster patch.
Tools needed: fishing line, light cardboard, paint-scraper, commercial plaster-mix, strong glue, sandpaper, sharp, strong knife.

PROCEDURE. First, use the knife to clean up the hole into a nice, regular shape with sharp edges. Next, cut a piece of light cardboard slightly larger all round than the hole in the plasterboard. Put two pinholes in the middle, about 4cm apart. Cut off a 40cm chunk of fishing line. Run it in through one pinhole, back out through the other, and tie the two ends into a loop.

Put a layer of glue around the edges of the cardboard, and another layer around the hole in the plasterboard, on the inside. Then fold up the cardboard, slip it into the hole, and unfold it again. Use the loop of fishing line to pull it tight against the hole, so the glue on the cardboard matches the glue you put inside the plasterboard. Tie the loop of fishing line to something, to keep the cardboard in place until the glue dries.

When the glue has set, follow the manufacturer's instructions and mix up a batch of plaster. Use the paint-scraper to smear it into the hole, which is now 'backed' by the sheet of glued cardboard. Fill the hole completely, and trowel the plaster as smooth as you can, using a gentle, upwards motion of the paint-scraper. It is better to slightly overfill the hole if you can, as there will be a certain amount of 'sag' in the plaster before it sets hard.

Once the plaster has set properly, use fine sandpaper to bring it back to the level of the rest of the wall.

6) BROKEN WINDOW

Probable cause: Indoor Test Cricket.
Solution: Replace the pane.
Tools needed: Sharp, strong knife, tape measure, glazier's putty.

PROCEDURE. If you're dealing with one of the modern, aluminium-framed windows, you're better off just calling a glazier. However, if you've got one of the old-style wooden-framed windows, it's cheaper and easier to do the job yourself.

First, remove all remaining glass from the window frame. Wear heavy leather gloves while doing this.

Next, use your knife to chip away all the old window putty from the wooden frame. When you have done that, you can accurately measure the dimensions of the window frame, so that you can order a replacement pane. Window glass is usually 3mm to 5mm in thickness.

When you have the replacement pane, gently slip it into place, and use a small amount of glazier's putty around all the edges to anchor it in position. Glazier's putty dries like rock, but until it has set, you'll need to support the window in its place. Duct tape will usually do the job quite nicely.

7) SQUEAKY FLOORBOARD

Probable cause: board is loose. May have warped with time.
Solution: Bang in a couple of extra nails.
Tools needed: Hammer, nails, drill with very fine bit.

PROCEDURE. Driving a nail isn't quite that simple. If you're worried about splitting the board (nailing near the edge) you should drill a fine pilot hole for the nail to travel down. Or just blunt the point slightly by tapping it against some concrete. Blunt nails don't split wood nearly so well.

Now hold the nail between your thumb and index finger, perpendicular to the board, and give it a sharp tap with the hammer to set it into the wood. Make it a good, sharp rap. Once it's set, then you can start giving it a really good belt. Hammer carefully, and if the nail bends, yank it out and start again. If you're dealing with nice, polished floorboards, don't whack the nail all the way down with the hammer. Drive it until it's about 4mm above the floor surface, and finish the job with a nail-punch.

8) Ugly graffiti on walls

Probable cause: Angst, drunkenness, Nikko pens.
Solution: Repaint the wall.
Tools needed: Paint scraper, spackle, sandpaper, primer, stain-sealant, dropcloths, masking tape, roller, roller-tray, paintbrushes, latex wall paint of appropriate colour.

Procedure. First, scrape off all loose paint using a paint scraper. Be thorough. Use the spackle to fill in holes and cracks. Now sand the hell out of any rough surfaces. Slap some primer over any sanded spots; it will save you two coats of paint later. Use the stain-sealant to paint over any water-marked or stained areas (like the graffiti, stupid). Dust down everything in sight, and use masking tape on all window sashes, door lintels, and trim. Lay out dropcloths to protect the floor and furniture. Now you can start painting.

Start from the top. Use a brush to paint a strip around the ceiling. Likewise around the doors and windows. Load the roller with paint, taking care not to overload it. Work in small patches, using a zig-zag motion. Once you have a patch of paint on the wall, start new roller-loads in the dry area, and work towards the painted patch. This keeps the paint at a fairly even thickness.

Wash out your brushes and rollers immediately after use. Latex paint washes off with water, fortunately.

9) Sticking door

Probable cause: Wet weather causes either the door or the frame to expand, so that it no longer opens or closes properly.
Solution: Clean up the area that sticks.
Tools needed: Hopefully, just sandpaper. May need a plane if things are really bad.

PROCEDURE. Examine the door carefully, opening it and closing it until you've identified the area which sticks. Grab your sanding paper and sandblock, and see if you can't take a millimetre or so of wood off the door. (Not the frame. It works better if you do it this way.) Hopefully, this will fix your

§

EASY HOME EXPLOSIONS

The following two recipes are unsafe, unsound, and reasonably likely to cause nasty accidents. On the other hand, they're also enormous fun, and positively guaranteed to enliven even the most boring of parties or meetings. Make up your own mind.

• YOUR OWN SMOKEBOMBS

You need: 200g sugar + 200g potassium nitrate (from a chemical supplier).

Dissolve the sugar and the nitrate in about half a litre of water, in a cheap saucepan. Over a medium heat, boil the mixture until you're left with a thick, waxy precipitate, usually a gooey yellow in colour. Wait for it to turn that yellowish colour. If it's still white, there's too much water in it, and it won't burn evenly.

Once you've got that yellow colour happening, scrape the stuff out of the pot and spread it out to cool on some alfoil. When it's bearably warm to the touch, roll it into long cylinders no more than 1cm thick. That's really important. If your smokebomb mix is too physically thick, it gets too hot when it's burning, and moves to a kind of secondstage burn with really enormous heat and not a lot of smoke.

A thumb-sized cylinder of this stuff will absolutely fill a small room with smoke at a startling rate. It's easiest to ignite with something like a cigarette. A bloke I know sticks chunks of sparklers into them while they're still waxy (they set hard when they cool completely) and uses the sparkler as a fuse. One warning: this stuff gives off a lot of heat when it burns. If you set it down on something flammable, it's your own look-out.

problem. If it doesn't, then you need to get a little more drastic. Borrow a plane. Try to shave the door down while it's still on its hinges; that way, you can test the fit as you go. Only if the bottom of the door is the problem will you really need to take the door off its hinges.

• HOME HINDENBURG DISASTERS

You need: A jar of Caustic Soda from the supermarket, a packet of round balloons (only round ones will do) a roll of aluminium foil, and a nice thick glass bottle.

Dissolve about half a cup of caustic soda in a litre or so of water and pour the mix into your thick glass bottle. Rip off a square of aluminium foil about 30cm by 30cm. Make it into three strips, and roll each of these strips into a rough cylinder. Now toss the cylinders into the bottle, and quickly stretch the neck of a round balloon over the bottle's mouth.

The caustic soda solution will now dissolve the aluminium, and release rather a lot of hydrogen in the process. This hydrogen will be trapped in your balloon, which is where you want it.

After a few minutes, all the aluminium will be gone. You'll know because the fizzing will have stopped, and the balloon will no longer be inflating. If you carefully take your balloon off the bottle now, and tie it off, it should rise to the ceiling. This is because hydrogen is considerably lighter than air.

Hydrogen is also extremely flammable. If you can tie a bit of soft woolly string into the knot of the balloon, you'll have a pretty good fuse. Take the balloon outside. Light the fuse. Watch the balloon rise until the flame burns through the skin and the hydrogen explodes with a dull 'whoof!' and a flash of yellow light. Scream 'Oh, the humanity!' and rush inside to make another one.

You know, it suddenly occurs to me that perhaps portions of my youth have *indeed* been mis-spent ...

§

COMMON HOUSEHOLD DISASTERS: IDENTIFICATION AND ELIMINATION

• **LIGHTS DON'T COME ON.** Did you pay the power bill? Assuming you did, there may have been a local power outage. Put your head round the corner and see if the neighbouring houses have electricity. If they do, check your fuse-box. (It will be on the exterior of your residence, somewhere that the meter-reader can get at it.) Check to see if the circuit-breaker switches are all in the 'on' position. If any of them are set to 'off', at least you know what happened. Go back through the house, turning off everything you can find. Then reset the switch, and see if you can work out what the hell you overloaded.

If it ain't the circuit-breakers, and the fuses are intact, and everyone else in the neighbourhood has electricity, turn your master switch off and contact an electrician immediately.

• **FREEZER COMPARTMENT RESEMBLES ANTARCTICA.** Well, you should have defrosted it, shouldn't you? Empty the fridge. Turn it off. Mop up the overflow as the ice melts. Refill and restart your fridge. Next time, pay more attention.

• **CLOTHING COMES OUT OF THE WASHING MACHINE SMELLING VILE** Clothing was left in the washing machine after the cycle finished. Wash the clothing again. This time, instead of detergent, throw in a handful of baking soda. And hang the clothing up immediately when it's done you lazy little prick.

• **DRAINS REFUSE TO EMPTY THE SINK. OR THE BATHTUB.** First, check that the plug-hole isn't blocked with something horrid. In the bathroom, that will always be hair. Especially if there are women in the house. Women have a remarkable talent for shedding tonnes of hair without ever going bald, and it all winds up in the drain of the shower. (Except for the stuff which wraps itself around dust and mintie papers in the lounge room, so that your vacuum cleaner gums itself up).

If the plughole is clear, you have a problem. Bail out the sink. Get one of those plunger-things that Wile E. Coyote was always shooting at the roadrunner. Clap the slurpy end over the drain, and schlock it up and down for all you're worth. With luck, this will get things moving. After that, you should mix up a nice, strong solution of either Draino, or caustic soda, and pour it down the drain. That should fix things. (*Read the instructions carefully*. Both Draino and caustic soda are very, very exciting chemical compounds which can cause no end of grief if you mess around with them.)

• **FIRES.** There are three kinds of fire. Plain, simple wood-and-paper type fires, which can happen anywhere; oil fires, which generally happen in the kitchen, and electrical fires, which (obviously) need something electrical to get going. The thing to remember is that ONLY THE FIRST fires want water. Water is very good at eliminating the kind of fire you get when the candle gets knocked over onto the bedsheets while you're too busy to notice. Oil fires, however, need different treatment. Oil floats on water, remember? If you throw water on an oil fire – supposing, for example, you turn your back on the wok and it bursts into flame – all you will succeed in doing is spreading and scattering the fire over a much wider area. If you are confronted with a (small!) oil fire, you must SMOTHER it. Throw a damp cloth over it. Put the lid on the wok. Grab a sheet, a towel, or a blanket and keep the oxygen away!

Electrical fires are one step up in the nasty stakes. If any of your appliances should begin spitting out sparks and smoke, don't throw water on it. Chances are you'll blow the power supply to the whole residence ... if you're lucky. And don't try to smother it with a cloth: the electric current is providing a heat source which may well eventually ignite your woolly blanket. No, what you do is find that fuse-box, and throw ALL the circuit-breaker switches to the off position. Next, smother any residual fire. Finally, unplug the appliance and throw it away. Don't try to plug something else into that particular outlet; it may not have been the appliance which was the source of your troubles. Owning a good multi-purpose fire extinguisher is also a useful idea. The yellow ones are okay for all kinds of fire.

• **REALLY BIG FIRES.** Get out of the residence. In areas of dense smoke, get down as low as you can, and crawl to the nearest exit. Before opening any door, touch it with the back of your hand. If the door (especially the handle, if it's one of those metal kinds that goes right through the door) is hot to the touch, back up and find another way out. It's a good idea to keep all your most important papers and documents (passports, birth certificates, investment records, chequebooks and the like) in a single, easily-grabbed bag or briefcase. Keep them close at hand, in your bedroom. Trust us on this one: if it comes down to it, having those few things survive the fire with you will make your life about a hundred thousand times less difficult than it might otherwise be.

• **COCKROACHES.** The big glossy brown ones (*Periplaneta americana* and *P. australasiae*) as often as not fly in from outdoors. Spray the ones you see with a pyrethrin household spray. Lay baits in likely areas, such as kitchen cupboards. If you make sure nobody leaves food scraps around the house, it shouldn't be too difficult to pretty much eliminate these blokes with this treatment.

The wee tan bastards are a real problem, though. They live and breed indoors, big-time. These days, spraying the little buggers just makes them high; they love it. If you've got a real problem with the little tan roaches (*Blatella germanica*) you might want to think about simply moving to a new residence. However, if you must deal with them, try the following.

The only time to do a general spray for roaches is during winter. Do it during summer, and the survivors breed back in no time, bigger and friskier than before. If you do it in winter, though, when their numbers are down, chances are good you'll knock them back for a year or more. Go to the supermarket and buy yourself one bug-bomb per room of the house. Make sure you get one for the crawlspace in the ceiling as well.

Open all cupboards. Pull everything out and lay it in the open. Close all windows and doors. Put one bug-bomb on the floor of the middle of each room, with a couple of sheets of newspaper spread under it. Trigger the bombs, and get out of the house for at least 36 hours.

When you come back, lay roach baits in every area you've ever seen the little bastards. Do an extra spray-job behind any kitchen cupboards, under the stove, and behind the hot-water system. If you follow these rules exactly, your future children will have two heads but you'll be as clear of the roaches as if you'd called in the professionals.

NOTE: Should you discover you have a brutal roach infestation during summer, fight a holding action until the temperature drops and they die off. Then hit them hard, as above.

• **MICE AND RATS.** You'll know they're around by the nibbled food and by their droppings. Keep an eye open, and see if you can't find where they're coming into the house. Then buy a whole bunch of traps. Cheese and peanut paste make an excellent bait for both mice and rats. Lay your traps in the areas the creatures frequent. Move the traps regularly, and don't expect to get too many catches in the same spot. They may be small, but they're not completely stupid.

When you've stopped getting anything in your traps, seal up any entrance holes you've found. Keep your kitchen and household absolutely free of foodscraps, and store all food in sealed containers. Lay baits in likely areas around the kitchen, taking care to put them out of reach of Fido, Pussykins or Junior. They don't much like Ratsak either ...

CHAPTER ELEVEN

Do Ya Wanna Live Forever?

WELL, YES, ACTUALLY. DON'T WE all? Death looks like the most boring proposition in the universe. Worse still, when you finally accept the invitation, you don't get to change your mind if you don't like it.

Science is making impressive strides in the direction of life extension. Cloning, for example. There's an interesting way of coming up with perfectly immunotyped transplant organs, eh? Bit rough on the clone, of course, but if you just grow one without any real brain to speak of, nobody suffers, right?

Then there's high, or Human Growth Hormone. Careful studies with this one seem to show that it can tip the metabolic balance back away from slow decay (where it's been ever since you were about 21) towards growth and renewal again, at least to a limited extent. And what about recent research in the role of telomerase in extending cell lifespans by up to forty percent? Translate that into a functional therapy, and you're suggesting that most of us should live to see our hundredth birthday.

There's a problem, though. It's called overpopulation. In the real world, these treatments will be developed, and they will be banned for reasons of 'ethics'. They will then become illegally available to rich bastards all over the world, and people like Mr Gates, Mr Packer and Mr Murdoch will be able to go on rogering us all senseless for another fifty years past their reasonable span.

Therefore, if you want to have a shot at living forever, you're going to have to become a Rich Bastard. Not only that, but since that's going to take some time, you're going to have to ensure to remain healthy until then. And here's the way to do it:

THE SINGLE MOST LIFE-PROLONGING DECISION YOU CAN MAKE

No prizes for guessing this one; it's a no-brainer. *Quit smoking*. Of the top ten medical killers of Men (non-accident related, that is), six are smoking-associated problems. These include heart disease and heart attack, hypertension, stroke, diabetes, emphysema, and lung cancer.

The damage done to your lungs by a pack-a-day habit is intuitive and obvious. Tobacco smoke is laced with all kinds of nasties, including tar, cyanide, carbon monoxide, sulphur dioxide, and a host of less pronounceable chemical irritants. Lungs are delicate, spongy bits of tissue that do all of your oxygen intake duties. Dump shit like that into them on a regular basis, and it's no wonder they pack it in.

The circulatory system stuff is a little less easy to understand on the surface, but it's simple to explain. Nicotine does a couple of things to you. Firstly, it's a stimulant, a bit of an upper. It gets your heart thumping and the blood pumping. On top of that, though, it's also what's called a *vaso-constrictor* – that is, it causes your blood vessels to contract. So suddenly, your heart is working harder, and at the same time, the blood is being pumped round in a tighter space ... bingo! Instant blood pressure surge. This is Not A Good Thing.

STEP ONE IN THE PLAN TO LIVE FOREVER: Throw the cigarettes away. Take the money you were spending and invest it somewhere.

OKAY, THE FAGS ARE GONE. NOW WHAT?

Step two on the road to immortality is getting your heart and circulatory system into condition. Heart disease is still the number one non-accident killer of men. Fixing this one is complicated. It needs attention from several directions.

• BOOZE. Heavy drinking is bad. Really bad. Binge drinking is even worse, so goodbye to Saturday nights with the lads down the pub. On the other hand, there's a growing body of evidence which suggests that teeto-tallers don't have it all their no-fun, fucked-up, anally retentive way. Apparently, two to three standard drinks taken on a daily basis significantly reduce the incidence of heart disease in Men. Better still, if you can make those standard drinks glasses of strong red wine, you gain an even greater protective effect. The jury's still out as to exactly what the cause could be, but candidates include a wide range of anti-oxidants found in red wines, and a couple of weird pseudo-vitamins that crop up in grape skins. Maybe it's just because it makes you feel good.

• GENERAL FITNESS. A fit, healthy frame includes a fit, healthy cardiovascular system. The simple rule is plenty of aerobic exercise, good nutrition, and good sleep.

• DIET. Saturated fats and Bad Cholesterol are Kryptonite to your potential Superman. Junk food is a vicious plot by the moneyed ruling classes to fatten up and kill the proles.

WHAT YOUR DIET OUGHT TO BE

Think back to school, or better yet, the last time you were in a doctor's waiting room. Remember that big poster on the wall, with all the pictures of fruit and vegetables and rice, and that pyramid-shaped thing next to them? They put it up there for a reason. The majority of your diet should not consist of grease, McBurgers, fried chicken and beer.

There are five groups of things you need from your food. These are carbohydrates, fats, proteins, vitamins and minerals. There's somewhere between forty and fifty different substances which you must have in your diet to sustain life, but they all boil down to being one of these.

- **CARBOHYDRATES.** These you get mostly from grains and cereals, as well as from things like potatoes. Starch is a carbohydrate. Carbohydrates are the major source of energy for your metabolism, as they are very easily converted to glucose. (You should think of glucose in your body as being something like petrol in a car.) Whole grains and cereals are better for you than potatoes and pasta, but in general, this is the stuff that should comprise most of your dietary energy intake. It's the bottom step, the broadest part of the food pyramid. Careful with the sugar, though. It's a carbohydrate too, but it is readily converted to fat, and Fat Is The Enemy.
- **MMMMMM, FATS.** These are long, complex molecules that store a whopping great amount of energy. Your own body produces fats to store energy. You've evolved to do exactly that, back from the days when meals were few and far between, and it made sense to eat up big when the food was there. For this reason, fats are also among the tastiest of foods. Pretty much all the stuff you really like to eat is laced with the things – burgers, fries, chocolate, pastries, crunchy snacks, cheese ...

  Problem is, you no longer have the kind of Tarzan lifestyle that requires this sort of energy. So here's your body, with two million years of evolution telling you that Fat Is Good! And there's your 20th century lifestyle, with foods rich in fat available at every hand ... witness the birth of the Love Handles. Or the Spare Tyre. Or even the Michelin Man, depending on how long you let the situation go on.

  What makes fats bad? Lots of things. For one thing, the fatter you are, the harder your poor heart has to work. Also, getting too much fat and cholesterol (which is a kind of fat) into your system leads to fatty, nasty deposits clogging your arteries – which kills you, if you let it go on long enough.

  Of course, you do need some fats. Some of the vitamins are fat-based, for example. And you need fats to produce the sheathing that protects your neural cells. Then there's evidence that some of the more complex oils play all kinds of weird biochemical roles in slowing the aging process. How much do you need? Well, think back to that poster with the pyramid on it. Remember the itty-bitty pointy bit way, way up top? That's it. Bugger-all, really. Most of us consume many, many times the amount of fat we actually need.

  The kinds of fats you ingest are quite important. Saturated fats –

§

How to be Robin Hood

Rule one: stick to sensible bows if you're a beginner. Gigantic, multi-pulleyed complex bows with 200lb draw weights are for deranged pig-hunters, not rank amateurs who want to look like they know something about archery. The bow you want is a 35lb single curve job made out of laminated wood.

The first thing to do is string the bow. If you can't string it, you can't fire it, and that's all there is to it. The bow is always strung in the opposite direction you think, on the side *away* from the natural curve of the wood. That's how it puts tension on the bow proper, you see.

Slip one loop of the bowstring over the end of the bow until the loop settles neatly onto the notches. Now tuck the curved end of the bow under the inside of your left instep, and tilt the upper end to your left. Keeping your foot in place, bend your left knee, and push it forward until it leans out across the middle of the bow. Now you can use your left hand to bend the middle of the bow across your knee, while your right hand slips the other end of the bowstring over the top end of the bow. When this loop has settled on the notches as well, relax your grip on the bow, and as the string pulls taut, straighten your knee again.

Now select a target. For a beginner, 25 – 30 metres is a good learning range. Much further than that, and you'll get depressed as you trudge about, looking for the arrows that missed the target. By the way: choose a nice, big open space to shoot in, and don't shoot towards people, cars, buildings, animals, or anything else that might be hurt. You may be

which are generally solid at room temperature, like lard, suet, butter, and the fats in chocolate – are absolutely the worst. Unsaturated vegetable oils, like sunflower oil, peanut oil and olive oil, aren't so bad. You can safely do a little stir-frying with these. The kinds of oils you get from fish, like cod liver oil for example, are positively good for you. Try shooting only 30 metres, but the bow and the arrow don't know that. Even a 35lb bow can send an arrow well over a hundred metres if you're careless.

Put your left shoulder towards the target. Stand facing exactly 90 degrees away from the target proper. Select an arrow, and turn the cock feather outwards. (The 'cock feather' is the differently coloured one. Facing it away from the bow helps the arrow sit properly.) Hold the bow in your left hand, by the grip in the middle, and place the shaft of the arrow on the rest, on the left-hand side of the bow. Slide the shaft forward until you can tuck the reinforced middle of the bowstring into the *nock* or notch in the feathery end of the arrow. Use your left index finger to hold the arrow in position on the bow as you raise your left arm to shoulder height. Hold the bow just shy of arm's length, with the wrist cocked fractionally inwards. If you don't do this, as the string snaps forward on release, you'll lose a big swatch of skin from the inside of your forearm. This is a Bad Thing.

With your right hand, draw on the bowstring, not the arrow. You should use the first two fingers of the hand, with the index finger curled around the string above the nock, and the middle finger curled below the nock. Keeping your body facing 90 degrees away from the target, draw the string back until the nock of the arrow is roughly opposite the point of your jaw, just under your right ear. Hold it steady here. Use your left hand to target the arrow. Now release the string. Don't pluck; let it roll off your fingertips.

It's a lot simpler than it sounds. Half a dozen practice shots, and you'll look smoother than Kevin Costner in leather tights.

§

to eat more fish, especially the oily, cold-water species. Also useful are a few of the weirdball oils from plants like linseed and soya, but as yet, nobody's quite sure of the best way to get them into your diet. Maybe you could eat some of those linseed-soy loaves. We've heard that chicks who eat that stuff put out.

- **PROTEINS.** These super-complicated compounds make up the bulk of muscle and tissue in your body. And in animal bodies in general, of course. Therefore, your sources of food protein are largely meat, eggs, fish and poultry. You've got to get protein to build your own muscle mass, of course, but also, proteins do almost all the really complex and tricky jobs in your metabolism. Hormones are proteins. So are enzymes. Most of the transmitter substances are proteins of one sort or another.

  You don't assimilate proteins straight up when you gobble down a rib eye fillet steak. In fact, you break them down and digest them, and turn them into their basic building blocks, called *amino acids*. There's about 20 of these amino acids that you actually use, but only eight that your body can't synthesise for itself. These are known as the essential amino acids, and the bad news for vegetarians is, it's damned difficult to get enough of all eight of these on an all-leaf diet you losers.

  So how much protein do you need? Not a lot. On our food pyramid, meats and poultry fall just below the fats, which are the topmost step, remember? And if you insist on vegetarianism, you can get most of your protein requirements from nuts, legumes, pulses and mushrooms. But it's not nearly as much fun as *killing* things.

- **VITAMINS.** These are a mixed bag of chemicals that do small but vital jobs all over your biochemistry. They are divided into fat-soluble vitamins (A, D, E and K) and water-soluble (C and all the various B vitamins). The fat-soluble vitamins are usually taken up with foods which contain fat, and if you get more than you need, the excess is stored in your own body fat, in your liver, and your kidneys.

  The water-soluble vitamins are a different matter. You can't store these, so you need to make sure you get them into you on a daily basis. Of course, in the affluent Western countries, vitamin supplements are available to anyone with a few bucks, and most processed foods have lots of vitamins added so that their manufacturers can claim they're 'nutritious'.

  Vitamins are best aquired from fresh fruit and vegetables, not expensive vitamin supplements. A quick breakdown of what vitamins do for you and where you get them looks like this

  - **VITAMIN A.** Acquired from eating liver, carrots, pumpkin. Important for skin and vision.
  - **VITAMIN B COMPLEX.** Obtained from yeast and liver. Important metabolic activators, prevent beri-beri and pellagra.
  - **VITAMIN C.** Found in fruit – especially citrus fruit. Important in the immune system, and connective tissues. Lack of Vitamin C causes scurvy.

- **VITAMIN D.** Acquired from exposure to sunlight. Helps regulate metabolism of phosphorous and calcium, vital to bone growth.
- **VITAMIN E.** Found in seed oils and wheat germ. Plays a role in skin, and possibly sex drive.
- **VITAMIN K.** Acquired from leafy green vegetables. Needed to allow coagulation of blood.

For a normal, even vaguely healthy person, vitamin supplements shouldn't be necessary if a reasonable diet is eaten. They may be of some value during periods of illness, or periods of intense activity. Maybe.

- **MINERALS.** These are inorganic nutrients that play a wide variety of roles in your body. Calcium for example, and phosphorous, both of which you get from dairy products, are necessary for your teeth and bones. Potassium, magnesium, and sodium (bananas, green vegetables and salt respectively) pretty much regulate your electro-chemistry. Iron you get most readily from meat. It forms the red pigment in your blood – haemaglobin – which actually carries oxygen around your body. Zinc crops up in seafood. You need it for your immune system, and in Men especially for the sexual function. Iodine (sea salt) is needed for thyroid hormones, which largely control your overall metabolic rate. There's a bunch of other trace elements needed, but nobody's quite certain what they do, or how they do it. We do know, though, that if you don't get them, you die.

The best source for minerals (except iron) and water-soluble vitamins are fruits and vegetables. Preferably taken raw, or at least, minimally cooked.

So: there, in one fell swoop, are your five nutrient types, as contained within the four main food groups – meats, fruit and vegetables, cereals and tubers, and fats. With this information, it's easy to plan a healthy diet. Just remember the proportions: at least half of what you eat should be cereals, grains and complex carbohydrates. A quarter to a third should be vegetables and fruit. Then about a sixth should be meats, eggs, proteins and low-fat dairy products, and only a tiny amount of fats and oils should go down your neck at all. That probably doesn't add up ... but if you call the rest fibre and roughage, to keep your bowels in action, you'd be pretty close.

Aside from the thing about not smoking, which is really just a step back from the Dark Side, changing your diet is the first good habit you need to develop on the road to living forever. The difference it will make to your overall health has to be experienced to be believed.

So what does a good, healthy meal look like? How about a plate of steamed jasmine rice, with a bowlful of lightly stir-fried vegetables and chilli, with a just a palmful of stir-fried chicken and cashews under a light oyster sauce? See? The good stuff doesn't have to taste like cardboard and batshit.

One final note on diet: of all the research done on the effects of diet on life expectancy, the most reliable and reproducible results can be stated very simply. Eat less. A whole lot less. Not just enough to lose weight. Get your food intake down to the bare minimum you need for sustenance and daily activities. In rats and other lab animals, this kind of food intake increases life expectancy by anywhere up to 20%. For a human, that's something like fifteen years. (Mr Birmingham demurs on this point, preferring not to live like an aged lab rat.)

HOW TO KEEP YOUR HEART PUMPING

AEROBIC EXERCISE

That's the key to getting your heart started, your arteries clean, and your blood pressure down. It won't do much for building muscle on you, but that's a different matter anyway.

Aerobic exercise doesn't mean wiggling into a leotard and legwarmers, then heading down to the local gym to bounce around the floor all morning. 'Aerobic' refers to working within your oxygen-carrying capacity.

Y'see, muscles do their job in two ways. Under conditions of moderate stress, your heart can pick up its rate and pump enough blood to the muscles to keep up with their oxygen demands. The muscles burn glucose, produce carbon dioxide, and you can keep going for quite a while. This is aerobic exercise. Keep it up for at least twenty minutes, your body runs out of stored glucose and starts converting fats ... which is exactly what you want it to be doing.

Under conditions of greater stress, such as in a quick sprint, or when lifting colossal weights, your body simply can't get enough oxygen to the muscles in time. It's no problem, though. Your muscles switch to a different metabolic pathway to produce energy, one which requires much less oxygen, but produces lactic acid (that 'burning' feeling you get in the muscles from heavy exercise is lactic acid buildup). This form of exercise, while it may help you build muscle, does *not* contribute much at all to either fat burning, or cardiovascular fitness.

The idea is to get your heart-rate up. For most relatively healthy, youngish men, you want to just about double the normal resting rate of 72 beats per minute. Good ways to do that include rowing, skipping rope, and swimming. Not so good ways include jogging and boxing, which certainly raise the heart rate, but can do you a deal of damage in the meantime. Lifting really heavy weights probably won't do it for you at all; you'll add muscle mass, but you won't burn fat or improve your cardiovascular fitness.

So, grab yourself a skipping rope. Half an hour a day, five days a week. Get plenty of bounce into your skipping, and make sure your heart rate goes up. And that's it!

Mind you, if you really want to go crazy-fit and maybe build up all those muscles as well, you'll want to go to a gym and get yourself a professionally assessed workout programme. On the other hand, if you're just doing this to impress the babes, don't get too worked up. It's only a small fraction of women that really go for the muscle-boy look. Most of them are happy if you're just reasonably fit. In fact, the hardbody musclebound look is a lot more 'in' for the gay community than for the straights ...

SECRET MEN'S BUSINESS: FOUR THINGS EVERY MAN SHOULD KNOW ABOUT HIMSELF.

ON THE WHOLE, MEN'S HEALTH and women's health are pretty closely allied. We're both human, right? (Well, probably, anyway.) Of course, we don't have all those plumbing problems they've got; and apparently there's only ever been one man who died of breast cancer – but there are a couple of things that go wrong with men that can't and don't go wrong for women.

1) MEN SHOULDN'T GET FAT. Okay, being bloated and obese is no good for anybody – but women are more likely to survive it than men. The key is in the *way* the two sexes get fat. Women are meant to carry a little fat, biologically speaking. After all, they're supposed to be walking food repositories for the next generation of Homo saps, right? They've got to store all that nutritious goodness somewhere, don't they? End result is that women tend to deposit fat around their arses and thighs, and just under their skin – in places where it doesn't do them a whole lot of harm.

Men, on the other hand, are meant to be dynamic Tarzanoid hunter-gatherers, who spend all day out there on the plains beating the snot out of mammoths and digging up gigantic tubers from the hard African soil. They're not supposed to be sitting around on their butts in front of computer screens. End result? When men pile on the blubber, it builds up around their bellies, and in their body cavities around the organs. That, apparently, is a bad thing. The upshot of it all is this: a woman carrying an extra ten kilos looks lush and ripe, and really isn't in particularly bad shape. A man carrying an extra ten kilos is flabby, and his body is under unnecessary stress. Stay thin if you want to live longer.

2) **PROSTRATE WITH THE PROSTATE.** Right, lads – the other area where we differ notably from women is of course, at the juncture of the thighs. Men's sex organs hang out in the breeze, rather than hiding discreetly away in the vicinity of the kidneys, and there are in fact a number of things that can go wrong in this department that you should consider being concerned about.

First, lets consider the key players in the system, and how they work together. Let's take it for granted that you know where to find your own scrotum, and are aware of the fact that it contains two testicles which really don't enjoy being knocked about. Likewise, you probably know how to locate your penis, that it acts as a conduit to the outer world for used beer which would otherwise bloat you up like a giant waterbed. You may even be aware that on occasion (okay – practically all the time) it rises up like a short pink steel fire hydrant, and in that condition can be used to great effect with members of the opposite sex. (Or your own, should you be thusly inclined. Or even with sheep, should you be from a neighbouring island nation which will remain nameless.) However, are you aware of the silent partner in the Holy Gooly Trinity?

We are, of course, referring to Mr Prostate Gland. This little devil is a vital part of the system, and proper functioning of the prostate is important to proper bladder control and normal bedroom calisthenics.

So, where the hell does Mr Prostate Gland get his mail delivered?

Mr Prostate Gland is a solid organ found immediately below your bladder. It surrounds the *urethra*, which is the tube connecting the bladder and the penis through which that aforementioned used beer is jettisoned. The normal prostate in a young adult man is about the size of a walnut. However, its size can change over time, and in many men the prostate gets larger as we get older, particularly once a man gets over the age of 40 or 50 years. This can affect the ability to urinate, among other things.

The prostate does a couple of important things: one is to help control urination and the other is to help sexual activity. The prostate has a so-called passive role in the process of urination. It helps to control the rate at which urine flows out of the bladder and into the urethra. It does this by the effect of muscle fibres in the prostate that surround the urethra.

The prostate has an active role in sexual activity. The prostate gland makes a whitish glandular secretion which collects within the prostate and is fed into the urethra during ejaculation. This glandular secretion helps the motility of the sperm in the urethra and makes up about a third of the seminal fluid, thus giving seminal fluid its whitish appearance.

The growth of the prostate and control over how it works are essentially based on the levels of the male sex hormone testosterone, which is produced by the testicles. The production of testosterone is itself controlled by another complex set of hormonal interactions. See how it all fits together?

Of course, where it all breaks down is in the heinously commonplace realms of prostate cancer. Lads, here is one of the great prices you pay for being able to stand up to piss: by the time you're seventy, something like eighty percent of you will have prostate trouble of one form or another. Quite a lot of you will have precursors to prostate cancer, and a very decent number of those will have prostate cancer proper. It comes with the territory.

On the plus side, prostate cancer is one of the slowest-moving, least aggressive cancers that there is. Even more weirdly, in most cases, the basic 'seed' of the cancer just sits there, doing nothing. It's usually not even noticed. For most of us, by the time a prostate cancer becomes serious enough to worry about, we've already thrown a massive hearty and gone belly-up from old age. On the minus side, it's a bastard to treat if you do get a case that warrants treatment ...

Nobody is too sure how or why some blokes get prostate cancer and others don't. However, we do know that it runs in families, so if your father or grandfather or uncles on either side of the family cop it, your chances of copping it too are much increased. Race may play a part as well. Japanese men don't get much prostate cancer, relatively speaking. Japanese men living in America seem to get prostate cancer about as often as everybody else, though. And Black American men get more prostate cancer than white Americans. And of course, the older you get, the more likely it is to show up – although cases are known to have occurred in men in their twenties.

Questions of diet and prostate cancer are unresolved. We know that it's clearly linked with your intake of saturated fats, but nobody knows why or how. Best bet is, once again, to stick to a low-fat, healthy diet.

Evidence linking vasectomies to prostate cancer has been shown to be flawed. Basically, more prostate cancer has been found in men who have had vasectomies because proportionately more men who have had vasectomies are concerned enough with their health to turn up regularly and allow their doctor to shove a finger up their butts – which is the standard method of examining a prostate gland, by the way.

It's probably worth knowing how to recognise the commonly accepted list of symptoms which may indicate prostate problems:

- Frequent urination (especially at night)
- Inability to urinate
- Trouble starting to urinate or trouble holding back urination
- Pain during ejaculation
- A weak or interrupted urine flow
- Pain or a burning feeling during urination
- Blood in the semen or in the urine
- Frequent pain/stiffness in the lower back, hips, or upper thighs.

However, you should also know that all of these symptoms are also commonly indicative of any one of a bunch of other problems. Any one of them is worth taking to the doctor, and if you get a number of them, move your appointment up, pronto!

3) **MR WOBBLY DOESN'T WANT TO PLAY TODAY.** Mr Birmingham insisted we put this section in – especially the bit about 'incidents of temporary impotence are perfectly normal and occur to practically all men at some stage in their lives ...' He seemed to think there was a point to make in there somewhere.

Of course, it is perfectly true. Chances are good that at some stage or another, your little purple soldier isn't going to want to come out and fight when you want him to. Don't worry about it, if you can manage that. Give the poor bastard a break, and do something else to entertain your partner. Chances are extremely good that the next time the opportunity comes, he'll don his lavender helmet and stand at attention like a Grenadier Guardsman.

Mind you, if this isn't the case, and your sex life starts to grind to an ugly halt, you might consider seeing a doctor.

A penis becomes erect because somewhere along the line, you got excited and your neurochemical system sent messages to certain receptor sites in the organ. Blood comes charging into the penis, filling a couple of spongy cavities which run down either side of the urethra, and a couple of small muscles lock up the veins which would ordinar-

BIG LOG

Its He-Man Aroma "WOWS" the Ladies!

ily let that blood out again … and bingo! Hydraulics in action: one bona fide boner, ready to go.

It's when that doesn't happen that you're looking at 'impotence'.

Now once upon a time, it was thought that most incidence of impotence was purely psychological, or as a result of encroaching age. Modern medicine has shot that one down in flames, however, and now the thinking is that roughly 85% of impotence has a physical basis – although it's almost never due to damage to the sexual systems proper. Usually, impotence occurs as a result of illness or injury to one of the other body systems, and therefore, keeping yourself in good health is the single best method there is of ensuring that your sex pistol remains loaded and ready for action. (How many more bad penis clichés do you suppose we can work into this text?)

What kinds of thing are likely to cause reduced sexual function? Usually, something to do with your circulatory system. Vascular disease. Diabetes. Hypertension. High cholesterol and arteriosclerosis. Heavy drinking and smoking.

Another possible source of problems is your endocrine – or hormonal – system. (Hormones are chemical messengers which rush around your body keeping things in order.) Low testosterone or low thyroid hormone can result in reduced sexual function.

Where does all this leave you? Relax. Take a visit to your local GP, and place your problem in their capable hands – as it were. These days, physical impotence can be treated with any one of a barrage of different treatments. In fact, it's quite possible for blokes who've had both their testicles and their prostate glands removed to work up a fully functional (well, not for producing children with) hard-on. It just takes a little bit more work. The 21st Century Man should be able to shag his way through the twilight of his life with perfect aplomb ...

4) **THE BEST ADVICE OF ALL: SEE YOUR DOCTOR.** Gentlemen, the sad fact is that one of the biggest medical killers of men is sheer laziness. For most of us, the only reason to see a doctor is to score a medical certificate so we can get Grand Final day off work. We don't go to regular physicals. We don't take our medication properly. And most importantly, we don't pay attention to the little warning lights on the control panel.

Men are supposed to be 'men', you see. A little pain, a little recurring dysfunction – who gives a rat's? Why go to the quack, anyhow? They're only going to tell you to knock back a couple of aspro and go to bed anyway, right? Go and see the bastard when you've got something *serious* to complain about.

Unfortunately, it doesn't work that way. There are many diseases and dysfunctions which can be dealt with quite easily – if they're caught early enough. If you wait until the symptoms are loud and clear before reluctantly dragging yourself to see the doctor, you've got no call to complain when they tell you that you've passed your use-by date and you're on your way out. That is not the way to live forever, friends.

Regular physical examinations, that's the ticket. Pay attention to the doctor's advice when they offer it. Ask intelligent questions. Listen to the answers. Take your medication. Go through the tests. Put up with the sampling and screening. Grin and bare it when they pull out the old rubber glove. Don't be a 'real man' if being a real man is going to get you killed! Remember a visit to the doctor can lead to all sorts of exciting drugs and the cops can't do a fucking thing about it!

First Aid

WELL, IT STANDS TO REASON you should know some, doesn't it? Let's do it alphabetically. That's as good an approach as any.

- **ABC.** This is a really important acronym. It stands for Airway, Breathing, and Circulation – and that's the order you deal with these things in any unconscious person. Put them in the lateral position. Next, with your finger, check to see that they have an unobstructed airway – that there's nothing in their mouth or throat for them to choke on. Now watch to see whether or not they're actually breathing. Next, try to find a pulse at the big artery in the side of the neck, next to the windpipe. No breathing? Time for some EAR, or Expired Air Resuscitation. No pulse? Time to consider CPR, or Cardio-Pulmonary Resuscitation.
- **ASTHMA.** The most common chronic childhood disease in Australia. Characterised by shortness of breath, wheeziness, or persistent cough. During an attack, the muscle tissue surrounding the air tubes in your lungs goes into spasm. The lining of the tubes becomes swollen and starts pumping out thick mucous, all of which results in a lot of difficulty for the person trying to breathe.

  Asthma can be very serious – even fatal, on occasion. If the person suffering the attack isn't carrying their medication (usually an inhaler of a drug such as Ventolin) seek medical assistance. In the meantime, sit the person in a quiet, warm place away from other people. If they do have a puffer, administer it – four puffs should do it. If there's no result within four minutes, try another four puffs. If that doesn't work, or if the victim starts to look really shabby, call an ambulance. Keep trying the puffer as above until the paramedics arrive. Apparently you can't OD from a puffer ...
- **BITES & STINGS.**

  A) NON-VENOMOUS – DOGBITE, HUMAN BITE OR WHATEVER. Wash the wound carefully with a mild antiseptic or soap and water. Cover it with a clean dressing and a bandage. Take it to a doctor – it may need stitches, and if it's a human bite, it's sure as hell going to call for antibiotics.

  B) MODERATELY VENOMOUS (BEES, WASPS). Remove the sting

(bees) by brushing sideways with a knifeblade or your fingernail. Wipe the area, apply a cold compress. Watch for an allergic reaction. If it occurs, get the victim to medical assistance quickly. Apply pressure immobilisation – a pressure bandage and splint – if the sting is on a limb. Signs of serious allergic reaction include an itchy rash or welts on the body, puffy eyelids and face, constriction of the throat and breathing difficulties. In severe cases, it may be necessary to undertake EAR while awaiting medical aid.

c) **SAVAGELY VENOMOUS (SNAKES, FUNNEL-WEBS, BLUE-RINGED OCTOPUS, CONE SHELL).** Point to note: unless you happen to be an expert in snake identification, *all* snakebites should be treated as life-threatening. Australian snakes are murderously toxic. If you delay in taking action, somebody's going to die.

FIRSTLY: Don't cut, cauterise, bite, suck, or otherwise disturb the bite. That bullshit only works in cheap Spaghetti Westerns; in reality, it can do a lot of harm. Don't apply a tourniquet. Don't wash the skin, either – the venom on the surface can aid in the identification of the snake (or whatever). What you do is lay the poor bastard down and keep them still. Do *not* elevate a bitten limb! Immediately apply pressure immobilisation to the bite – wind a tight (but not constrictive) bandage immediately over the bite area. Next, apply a second tight bandage from the toes or fingers all the way to the base of the bitten limb. Splint the limb, and keep the victim as quiet and immobile as possible. If done quickly and correctly, this treatment can delay the onset of symptoms for a period of hours.

Now get medical help. And do it *fast*.

d) **OTHER NASTIES.** Stings from stonefish and bullrout don't want pressure immobilisation. Best treatment here is to soak the stung part in the hottest water the victim can stand, while waiting on medical assistance. For red-back spider bite also, pressure bandaging is no good. Apply a cold compress or ice-pack to the bite, and get help. In case of jellyfish sting, douse the sting liberally with household vinegar. Then peel away the clinging tentacles with your fingers. Don't rub the area. If it happens to be a leg or arm, you can use a pressure bandage, once you've removed the tentacles. Note: if it's a serious sting, it's very likely you're going to have to perform EAR and CPR. These two are more important than removing the tentacles from the sting, so make sure they're not interrupted. Now get help. Lots of it.

- **BLEEDING.**
  A) EXTERNAL. Lay the victim down. Check for foreign bodies or protruding bone in the wound. If present, don't mess with it. Apply a ring pad bandage – a bandage which doesn't press or disturb the foreign matter. If there's nothing nasty in the wound, apply direct pressure immediately. If you can't improvise a bandage, then use your hands to control bleeding until you can apply a clean dressing and bandage. When you can, bandage the wound firmly. If it's on a limb and there's no evidence of fracture, raise the limb. If blood soaks through the bandage, leave the dressing in place, but replace the pad. Do not remove the dressing, pad or bandage when the bleeding stops. Don't give the victim anything to eat or drink.

  B) INTERNAL. Identifiable by coughing or vomiting up blood, passing of black or red faeces, passing of red or smoky urine, or pain, tenderness and muscle rigidity of the abdomen. Lay the casualty down comfortably; loosen clothing. Raise or bend the legs – unless they're broken. Get help. Fast.
- **BRUISING.** Rest, Ice, Compression and Elevation (RICE – a good acronym to know). Lay the victim down. Apply an icepack to the bruised area. Apply a firm bandage when pain has subsided to a degree, and elevate the bruised area – if possible.
- **BURNS.** Remove the victim from danger – get them away from the heat source! If their clothing is alight, smother the flames with a cloth or a blanket. If you have to use water to put out the flames, don't throw it – pour it carefully and accurately from as close as feasible. If the victim is unconscious, place them in the lateral position, check the ABC (Airway, Breathing and Circulation, or the pulse), and begin EAR or CPR if necessary.

  Remove burnt clothing except where it is adhering to skin. Cool the burnt area with cold – not icy – water. (Place the burn under gently running water for ten minutes.) Now cover the burn with a sterile, nonadherent dressing, and bandage lightly. Don't apply any medications or ointments. Give no alcohol to the patient; they can sip water if they're thirsty. Get medical assistance for all but minor burns.
- **CHEST INJURIES.**
  A) FRACTURED RIBS. Identified by pain which worsens when the victim coughs, breathes or laughs; breathing difficulty, coughing up of bloody froth, or unusual tenderness in the area of the injury.

  If the victim is unconscious, go to the lateral position, check ABC, and commence EAR or CPR as necessary. If conscious, put them in a half-sitting position, leaning downward on the injured side. Pad the injury, bandage the upper arm, and immobilise the arm. Get help.

B) SUCKING WOUNDS. (Isn't that a really great term?) Not hard to identify. Blood bubbling from the wound, bluish lips, increasing difficulty breathing, sucking noises ... eeyeechh.

If the victim is unconscious, go through the usual routine. (Lateral position, ABC/EAR/CPR) If conscious, place them in a half-sitting position, leaning downwards towards the injured side. Remove any clothing from the wound, and place your hand over the wound. Cover the wound with a sterile dressing as soon as possible, or make an airtight dressing out of plastic or alfoil or the like. Use tape to anchor three edges of the dressing – but **NOT** the bottom edge. You have to leave that open so that air under pressure can escape. Now scream for help ...

- **CHOKING.**

  A) PARTIAL BLOCKAGE. Coughing, difficulty breathing, blueness in face, neck and extremities, or even unconsciousness.

  DON'T SLAP THEM ON THE BACK! Chances are you'll just send the blockage careening into what's left of the airway, and choke the poor swine to death. If they're out cold, put them in the lateral position and yell for help. If they're conscious, encourage them to relax, allow them to cough. Maybe they'll spit out the obstruction. Get help if they pass out, or if they don't start breathing more freely.

  B) COMPLETE BLOCKAGE. No coughing. No breathing. Rapid passage into unconsciousness. Blueness. Lots of waving of hands and bulging eyes ... it's not a pretty sight. Note: if the airway resists air, and the chest doesn't move during attempts at EAR on an unconscious person, you've probably got a blocked airway.

  Position the victim so that the head is slightly lower than the chest. (Actually, if they're small enough for you to do it, tip the bugger completely upside down ...) Give three or four sharp slaps between the shoulder blades with your hand. If that doesn't work, keep their head down, put your hands on either side of the chest at the short ribs, and squeeze sharply, once or twice as necessary. If there's no improvement, go to EAR. And get help, very, very quickly.

- **COLD/EXPOSURE.** Mild exposure – shivering, extreme fatigue or drowsiness, cramps, blurred vision, slowing of faculties, slurred speech and confusion. If they're unconscious, run the lateral position/ABC/EAR/CPR drill. Then move them to a dry, sheltered spot – preferably a warm one. Get rid of any wet clothing. Insulate the person to prevent further heat loss; use dry clothing, blankets, or a sleeping bag. Wrap them up in something windproof too, if possible – a space blanket, plastic sheeting, or a tarpaulin. Strip a volunteer to their underwear and put them in with the victim; the shared body heat is a valuable aid. Call for medical assistance. If the person is conscious, warm drinks are in order. **ALCOHOL IS NOT A GOOD IDEA.**

Extreme exposure results in hypothermia – a dangerous reduction in the body's core temperature. The victim may display cold skin, slow and shallow breathing, a slow pulse, listlessness or even unconsciousness. The trick with hypothermia is not to warm them too quickly. No hot baths. No electric blankets, hot-water bottles. Not even a comfortable seat next to a fire. Dry them off, bundle them up, put a volunteer in with them, and if they happen to be conscious, give them warm – not hot – drinks. And get medical assistance as soon as possible.

Frostbite is pretty nasty too. It usually occurs in the extremities – toes, fingers, ears, and nose. The small blood vessels constrict, and the area gets really, really cold. May even start to freeze up. In extreme cases, gangrene can set in, which calls for amputation – and you know how much we hate that, don't you? Look for tingling and numbness in the affected part. The skin will be waxy, almost chalk-white, and firm to the touch. There will be no pain until the part is warmed up again, but there may be some surface blistering. **DO NOT** rub or massage the affected part. **DO NOT** give alcohol. **DO NOT** apply direct heat, snow, or cold water. Get the victim to a warm, dry spot. Warm the affected area slowly, using body heat. Treat any blisters with dry, sterile dressings, and get medical help.

- **CONCUSSION:** Occurs when the head is severely struck or shaken. Watch for pale, clammy skin, shallow breathing, nausea, dizziness, unconsciousness – even if only momentary, loss of short-term memory, double vision, persistent and intense headache.

  Lay them down. Give no food or drink. Apply a cold compress to the site of the injury if possible. Watch for any worsening of the condition. If they lose conscious, go to the lateral position ABC/EAR/CPR drill. Get medical aid if concussion is apparent or suspected.

- **CONVULSIONS:** Protect the victim from injury by removing any dangerous objects in their vicinity. Don't forcibly restrain them, and for the love of crap, **DON'T STICK YOUR FINGERS IN THEIR MOUTH.** Their tongue will be just fine. If you stick your fingers in there, you're likely to have them really savagely bitten. When the convulsions pass, put the victim into the lateral position. Reassure them when they come around, and help them get to somewhere quiet to rest. Seek medical aid if the seizure lasts longer than ten minutes – or if associated with a high fever.

- **CPR.** Cardio-Pulmonary Resuscitation – what you do when they've got no pulse. (For crap's sake, be certain they need it first. In a cold, sick person, that heartbeat can be very hard to locate, and you can do them serious harm by buggering about with the rhythm of their functioning heart. Anyone who is capable of noticing you performing CPR on them **DOESN'T NEED IT!**) It's a combination of EAR and external cardiac compression, and ideally, it keeps circulation going in the victim until real help arrives on the scene. It's tiring as all hell; usually, two people do it to keep the rhythm going nicely.

Kneel beside the head and upper body of the victim. Lie them on their back. Find the middle part of the breastbone: trace the fingers of both your hands along the lowest rib on either side of their chest, moving inwards until they meet in the middle. Leave one of your index fingers positioned here as a marker. Put the other index finger in the notch in the middle of the collarbone. Now bring your thumbs together in the centre of the chest. This marks the middle of the breastbone.

Leave the hand which is nearer the victim's head in place. Slide your other hand underneath it, so the heel of the lower hand rests on the victim's chest. Lace your fingers together. Keeping your arms straight, firmly and sharply depress the breastbone about 5cm, trying not to put any pressure on the ribs. (This is a futile exercise. Anyone who's ever done good, effective cardiac massage will tell you that the victim almost always comes out with a few cracks and bruises. Still, it's better than being dead, right?) Release the pressure, allowing the chest to rise again, but keep your hands in place. Repeat the compressions rhythmically.

If you're on your own, you should compress the breastbone about 15 times in 10-12 seconds, then give EAR at the rate of 2 breaths in 3-5 seconds. If you've got help, then one person (the stronger) should handle the cardiac compression, and the other the EAR. The rate here is 5 compressions and one breath in five seconds. Keep a count, so that the rhythm is maintained easily.

Check for a pulse after one minute, then after every two minutes. If there is no pulse, keep up the CPR. If you get a pulse but no breathing, go to EAR only. When you've got both pulse and breathing, put them in the lateral position and keep a close eye on them.

CPR is tricky stuff to do and to keep doing. However, once you get started on it, you shouldn't stop until either you've got a pulse and breathing in the victim, or professional help arrives. Especially in the case of someone pulled out of cold water: intense cold does tricky things to the human metabolism. There have been people revived after forty minutes without breathing, where they've been trapped in ice water. You can't just give up after five or ten minutes and call it quits.

CPR is not really something you should be doing from a vaguely worded description in a book. If you think you're ever likely to be in the situation where you might want to know how to administer CPR, take a St John's Ambulance course, and learn to do it right.

- **CUTS/ABRASIONS.** Wash your hands thoroughly. Gently brush away any foreign matter on the surface – such as gravel or glass. Clean the wound and the surrounding area, wiping away from the wound, using sterile swabs, warm water, and a mild antiseptic. Apply a sterile, non-adherent dressing, if necessary. Consider a tetanus injection if the wound is deep, or dirty, or caused by a rusty object.

If there is an object embedded in the wound, apply a ring pad bandage. Apply no pressure to the object proper, and seek medical attention.

- **DROWNING.** Don't go after anyone in deep water unless you can *really* swim. People on their way to drowning get panicky and difficult to handle, so unless you want two drownings, either toss them a line – or if you can't do that, and there's nobody else around to help, wait until they stop thrashing before you go in to get them.

Once you've got them, check and clear their airway. You may well need to begin EAR while still bringing the victim ashore. **DON'T** try it in deep water unless you've been trained for it. Wait until you can stand safely.

When you're out of the water, place the victim in the lateral position and clear the airway again. If necessary, start EAR/CPR. Once they've started breathing on their own, keep them in the lateral position, and cover them with a towel or blanket, for warmth. Anyone who has lost consciousness or required resuscitation warrants a visit to hospital as soon as possible.

- **DRUG OVERDOSE.** Look for dizziness, faintness, convulsions, weak or thready pulse, breathing difficulties, vomiting, slurred speech, disorientation or loss of consciousness. If they're unconscious, put them in the lateral position and go through the ABC/EAR/CPR routine. Try to establish what drug has been taken – get empty containers, leftover tablets, syringes, or even samples of vomit, and send them to the hospital along with the victim.

- **EAR.** Expired Air Resuscitation, also known as mouth-to-mouth resuscitation. Mouth-to-mouth is easiest, of course, but in the case of serious jaw injury, mouth-to-nose works as well. Mouth-to-nose is also used for babies and small children, where your mouth actually covers both their mouth and nose. Note that the risk catching of HIV is quite low, and EAR is a life-saving technique.

  Once you're sure the victim isn't breathing on their own, kneel beside them. Roll them gently onto their back, ensuring the airway is clear. Gently tilt the head back, supporting the jaw with your fingers. For crap's sake – **DON'T PRESS ON THE THROAT!**

  Place your cheek on the victim's nose to seal it, and take a deep breath. Place your mouth over theirs, making a tight seal. Keeping their head tilted, breathe gently and completely into their airway, watching for their chest to rise. **DON'T OVERDO IT.** It doesn't take as much effort as you might think – certainly not as much pressure as is required to inflate a balloon. Deliver five full breaths in ten seconds, then check the pulse at the carotid, in the side of the neck. If there is no pulse, commence CPR. If a pulse is present, but breathing hasn't started on its own, keep up the EAR. Give one breath every four seconds. Check pulse and breathing every two minutes. When the victim is breathing on their own, place them in the lateral position to recover.

- **EARS.** Bleeding from the ear is bad. There may be a serious head injury involved. Place the person in the lateral position with the injured ear tilted downwards on a clean dressing. **DON'T** plug the ear, or put in any damned eardrops. Now get help at once.

  Foreign bodies in the ear are kind of annoying. **DON'T** go probing the ear. **DON'T** try to get the object out – unless it's an insect. If it is an insect, tilt the victim's head away from you and let a little warm oil or water into the ear, then tilt the head back towards you so the insect can float out. If it's anything other than an insect – or if the damned bug won't float out – go see a doctor.

- **ELECTRIC SHOCK. DON'T** touch the victim until you're sure you are safe. Turn off the current at the mains, or the power point – and pull out the plug, too, if that's feasible. If we're talking high-voltage stuff like electric train lines, overhead lines or heavy machinery, get clear, call for help, and wait for someone trained to disconnect the power. Electricity is sneaky, dangerous stuff that will gang up on you if it gets the chance.

  In the case of normal household voltages, if you can't shut off the power, move the victim clear using something dry and non-conducting, like a wooden broom-handle. Stand on a non-conducting surface, too – like a dry newspaper, or a rubber mat. Once they're clear, smother any flames. If they're unconscious, place them in the lateral position and commence ABC/EAR/CPR drill. Treat any burns. Get medical help.

- **EYES.** In case of chemical or simple heat burns, open the eyelids gently with your fingers, and flush with cool running water for at least 20 minutes. Gently pad and bandage the eye, and get to a doctor.

  In the case of flash burns, which can be caused by the light of an arc welder, don't flush the eye with water. Just pad it gently, and get to a doctor.

  Foreign bodies on the surface of the eye can also be flushed away in this manner – though it shouldn't take 20 minutes. Where the eyeball is actually wounded, however, or where a foreign body is embedded in the eyeball, be very careful. Don't touch the eye. Don't let the victim touch their eye. Don't try to remove the object yourself. Lay the person down, place thick padding above and below the eye, and put a dressing over that. **DON'T** allow the covering to press on the injured eye at all. Get medical help.

  BLACK EYES. Check to see the eye itself is uninjured. Apply an icepack to the general area – but not to the eye itself. Consider checking with a doctor if the eye swells and closes.

- **FAINTING.** Lay the person down with their feet raised. Loosen any tight clothing, ensuring they get adequate fresh air. Check breathing and pulse, and look for any signs of injury. A person who doesn't recover consciousness quickly may have something much more serious to worry about than a fainting spell. Get medical help quickly.

- **FRACTURES.** A fracture is a broken bone. Where a bone pierces the skin, you have a compound fracture, which is quite serious: susceptible to infection, and prone to lots of exciting blood loss. If the skin is still closed, it's a closed fracture.

  You can identify a fracture by: the sound or feel of breaking bone; intense pain around the break; deformity of a limb, or inability to move naturally; excessive tenderness to light pressure; swelling – or the truly nasty noise which occurs when two broken bone ends grate across one another (crepitus). Don't ask how this sounds. You'll know if you ever hear it.

If possible, don't move a broken bone. Don't even shift the victim, unless it's essential to their safety. (Point to note: outside of Hollywood, cars are rarely known to explode. Don't move somebody from a crash unless there's a serious fire danger – leaking petrol, or live flames. Okay?) And don't give them anything to eat or drink. They may be looking down the barrel of a general anaesthetic in the near future, and it's bad karma to go under when you've got a load in your guts.

If there's an open wound, control the bleeding and cover the wound with a sterile dressing. Use a ring pad to prevent pressure on any foreign objects or protruding bones. Support a fractured limb in the most comfortable position – raise a broken foot or ankle on pillows or folded blankets. **DON'T** try to straighten a fractured limb. If necessary, immobilise it with a splint.

- **HEART ATTACK.** Occurs when the blood supply to the heart is blocked by a blood clot or other obstruction in the coronary artery. This is an occasion for rapid first aid and immediate, specialised medical attention. Heart attacks are characterised by severe pain in the centre of the chest, which can spread to the arms (especially the left), the neck and jaw. Occasionally mistaken for really savage indigestion. May also cause nausea, shortness of breath, pale, cold and clammy skin, confusion and disorientation, or complete collapse – leading to loss of pulse.

  Heart failure is even nastier, but the symptoms are similar (although there may be some excitingly swollen neck veins, blood-stained mucus, and a blue tint to the lips and the extremities) and you do exactly the same thing for it.

  If the person is unconscious, put them in the lateral position, check the ABCs, and start EAR/CPR if required. If they're still with you, sit them up, and loosen their clothing. Call an ambulance immediately, and specify that you think the victim has had a heart attack.

- **HEAT.** Heat exhaustion is the result of excessive fluid loss through perspiration. The victim feels hot and exhausted (wow, hey?), usually has a killer headache, probably feels faint, giddy and nauseous, is thirsty as hell, may get muscle cramps and weakness, may turn pale and clammy, sweat heavily; their pulse is quick, and they may become uncoordinated and confused. Take them somewhere nice and cool – black shade at the very least. Lay them down, get rid of any excess clothing. Sponge them with water. Get them to drink a little water – or better still, one of those sports electrolytic drinks. If they don't perk up pretty well on the spot, get them to medical assistance.

Heat Stroke is much nastier. It occurs when the body's heat-regulation mechanisms just plain give up. Look for hot, flushed, dry skin; headache; dizziness; sharp rise in body temperature – up to 40C or more; rapid pulse; nausea and vomiting; disorientation, and even unconsciousness. If the victim is unconscious, place them in the lateral position and run the ABC/EAR/CPR drill. Then get them into a cool place – again, black shade at an absolute minimum – and get rid of all but the essential garments. Cool them down as quickly as you can: apply ice packs to the armpits, neck and groin. Wrap them in a wet sheet and fan them. Now call for medical help. Keep an eye on the temperature of the victim; as soon as the skin feels cool to the touch, get rid of the ice-packs and the wet sheet. Once they're conscious, give them small, frequent mouthfuls of liquid, as for heat exhaustion.

- **ICEPACKS.** Always wrap ice in cloth. Never apply ice to bare skin. Apply ice-packs for about 20 minutes every two hours for the first 24 hours after an injury, then every four hours for the next 24 hours.

- **LATERAL POSITION.** Also called the Recovery Position. Wherever possible (ie, so long as their injuries don't make it a bad idea), this is how you lay out an unconscious person. Kneel beside them. Place their far arm straight out, at right angles to their body. Take the near arm, bend it at the elbow, and place it across the chest with the fingers close to the other shoulder. Bend the near leg up at right angles to the body, allowing the knee to flex naturally. Holding the shoulder and hip nearest you, gently roll the victim away from you, onto their side. The top leg lies, bent at the knee, on the ground with the thigh at right angles to the body and the calf parallel to the straight leg. Now rest that uppermost (bent) arm across the elbow of the straight arm. Gently tilt the head backwards. The face should be turned slightly downwards to allow any fluid to drain from the mouth, and the tongue to fall forward, clearing the airway.

- **NECK AND SPINE INJURIES.** These are always to be treated with utmost respect. Look for intense pain at or below the site of the injury; tenderness at the site; tingling in the extremities, or loss of movement/feeling at or below the injury. There may also be loss of bowel or bladder control, and possible breathing difficulty.

DON'T MOVE THE VICTIM. If they are unconscious, you may run the lateral position/ABC/EAR/CPR drill – but only while very carefully supporting the head and neck with your hands. The spine must not twist at all. Other than this, and possibly supporting the head and neck with your hand if the person is trapped, do absolutely nothing. Get help. Let the paramedics handle the ticklish task of moving somebody who may well have life-threatening injuries ...

- **NOSEBLEED.** Tell the person not to blow their nose. They should breathe through their mouth. Sit them down, lean them slightly forward, and get them to pinch their nostrils shut for about ten minutes. That should do the job. If the bleeding continues, repeat the process. The victim should avoid blowing their nose for several hours afterwards. If the bleeding persists, get somebody medical on the case.

- **POISONING.** Poisons can be inhaled, absorbed, swallowed or injected. There are many, many different kinds of poisons, with all sorts of exciting symptoms. For specific poisons information, phone 131 126. The Poisons Information Centre (PIC) can be reached at that number from any town in Australia.

  In general, for an unconscious victim, you should undertake the lateral position/ABC/EAR/CPR drill. Make sure you wipe away any poisonous substances from the victim's mouth and nose first. If the victim is conscious, the treatment is poison specific. Always call for medical assistance as soon as possible.

  A) DRUGS, MEDICINES AND STUFF. (Including plants, mushrooms, and detergent.) Don't induce vomiting if the victim is unconscious, or lying on their back. There's few things nastier than choking on vomit ... If the PIC or a doctor tell you to do so, administer syrup of Ipecacuanha (Ipecac Syrup) – which is guaranteed to make the victim woof their cookies faster than a Brady Bunch Charity Variety Special. **DON'T** use saltwater or detergent to induce vomiting.

  B) CORROSIVES, PETRO-SOLVENTS, OR UNKNOWNS. Don't induce vomiting at all. Wash the face and mouth. Give nothing by mouth at all. Get help.

  C) INHALED POISONS. Carbon monoxide, industrial gases, solvent fumes: avoid getting a snootful yourself. Cover your mouth and nose with a wet cloth. Ventilate the area, or move the victim to fresh air. Run the lateral position/ABC/EAR/CPR drill if the victim is unconscious. Get medical aid.

  D) ABSORBED POISONS. These are totally bad karma, and include most of the pesticides. The worst thing about it is, the action can be quite delayed – they may develop symptoms hours after exposure. First, get them to remove any contaminated clothing. Wear protective gloves if you're going to help them. Now wash the contaminated skin thoroughly with soap and water. Call for medical aid. If the victim passes out, run the lateral position/etc drill.

- **PULSE.** The pulse rate is the rate of the heartbeat. 60-80 strong, regular pulses per minute is normal for adults. Children range up to 100 per minute, and babies up to 140. If the victim is unconscious, the place to check for a pulse is the carotid artery, in the side of the neck. Lightly place the tips of your middle two fingers on the victim's windpipe, and slide them into the groove between the windpipe and the big neck muscle. Check only one side when you check the pulse. Check for five seconds. If you don't get a pulse in that time, start straight in on CPR.
- **RICE.** Rest, Ice, Compression and Elevation – standard first aid for bruising, muscular strain or sprain. The compression refers to a tight, but not constrictive bandage, while 'elevation' refers to the damaged limb itself.
- **SEVERED BODY PARTS.** If you're quick, you may be able to save the severed bit. First priority, though, is to save the person. No good saving an arm if the body you were going to re-attach it to happens to be dead ... First, lay the victim down. Firmly press a large piece of gauze or cloth to the bloody stump to prevent bleeding. Bind the dressing in place. Now yell for help.

  In the meantime, keep the victim still. Now grab the missing part, and wrap it in clean gauze or cloth. **DON'T WASH IT**. Put it in a watertight container – like a plastic bag, preferably. Put the bag into cold water – preferably, ice water. Don't let the part come into contact with the ice, though. Send the bag off to the hospital with the victim. Vomit copiously.

- **SHOCK.** Clinical shock – as opposed to electrical – is a weird condition. It can follow extreme pain, severe bleeding, or heavy fluid loss. It's a serious, even life-threatening matter, so watch for: pale, cold, clammy skin; weak, rapid pulse; dizziness, faintness, or greying of vision; nausea; rapid breathing; drowsiness and confusion, possibly leading to unconsciousness.

  If the victim is unconscious, perform the lateral position/etc drill. If they're conscious, lay them down and try to elevate their legs – if they aren't broken, of course. Keep the head low. Identify the cause of shock, and treat it. Keep them warm. Call for medical help. Give no food or drink. If the victim complains of thirst, do no more than moisten their lips. Keep an eye on the ABC at regular intervals.
- **SPRAINS AND DISLOCATIONS.** A sprain occurs when a joint is forced

beyond its normal range of movement, stretching or tearing the ligaments that hold it together. Look for pain and tenderness around the joint, restricted movement, swelling and bruising. Don't move the joint if you suspect a fracture. Apply RICE. Most common sprains occur at the ankles, but it is entirely possible to sprain wrists, elbows, and other joints.

Dislocation occurs when the bones are forced all the way out of contact with one another. Usually, there will be intense pain and local sensitivity, deformity of the joint, inability to move the joint, and considerable swelling and bruising. Don't try to 'pop' the joint back into place. Leave that for the doctor. Support and rest the joint as best you can, apply icepacks, and get medical help.

- **STROKE.** Refers to a blocked or ruptured artery in the brain, causing brain damage. Look for severe headache, difficulty swallowing, red face, pounding pulse, seizures, difficulty speaking, confusion, weakness or partial paralysis – especially down one side of the body, or unconsciousness.

There's not a whole lot you can do about a stroke except practise your lateral position/etc drill on an unconscious victim, or make conscious victims more comfortable. Call for help. Strokes are serious events.

- **TEETH.** A tooth which has been knocked out should be cleaned by having the victim suck on it. If this can't be done, use a little spit, or cold milk. Tap water is a last resort. And definitely no detergents or antiseptics! Now replace the tooth in its socket and hold it there for two minutes. Use a ball of alfoil molded over the tooth and its neighbours as a splint. If you can't get the tooth back in the mouth immediately, keep it moist in milk or saliva. Call on a dentist, pronto.

- **TEMPERATURE.** Standard body temperature alters during the course of the day, and can be affected by exertion, different foods, hot drinks and a bunch of other things. The normal range is between 36.1 and 37.1C. Low temperatures can indicate shock, heavy bleeding, or hypothermia. High temperature may be a result of severe infection or heat stroke.

To take the temperature accurately, wash and dry a mercury thermometer. Shake it down until the reading is below 34C. Place the bulb of the thermometer under the tongue, in the armpit, or in the fold of the groin. Leave it there for three minutes before taking a reading.

Index